Financial Accounting

FOR DUMMIES®

A Wiley Brand

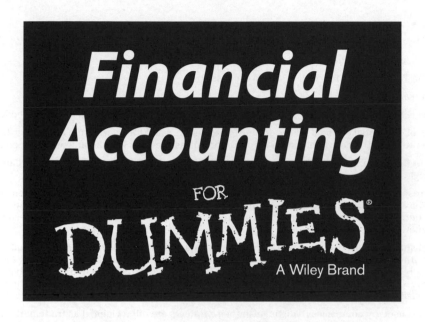

Financial Accounting

FOR DUMMIES®

A Wiley Brand

by Steve Collings and Maire Loughran

FOR DUMMIES®

A Wiley Brand

Financial Accounting For Dummies®

Published by: **John Wiley & Sons, Ltd.,** The Atrium, Southern Gate, Chichester, www.wiley.com

This edition first published 2013

© 2013 John Wiley & Sons, Ltd, Chichester, West Sussex.

Registered office

John Wiley & Sons Ltd, The Atrium, Southern Gate, Chichester, West Sussex, PO19 8SQ, United Kingdom

For details of our global editorial offices, for customer services and for information about how to apply for permission to reuse the copyright material in this book please see our website at www.wiley.com.

The right of the author to be identified as the author of this work has been asserted in accordance with the Copyright, Designs and Patents Act 1988

Wiley publishes in a variety of print and electronic formats and by print-on-demand. Some material included with standard print versions of this book may not be included in e-books or in print-on-demand. If this book refers to media such as a CD or DVD that is not included in the version you purchased, you may download this material at http://booksupport.wiley.com. For more information about Wiley products, visit www.wiley.com.

Designations used by companies to distinguish their products are often claimed as trademarks. All brand names and product names used in this book are trade names, service marks, trademarks or registered trademarks of their respective owners. The publisher is not associated with any product or vendor mentioned in this book.

For general information on our other products and services, please contact our Customer Care Department within the U.S. at 877-762-2974, outside the U.S. at (001) 317-572-3993, or fax 317-572-4002. For technical support, please visit www.wiley.com/techsupport.

For technical support, please visit www.wiley.com/techsupport.

A catalogue record for this book is available from the British Library.

ISBN 978-1-118-55437-1 (hardback/paperback) ISBN 978-1-118-55434-0 (ebk)

ISBN 978-1-118-55435-7 (ebk)   ISBN 978-1-118-55436-4 (ebk)

Printed in Great Britain TJ International, Padstow.

10 9 8 7 6 5 4 3 2 1

Contents at a Glance

Table of Contents

Part II: Looking at Some Accounting Basics 65

Part IV: Investigating Income and Cash Flow.............. 143

Chapter 10: Understanding Profit or Loss........................145

Chapter 11: Figuring Out the Statement of Cash Flows under UK GAAP and IFRS 165

Introduction

*A*ccountancy is known as the language of business because it communicates financial and economic facts about a business to all sorts of interested parties – both *internal* (employees of the company) and *external* (people not employed by the company in question). External users include investors, creditors, banks and regulatory agencies such as HM Revenue and Customs and the stock markets.

Focusing on the external users of accounting information, this book is about financial accounting. *Financial* accounting serves the needs of external users by providing them with understandable, materially correct financial statements. Three financial statements exist: the income statement (often termed the *profit and loss account* in the UK and also known internationally as the *statement of comprehensive income* or *statement of profit or loss*), balance sheet (known internationally as the *statement of financial position*) and the cash flow statement (known internationally as the *statement of cash flows*). This book is a step-by-step guide on how to prepare all three.

You also find out the purposes of the financial statements:

- ✔ To report on the financial position of the company – what types of assets the company owns and what types of liabilities it owes.

- ✔ To show how well the company performs over a period of time, which is referred to as an *accounting period*. You measure performance by seeing whether the company made or lost money during the accounting period.

A lot of people considering starting out in the world of accountancy are often afraid they won't do well in their accountancy studies because they haven't done well in maths. Forget about the maths – that's why you have a computer and a calculator! Financial accounting is less about adding and subtracting and more about using logic-based skills. Added to the mix is the importance of gaining a working understanding of the standards set in place by authoritative accountancy bodies.

The reason I've written this book is to breathe some life into the subject of financial accounting and make it more understandable to students, trainee accountants and those seeking a career change into the world of accountancy.

About This Book

This book, like all *For Dummies* books, is written so that each chapter stands on its own. I always assume that whatever chapter you're reading is the first one you've tackled in the book. Therefore, you can understand the concepts I explain in each chapter regardless of whether it's your first chapter or your last.

However, certain terms and concepts are relevant to more than one subject in this book. To avoid writing the same explanations over and over, whenever I refer to a financial accounting term, method or other type of fact that I fully explain in another chapter, I give you a brief overview and direct you to the chapter where you can get more information. For example, I may suggest that you 'flick to Chapter 13' (which, by the way, discusses the statement of cash flows).

Also, in this book I break financial accounting down to its lowest common denominator. I avoid using jargon that only accountants with several years' experience already under their belts will understand. Please keep in mind that the list of financial accounting topics and methods I present in this book isn't exhaustive. I simply can't cover every possible transaction and event related to preparing financial accounting data and statements. This book is meant to give a basic introduction to the world of financial accounting in a down-to-earth, easy-to-understand and light-hearted manner.

Conventions Used in This Book

Following are some conventions I use that you need to bear in mind while reading this book:

- ✔ I introduce new terms in *italic* with an explanation immediately following. For example, *liquidity* refers to a company's ability or lack thereof to meet current financial obligations. To put it even more simply, does the company have enough cash to pay its bills?

- ✔ Many accounting terms have acronyms (which you'll soon be bandying about with your fellow novice accountants after you gain some familiarity or experience with the topic). The first time I introduce an acronym in a chapter, I spell it out and place the acronym in brackets. For example, I may discuss the Association of Chartered Certified Accountants (ACCA).

- ✔ I use **bold** text to highlight key words in bulleted lists.

- ✔ All web addresses are in monofont typeface so that they're set apart from the rest of the text.

What You're Not to Read

It would be great if you read every word of this book, but I realise that people lead busy lives and sometimes just want to get the specific information they need. So if you're short on time, you can safely skip the following without jeopardising your understanding of the subject at large:

- ✔ **Material marked with a Technical Stuff icon:** These paragraphs contain extra financial accounting information that, while useful, isn't critical to your understanding of the topic at hand.
- ✔ **Sidebars:** These grey-shaded boxes contain asides that I think you'll find interesting but that, again, aren't vital to understanding the fundamental concepts of a certain accountancy topic.

Foolish Assumptions

I assume you don't have more than a basic understanding of accountancy, and I'm guessing you're one of the following people:

- ✔ A financial accounting student who just isn't getting it by reading (and rereading) the relevant textbook.
- ✔ A non-accountancy student currently enrolled in either business or another course who's considering changing direction to go down the accountancy route.
- ✔ A business owner (particularly someone operating a small business with a relatively small/modest turnover) who wants to attempt preparing her own financial statements or just wants to have a better understanding about the financial statements prepared by the in-house or external accountant.
- ✔ A brand-new accountant working in financial accounting who needs a plain-English refresher of accountancy concepts.

How This Book Is Organised

To help you find the financial accounting facts you need, this book is organised into parts that break down the subject of financial accounting into easily digestible portions that all relate to one another.

Part 1: Getting Started with Financial Accounting

This part introduces you to the world of financial accounting. You receive an initiation into the purpose, constraints and responsibilities of financial accountants; various financial accounting career options; and the sorts of professional courses you need to pursue these careers. I also provide an overview of the three financial statements. For the business owner, it provides information about the education, training, certification and experience of the stranger who comes into your business asking about private accountancy-related facts.

Part 11: Looking at Some Accounting Basics

In this part, I lay the foundation of the basics of financial accounting that you're likely to come across in your day-to-day working life as a financial accountant or as an accountancy student. You discover how to enter accounting transactions into a company's books through the use of journal entries. You also find out about the general ledger, which is the place where accountants record the impact of transactions taking place in a business during a particular accounting period. Finally, you find out about the two different methods of accounting, the cash-based method and the accruals-based method – though I concentrate on the accruals method because this is the one financial accountants use.

Part 111: Bonding with the Balance Sheet

This section contains three chapters, each explaining a different section of the balance sheet. The three sections of the balance sheet are assets, liabilities and equity, and together they show the financial position of a company. *Assets* are resources a company owns, *liabilities* are what a company owes and *equity* is the difference between assets and liabilities, which equals the total of each owner's investment in the business.

Part IV: Investigating Income and Cash Flow

This part looks at the income statement and the statement of cash flows. The *income statement* shows a company's revenue and expenses, the end result of which shows whether a company made or lost money during the accounting period. The *statement of cash flows* shows the cash received by a company and the cash paid by a company during the accounting period. It tells users of the financial statements how well the company is managing its sources and uses of cash.

Part V: Analysing the Financial Statements

After all your hard work preparing the financial statements, in this section you find out about key measurements that users of the financial statements perform to gauge the effectiveness and efficiency of the business. I provide the complete picture on a company's *annual report*, which informs the shareholders about the company's operations for the past year. And you get an overview of corporate governance and interpretations of the explanatory notes and other information found in most companies' annual reports.

Part VI: Tackling More Advanced Financial Accounting Topics

Here, I delve into other financial accounting topics, like accounting for income taxes and leases. Knowing about these topics makes your financial accounting experience well-rounded, preparing you in case you decide to continue on your journey through the world of accountancy and, perhaps, enrolling on one of the chartered qualification courses.

Part VII: The Part of Tens

I wrap up the book by explaining ten financial statement deceptions to look out for when preparing financial statements. These include ways to inflate income by understating expenses and hiding unfavourable information from the users through use of accountancy lingo. I also provide some helpful information about industries that may deviate from generally accepted accounting practice (GAAP) while doing their bookwork and preparing their financial statements.

Icons Used in This Book

Throughout the book, you see the following icons in the left-hand margin:

Text accompanied by this icon contains useful hints that you can apply during your studies (or on the job) to make your studies (or work) a bit easier and more successful.

When you see this icon, get those brain cells in gear, because it sits next to information you want to commit to memory.

Looking for what not to do in the world of financial accounting? Check out paragraphs next to this icon because they alert you to what can trip you up during your studies or working in the field.

This icon includes information that enhances the topic under discussion but isn't necessary to understand the topic.

This icon shows you that a financial accounting concept is demonstrated by working through an example.

Where to Go from Here

Each chapter stands on its own, so no matter where you start, you won't feel like you've missed anything fundamental beforehand. Your motivation for purchasing this book will probably dictate which chapters you want to read first and which you'll read only if you have some spare time in the future.

If you're an accountancy student, flip to the chapter explaining a topic you're a little confused with after reading your textbook. Business owners can get a good overview of the financial accounting process by starting with Chapters 1 and 3; these two chapters explain the nuts and bolts of financial accounting and its concepts. Otherwise, check out the table of contents or index for a topic that interests you, or jump in anywhere in the book that covers the financial accounting information you're wondering about.

Part I

Getting Started with Financial Accounting

getting started with

with

Financial Accounting

Go to www.dummies.com/extras/financialaccounting for online bonus content.

In this part . . .

✔ Understand why financial accounting is so important to many different individuals and businesses.

✔ Come to grips with the key characteristics of financial accounting.

✔ Chart a career in financial accounting.

✔ Get a handle on the primary financial statements.

✔ Go to www.dummies.com/extras/financial accounting for online bonus content, including an extra Part of Tens chapter: 'Ten Differences Between Some National Standards and IFRS'.

Chapter 1

Seeing the Big Picture of Financial Accounting and International Accounting

I assume that you have a very good reason for buying this book; most people don't randomly buy a title like *Financial Accounting For Dummies*. The chances are you're embarking on your first accountancy course and want to be sure you do well in it, but it might be the case that you're a business owner wanting to get a better grip on the way your financial statements are prepared or to improve your bookkeeping. Whatever your reasons, this chapter is your key to the car to start the journey on the road of financial accounting.

I explain what financial accounting is and why it's so important to many different individuals and businesses. I identify the various users of financial information and explain why they need that info. Finally, I briefly introduce four all-important characteristics of financial information: relevance, reliability, comparability and understandability. Whether you're a financial accounting student or a business owner, you need to understand these crucial financial accounting terms from the very beginning as they underpin everything to do with financial statements right from the word 'go'. For those of you reporting under IFRSs, these principles are also relevant but are split between fundamental qualitative characteristics and enhancing qualitative characteristics; I offer a run through of these for you too.

Knowing the Objective of Financial Accounting

Broadly speaking, *accounting* is the process of organising facts and figures and communicating the results of that organisation to any parties interested in that information. This process doesn't just relate to numbers churned out by a computer software program; it pertains to any type of reconciliation.

Here's an example that a parent could possibly relate to that doesn't involve numbers or money: a teenager sneaks in after a curfew set by his parents, and his parents ask for a complete account of why he's late. When the teenager tells them the facts, we have information (his car broke down in an area with no mobile phone signal), the individual producing the information (the mischievous teenager) and the interested party, also known as the user of the information (the worried parents).

The subject of this book, financial accounting, is a subset of accountancy. *Financial accounting* involves the process of preparing financial statements for a business. (Not sure what financial statements are? No worries – you find an overview of them in the next section.) Here are the key pieces of the financial accounting jigsaw:

- **Information:** Any accounting transactions taking place within the business during the accounting period. These include generating revenue from the sales of company goods or rendering of services, paying business-related expenses, buying company assets and incurring debt to run the company.
- **Business entity:** The company incurring the accounting transactions.
- **Users:** The persons or businesses that need to see the accounting transactions organised into financial statements to make informed decisions of their own. (You can find more about these users in the 'Getting to Know the Users of Financial Statements' section of this chapter.)

Preparing financial statements

If you're starting an accountancy course, your entire course could well centre on the proper preparation of financial statements: the income statement (profit and loss account), balance sheet (statement of financial position) cash flow statement (statement of cash flows) and statement of changes in equity. Financial accountants can't just stick accounting transaction information in the financial statements wherever they feel like. Many, many rules exist that dictate how financial accountants must organise the information in the financial statements; these rules are called *generally accepted accounting practice* (GAAP), and I discuss them in Chapter 4. The rules pertain to both how the financial accountant shows the accounting transactions and in which financial statements the information relating to the transactions appears.

Curious about the purpose of each financial statement? Here's a run through of each one:

- **Income statement:** This financial statement shows the results of business operations consisting of revenue, expenses, gains and losses. The end product is net profit or net loss. I talk about the income statement again in Chapter 3, and then I cover it from start to finish in Chapter 10. For now, here are the basic facts on the four different income statement components:

    - *Revenue:* Sales earned by the company selling its goods or services.

    - *Expenses:* The costs to the company to earn its revenue.

    - *Gains:* Income from non-operating-related transactions, such as selling a company asset.

    - *Losses:* The flip side of gains, such as losing money when selling a company car.

    A lot of accountants call the income statement a *statement of profit or loss*, especially when they're working to international standards (International Financial Reporting Standards), or simply a *P&L* (as it's commonly known in the UK). These terms are fine to use because they address the spirit of the statement.

- **Balance sheet:** This statement has three sections: assets, liabilities and equity. Standing on their own, these sections contain valuable information about a company. However, a user has to see all three interacting together on the balance sheet to form a reasonably reliable opinion of the company.

    Part III of this book is all about the balance sheet, but for now here are the basics about each balance sheet component:

    - *Assets:* Resources owned by a company, such as cash, equipment and buildings.

    - *Liabilities:* Debt the business incurs for operating and expansion purposes.

    - *Equity:* The amount of ownership left in the business after deducting total liabilities from total assets.

- **Statement of cash flows:** This statement contains certain components of both the income statement and the balance sheet. The purpose of the statement of cash flows is to show cash sources and uses during a specific period of time – in other words, how a company brings in cash and for what costs the cash goes back out the door.

✔ **Statement of changes in equity:** This statement shows any movements in the equity accounts of the statement of financial position (balance sheet) – namely: share capital, share premium, revaluation reserve account and retained earnings. So if a company issues additional share capital, the additional capital it has issued during the accounting period will be shown within the statement of changes in equity.

Showing historic performance

The information reflected in the financial statements allows its users to evaluate whether they want to become financially involved with the company. But the financial statement users cannot make informed decisions based solely on one set of financial statements. Here's why:

✔ The income statement is finite in what it reflects. For example, it may report net profit for the 12-month period ending 31 March 2013. This means any accounting transactions taking place prior to or after this 12-month window do not show up in the report.

✔ The statement of cash flows is also finite in nature, showing cash ins and outs only for the reporting period.

✔ The statement of financial position only shows a 'snapshot' of the state of a company's affairs *as at* the close of play on the last working day of the accounting period.

All three financial statements are needed to paint that picture.

Savvy financial statement users know that they need to compare several years' worth of financial statements to get a true sense of business performance. Users employ tools such as ratios and measurements involving financial statement data (a topic I cover in Chapter 14) to evaluate the relative merit of one company over another by analysing each company's historic performance.

Providing results for the annual accounts

After all the rigmarole of preparing the financial statements, *publicly traded companies* (those whose shares are bought and sold in the open market) employ independent professionally-qualified accountants to audit the financial statements for their inclusion in reports to the shareholders. The main thrust of a company's annual report is not only to provide financial reporting but also to promote the company and satisfy any regulatory requirements.

The preparation of an annual report is a fairly detailed subject and if you're a student accountant, you probably won't be expected to prepare a full annual report for your course but may need to know what goes in one. I provide a more expansive look at annual reports in Chapter 16.

Getting to Know the Users of Financial Statements

Well, who are these inquisitive financial statement users I've been referring to so far in this chapter? If you've ever purchased some shares in a company or invested money in a retirement plan, you are one of these users. In this section, I explain why certain groups of people and businesses need access to reliable financial statements.

Identifying the most likely users

Financial statement users fall into three categories:

- ✔ Existing or potential investors in the company's shares or bonds.

- ✔ Individuals or businesses thinking about extending credit terms to the company. Examples of creditors include banks, finance companies and the suppliers from which a company purchases its stock (sometimes called *inventory*) or office supplies.

- ✔ Governmental agencies, such as HM Revenue and Customs, which will want to make sure the company is paying the right amount of corporation tax on its profits.

Recognising their needs

All three categories of financial statement users share a common need: they require assurance that the information they're looking at is both materially correct and useful. *Materially correct* means the financial statements don't contain any serious or substantial misstatements. In order to be useful, the information has to be understandable to anyone not privy to the day-to-day activities of the company.

Investors and creditors, though sitting at different ends of the table, have something else in common: they're looking for a financial return in exchange for allowing the business to use their cash. Governmental agencies, on the other hand, don't have a profit motive for reviewing the financial statements; they just want to make sure the company is abiding by tax legislation, regulations or generally accepted accounting practice.

Providing information for decision making

The onus is on financial accountants to make sure a company's financial statements are materially correct. Important life decisions may hang in the balance based on an individual investing in shares in one company rather than another. Don't believe me? Talk to any individual close to retirement age who lost his whole nest egg in the Enron debacle.

Two of the three groups of financial statement users are making decisions based on those statements: investors and creditors. Creditors look to the financial statements to make sure a potential debtor has the cash flow and potential future earnings to pay back both principal (sometimes called *capital*) and interest according to the terms of the loan.

Investors fall into two groups:

- ✔ **Those looking for growth:** These investors want the value of their shares in a company to increase over time. Here's an example of growth at work: you do some research on a fairly unknown company that's poised to introduce a ground-breaking new computer into the market. You have £1,000 sitting in a bank account that pays no interest. You believe, based on your research, that if you purchase some shares in this company now, you'll be able to sell the shares for £2,000 shortly after the company releases the new computer.

- ✔ **Those looking for income:** These investors are satisfied with a steady share price that weathers ebbs and flows in the market. The share price neither increases nor decreases in value per share by an enormous amount, but it pays a consistent, reasonable dividend. (Keep in mind that reasonableness varies for each person and her investment income goals.)

Remember that two ways to make money exist: the active way (you work to earn money) and the passive way (you invest money to make more money). Passive is better, no? The wise use of investing allows individuals to make housing choices, maybe educate their children, and make provision for their retirement. And wise investment decisions can be made only when potential investors have materially correct financial statements for the businesses in which they're considering investing.

Understanding the Key Characteristics of Financial Accounting Information

Now that you understand who uses financial accounting information, I want to discuss the substantive characteristics of that information. If financial accountants don't make sure that financial statement information has these characteristics, the financial statements aren't worth the paper on which they're printed.

The information a company provides must be relevant, reliable, comparable and consistent. In this section, I define what each characteristic means.

Relevance

Relevance is a hallmark of good evidence; it means the information directly relates to the facts you're trying to evaluate or understand. The inclusion or absence of relevant information has a definite effect on a user's decision-making process.

Relevant information has *predictive value*, which means it helps a user look into the future. By understanding and evaluating the information, the user can form an opinion as to how future company events may pan out. For example, comparing financial results from prior years, which are gleaned from the financial statements, can give investors an idea as to the future value of a company's share price. If assets and revenue are decreasing while liabilities are increasing, that's a pretty good indicator that investing in this company may not be such a good idea.

Relevant information also has *confirmatory value*, which means that new relevant information either confirms or rebuts the user's prior expectations. For example, you review a company's financial statements for 2012, and your analysis indicates that the company's sales should increase two-fold in the subsequent year. When you later check out the 2013 income statement, the company's revenue has, indeed, doubled. Woohoo! With the relevant information in hand, you see that your prediction was right.

Timeliness goes hand in hand with relevance. The best and most accurate information in the world is of no use if it's no longer applicable because so much time has elapsed that facts and circumstances have changed. Look at it this way: if you were in the market to replace your flat-screen TV, and you found out about a killer sale at the local electronics shop the day after the sale ended, this information is utterly useless to you. The same thing is true with financial information.

Independent verification of accounts receivable

Many companies sell goods or services to customers *on account*, which means the customer promises to pay in the future. When this happens, the amount of unpaid customer invoices goes into an account called trade debtors (or *accounts receivable* in international terms). (See Chapters 7 and 10 for detailed information about accounts receivable.) For a business carrying a sizeable amount of accounts receivable, an error in this account can have a material effect on the reliability of the income statement and balance sheet.

Independent confirmation of the accounts receivable balance is done by sending requests for confirmation. *Confirmations* (referred to as *debtors' circularisations*) are letters sent to customers listed in the accounts receivable subsidiary ledger (a listing showing all customers with a balance owed). The letters seek to verify the facts and figures contained in the company's books. The letter is usually brief, listing the total that the company's records show the customer owes at a certain date.

Some confirmation letters ask for a response; others ask the customer to respond only if the information on the confirmation form is incorrect. The company's external auditor then tallies the results of the confirmations and either confirms or refutes the amount the company asserts that its customers owe.

Reliability

Reliability means you can depend on the information to steer you in the right direction. For example, the information must be free from material misstatements (meaning it doesn't contain any serious or substantial mistakes). It also has to be reasonably free from bias, which means the information is neutral and not slanted to produce a rosier picture of how well the company is doing.

Here's an example of how a company would create biased financial statements. Say that a company has a pending lawsuit that it thinks will probably damage its reputation (and, therefore, its future performance). In the financial statements, the company doesn't include a disclosure note that mentions the lawsuit. The company is not being neutral in this situation; it's deliberately painting a rosier picture than is actually the case. (See Chapter 15 for my explanation of the purpose of financial statement notes.)

Reliable information must be neutral, have representational faithfulness, be free from material error, be complete and be prudent. Here's what I mean:

- ✔ A hallmark of *neutrality* is that information must be free from deliberate or systematic bias. Financial information will not be neutral if it's been selected or presented in such a way as to influence the users' decision-making process.

- ✔ *Representational faithfulness* means that if the company says it has sales of £200,000 in the first quarter of 2012, it actually has sales of £200,000 – not any other amount.

✔ *Free from material error and complete* means that the financial statements aren't significantly incorrect. Financial information that's been omitted (for reasons other than materiality) or contains a material error will mean the financial statements are misleading. For example, under-stating liabilities by £50,000 will more than likely be material in a smaller company, but under-stating liabilities by £5 probably won't influence the users' decision-making process because £5 will be immaterial (not significant).

✔ *Prudence* in UK GAAP (but not seen in the world of IFRSs) recognises that uncertainty will often surround many events and circumstances that are reported in the financial statements and uncertainty is dealt with by exercising care.

Comparability

Comparability means the quality of the information is such that users can identify differences and similarities among companies they're evaluating – or among different financial periods for the same company. For example, users need to know what particular GAAP the different companies they're examining are using to depreciate their assets. Without this knowledge, the users cannot accurately evaluate the relative worth of one company over another.

Seeing how depreciation affects the bottom line

Depreciation is the process of systematically reclassifying the cost of an asset from the balance sheet to the income statement over its useful life – a topic I discuss at length in Chapter 12. A few different methods of depreciation are allowed by GAAP, so unless you know which method the company is using, you can't effectively compare one company to another.

Consider an example. For the same asset, here is the amount of depreciation a company can charge for the asset's first year of use depending on which commonly used depreciation method it employs:

✔ Straight-line depreciation: £54,000

✔ Reducing balance method: £120,000

The difference between the two methods is a whopping £66,000 (£120,000 – £54,000)! Now imagine depreciating equipment that costs millions of pounds; the effect on the company's bottom line net profit of choosing one depreciation method versus another would be even more astonishing.

Luckily for the financial statement users, to aid in comparability, the depreciation method in use by a company must be disclosed in the notes to the financial statements. For much more info about depreciation, jump to Chapter 12. For the lowdown on what financial statement notes are, head to Chapter 15.

Consider a personal example: think about the last time you purchased a laptop. To the novice computer buyer, the shiny black cases and coloured displays all look pretty much the same. But the price of each model varies – sometimes substantially. Therefore, you have to dig out the facts about each model to be able to compare models and decide on the best one for your needs. What do you do? You check out the manufacturer's specs for each laptop in your price range, comparing such important facts as the size of the hard drive, processing speed and (if you want to be truly mobile) the laptop's size and weight. By doing so, you're able to look beyond outward appearance and make a purchasing decision based on comparative worth among your options.

Consistency

Consistency is a subset of comparability. It means the company uses the same accounting treatment for the same type of accounting transactions – both within a certain financial period and among various financial periods. Doing so allows the user to know that the financial accountant is not doing the accounting equivalent of comparing a dog to a cat. Both are animals, both are furry, but as any pet owner knows, you have a basic lack of consistency between the two.

Keep in mind that a company *is* allowed to switch accounting methods if it has a valid reason for doing so; the company isn't stuck with using only one method throughout its existence. An example of a good reason for a switch in methods is if using a different accounting method presents a more accurate financial picture. But a change in methods can't be done willy-nilly whenever the business feels like it. I provide a complete picture on changes in accounting policies and estimates in Chapter 20. Also, the company has to disclose such changes in its notes to the financial statements; see Chapter 15.

Consistency is crucial when it comes to depreciation. If the company lacks consistency – for example, it uses different depreciation methods when accounting for the same asset in different years – you cannot create truly useful financial statements.

Understandability

UK GAAP recognises that it isn't always possible to present a piece of relevant, reliable and comparable information in a way that a user can fully understand. Now that doesn't mean that if a piece of information is complex it can be left out – because it most certainly can't! Something that is material and left out because users won't be able to understand it will result in the financial statements being misleading. Therefore, UK GAAP requires information that's relevant and reliable to be included in the financial statements and not to be excluded just because it's too difficult for some users to understand.

Setting out qualitative characteristics under the IASB's Conceptual Framework

Financial statements prepared to IFRS GAAP have the same characteristics as those described above, but are set out in different ways under the *Conceptual Framework for Financial Reporting* of the International Accounting Standards Board (IASB). These characteristics are split into two bits:

- ✔ **Fundamental qualitative characteristics:** Financial information is:

  - **Relevant:** The information is capable of making a difference in the decisions made by users.

  - **Faithful in its presentation:** The information is complete, neutral and free from error.

- ✔ **Enhancing qualitative characteristics:** Financial information is enhanced when it's comparable, verifiable, timely and understandable.

The *Conceptual Framework* also includes materiality as a sub-section of relevance. Don't forget that an item is *material* if its omission or misstatement may cause the user of the financial statements to arrive at the wrong conclusion.

Understanding the Limitations of Financial Accounting

While preparing financial statements, accountants realise that time is money and a limit exists to the amount of cost that should be incurred for any reporting benefit. The bodies that set the standards for accountancy practices (which I introduce in Chapter 4) always perform a cost–benefit analysis before finalising any reporting requirements. Associated with this financial accounting limitation is the concept of materiality.

Materiality is the importance you place on an area of financial reporting based upon its overall significance. What is material for one business may not be material for another. You have to consider the size of the company, the size of the financial statement transaction, the particular circumstances in which the transaction occurred and any other factors that can help you judge whether the issue is truly significant to the financial statement users.

Cost–benefit lost in the woods

It's not unheard of for some bookkeepers to spend hours tracking down the reason why the company bank reconciliation has a difference of £2.00 to make sure the bank hasn't made a mistake. (Preparing a *bank reconciliation* means you take the balance in the bank account per the bank as at a certain date, add in any deposits that got to the bank too late to hit the statement, and subtract any cheques the company has written that have not yet cleared.)

Now, is this an effective and efficient use of the bookkeeper's time and salary expense? No, of course not. Let's say she was paid £10 per hour. It cost the company £50 for her to confirm that the bank account balance was indeed out by £2, and it wasn't just a mistake on the part of the bank.

For example, an expense totalling £10,000 would be material if the total expense amount is £50,000 but would likely be immaterial if the total expense was £500,000. But the nature of the transaction may make the difference material even if the comparative size is immaterial. For example, £10,000 that's deliberately – not accidentally – excluded from income may be material even if the amount is a small percentage of overall income. That's because the deliberate exclusion may be an attempt by the owner of the company to avoid paying tax on the income.

Conservatism is very important in financial accounting. It means that when in doubt, the financial accountant should choose the financial accounting treatment that will cause the least effect on revenue or expenses.

Considering Your Ethical Responsibilities

Every professional – and, frankly, every individual – should operate using a code of conduct. This means you should always attempt to act in an ethical manner and do the right thing, regardless of whether doing the right thing is the best choice for you personally.

In this section, I give you the nuts and bolts of the code of conduct that financial accountants must follow. Plus, you find out about the goals toward which financial accountants strive: integrity, objectivity and independence.

Following the accountant's code of conduct

When you're looking into becoming a financial accountant you'll see lots of different options available (I discuss some of these options in Chapter 2). Financial accountants who are serious about their profession normally become *chartered* or *chartered certified accountants* with the various professional bodies, which means they have to take several accountancy, audit and tax exams and have a certain number of years' practical work experience under their belts in order to become fully-fledged members of a professional body such as the Institute of Chartered Accountants in England and Wales (ICAEW), the Association of Chartered Certified Accountants (ACCA) or the Chartered Institute of Management Accountants (CIMA), to name just a few.

All professionally-qualified accountants at any level have to abide by their country's code of conduct and also follow the code of conduct established by their respective professional body. The Financial Reporting Council's Accounting Council is responsible for establishing accounting and auditing standards for companies in the UK that report under UK GAAP, and professional bodies are responsible for enforcing a code of professional conduct for their members. The International Accounting Standards Board (IASB) is responsible for establishing the International Financial Reporting Standards (IFRSs). In Chapter 4, I outline the code of conduct in detail.

But what if you're a financial accountant who isn't a member of a professional body? Do you still have to worry about abiding by a code of conduct? Of course you do! Any profession lacking ethical behaviour descends into chaos. Financial accountants must have high professional standards, a strict code of professional ethics and a commitment to serving the public interest. They achieve these goals through their integrity, objectivity and independence.

Having integrity

In the world of financial accounting, *integrity* means you act according to a code or standard of values. You demonstrate integrity when you do the right thing, regardless of whether doing so is best for you personally.

Specifically, having integrity means that you serve, to the best of your ability, your employer and/or the client for whom you're preparing financial statements, keeping in mind that doing so may not be the same thing as completely agreeing with the way the employer or client wants you to prepare the financial statements. You can't be worried that your employer or client is going to be mad at you or fire you if you disagree with him.

Maintaining objectivity

Whether you work in public practice (you have multiple clients) or for a company (you provide accountancy services only for your employer), you must be *objective*, meaning impartial and intellectually honest:

- Being impartial means you're neutral and unbiased in all decision-making processes. You base your opinion and reporting only on the facts, not on any preconceived notions or prejudices.
- Being intellectually honest means you interpret rules and policies in a truthful and sincere manner, staying true to both their form and spirit.

If you're objective, you keep an open mind until all facts are revealed, despite what you hear from your client's managers, employees or anyone else privy to the work you're doing.

Financial accountants must be objective, and the users of the financial statements must perceive that the accountants are objective. You never want to compromise your objectivity because doing so means you risk creating the perception that your work – and the financial statements that result from your work – cannot be trusted.

Achieving independence and objectivity

Many types of accountancy services, such as auditing, require the financial accountant to be independent in both mind and appearance. Being *independent* while providing services means that you have no special relationship with, or financial interest in, the client that would cause you to disregard evidence and facts when evaluating your client.

What does it mean to be independent in both mind and appearance? The biggie is that you avoid any real or perceived conflicts of interest: you don't perform services for any client with whom you have either a personal or non-audit-related business relationship. For example, if you have a significant financial interest in a major competitor of your client, your client may question whose best interests you have in mind while performing the services.

Financial accountants providing tax and consultancy services don't necessarily have to be independent; however, they still have to be objective.

The concepts of independence and objectivity differ somewhat depending on whether you work in public practice or for a company. *Public practice* is when a financial accountant, most likely an accounting technician, chartered or chartered certified accountant, works for an accountancy firm providing services such as auditing or financial statement preparation for clients. *Working for a company* is when you do accountancy work for your own employer rather than for a client. Obviously, you can't strive for independence when you're doing accountancy work for your own employer. So when you're working for a company, objectivity is key.

Making sure that you're professionally competent and take due care

To work for a client, or a company, you have to ensure that you're competent to do the work, are up-to-date with technical developments (such as accounting standard changes or changes in tax laws) and act in accordance with applicable technical and professional standards.

Keeping information confidential

During the course of her work, a financial accountant must ensure she keeps all information she acquires confidential and does not disclose it to third parties without express authority from either the client or a responsible individual within the company. A financial accountant must never disclose confidential information for personal advantage.

Behaving professionally

A financial accountant must make sure that she behaves in a professional manner at all times and does not undertake any action that discredits the accountancy profession.

Introducing the Conceptual Framework of Financial Accounting

Every profession needs a roadmap to help the people employed in the field provide the best possible service while doing their jobs. For example, an airline pilot has a detailed checklist he must follow each and every time he gets in the cockpit, regardless of how many years of experience he has.

For financial accountants, the UK's Accounting Standards Board (now the Financial Reporting Council's Accounting Council) started work on providing the *Statement of Principles* – a structure of financial accounting concepts – back in the 1970s. The Statement of Principles covers the financial accounting topics of objectives, characteristics, elements and financial statement recognition and measurement. Not sure what each of these terms means? I discuss this topic in detail in Chapter 6. For now, just remember that this financial accounting conceptual framework exists – or jump to Chapter 6 right now to read all about it!

The International Accounting Standards Board (IASB) has an international equivalent to the UK's Statement of Principles: the *Conceptual Framework for Financial Reporting*. You can check out this document at `www.iasb.org.uk`; click on 'Standards and Interpretations' and then scroll down until you see the word 'Framework'. You may have to register to view the Conceptual Framework, but to do so is free!

Chapter 2

Making a Career in Financial Accounting

*T*his chapter gives you the lowdown on the making of a financial accountant. If you're wondering about the types of college courses you might take in addition to a degree in accountancy, you've come to the right place! I outline the various business and nonbusiness courses you can expect to take to achieve a degree in accountancy and other courses that offer a springboard into the world of financial accounting.

Also, I describe the many different career paths a financial accountant can follow, from being self-employed to working for a large accountancy firm to working for nonbusiness entities such as charitable organisations.

In this chapter, you find out how much you can expect to earn as a financial accountant fresh out of college. You also get some perspective on the changing nature of business and the effect of that change on financial accounting.

The Making of a Financial Accountant

Personally, I believe that if you have an interest in the world of business, being a financial accountant is a pretty good gig. A plethora of career options is open to you, whether you dream of setting up your own business or see yourself working for a larger business, and whether your dream job is part-time or full-time.

Before you consider your employment possibilities, I want to walk through the education and licensing requirements for financial accountants so you know what to expect if you pursue this career path.

Getting educated

Some students interested in financial accounting attend a university, receiving a degree in accounting. Keeping in mind that each college or university has different accounting degree requirements, here's an example of the courses often required for a degree in accounting:

- **General education core requirements:** You'll generally need basic subjects under your belt such as maths and English. Degree courses will often require additional qualifications, such as A-levels with minimum grades.

- **Business subjects:** These courses generally apply to all business subjects, regardless of specific degree:

  - *Financial Accounting:* Focuses on the preparation of financial statements – the topic of this book!

  - *Management Accounting:* Approaches accounting from the business management angle and focuses on how accounting is used for internal reporting and decision making.

  - *Business Law and Ethics:* Covers the routine legal problems encountered in the business environment, such as contracts and employment law. The ethics section covers how all accountants should behave and how to handle varying degrees of threat to things like independence and objectivity.

  - *Principles of Management:* Introduces the basic processes and concepts of business management, such as planning, leading, controlling and organising business processes.

  - *Economics:* Introduces supply and demand and marketplace forces and how they affect business and individual decision-making.

  - *Finance:* Provides an introduction to the sources of business and financial market information, including the time value of money, the nature and measurement of risk, financial institutions, investments and corporate finance, and financial statement analysis.

  - *Marketing:* Introduces the planning and implementation of business activities designed to bring a buyer and seller together.

✔ **Accountancy subjects:** Here's a typical list and brief descriptions of the required accountancy subjects you may encounter. Once again, keep in mind that requirements may vary from college to college and university to university:

- *Intermediate Accounting:* More in-depth accountancy courses than the Financial Accounting or Management Accounting courses. Accounting theory is taught, along with the development of generally accepted accounting practice (GAAP, which I discuss in Chapter 4).

- *Taxation:* Covers both business and individual taxation. Topics include corporation tax, personal tax, inheritance tax, capital gains tax and value added tax (VAT).

- *Accountancy Information Systems:* Looks at how accounting data is managed from the point of view of how a typical company's financial organisation is handled.

- *Auditing:* Studies the process involved in auditing both a for-profit and not-for-profit entity, including the planning, internal control review, evidence gathering and procedures to audit the financial statements. Also covered are professional standards, ethics and liabilities of chartered/chartered certified accountants.

Depending on the university you attend, a bachelor's degree with a concentration in accounting can either be a Bachelor of Science or a Bachelor of Arts.

Aiming for chartered or chartered certified status

Many students often wonder what their next educational step after undergraduate graduation could potentially be. You can get a job in financial accounting with a bachelor's degree. But to stand out from the crowd, I recommend studying for one of the chartered qualifications (such as those offered by the Association of Chartered Certified Accountants (ACCA), Chartered Institute of Management Accountants (CIMA), Chartered Institute of Public Finance and Accountancy (CIPFA), Institute of Chartered Accountants in England and Wales (ICAEW) and such like).

Another popular qualification is that offered by the Association of Accounting Technicians (AAT). The AAT is a professional qualification within its own right and is very flexible to study for. As an added bonus, even if you don't go on to chartered qualifications after qualifying with the AAT, you still have a respected qualification under your belt.

TIP

Piggybacking your degree and chartered courses

Passing a chartered qualification course is the Holy Grail for financial accountants, so if you plan to work in *public practice*, which means doing accounting or auditing work for businesses that don't directly employ you, I think earning your degree and becoming a chartered or chartered certified accountant is a good move. The chartered qualifications require you to pass a set number of examinations (you may get exemptions depending on the degree courses you've already done and the relevance of those courses to the specific chartered qualification you're planning to study). Some qualifications, such as ACCA, also require both the completion of an ethics module and a minimum number of months' work experience in order to qualify with their professional body. The ICAEW, on the other hand, prefers to integrate ethics throughout its syllabus.

You could add in that ICAEW prefers to integrate ethics throughout the syllabus CF. Done and changed. SC. Certain qualifications, such as the ICAEW, require students to have a training contract in place with an employer before being able to qualify. Many of the large accountancy practices have a set number of places to offer to graduates; they put them through chartered or chartered certified qualifications whilst simultaneously allowing them to gain valuable work experience that will then enable them to qualify with the relevant accountancy body.

In relation to qualifications, a familiar pattern is that students leave school or college with GCSEs or A-levels, and then pursue the AAT qualification. Why do this and not just go straight on to chartered qualifications, I hear you ask? Well, the AAT is a fantastic springboard onto the chartered qualifications because it starts with the very basic fundamentals and you work your way through the qualification gaining valuable study experience at accounting technician level before going on to the higher advanced chartered courses. In my experience (having completed both the AAT and ACCA myself), I find that students tend to handle the chartered qualifications better having been through the AAT mill.

Looking at some alternative qualifications

In addition to the chartered qualifications, you may want to earn other professional qualifications that can improve your professional reputation as well as provide opportunities for advancement:

- **Certificate in international auditing:** Some of the professional bodies now offer the certificate in international standards on auditing (ISAs). Some of these qualifications can be studied for online and at your leisure. The course itself is designed to test your ability to apply the ISAs to given situations and requires a high degree of technical knowledge.

So, if you're an auditor who conducts audits according to the ISA process, this type of additional qualification might be for you.

✓ **Diploma in IFRS:** Some of the respected professional bodies also offer a diploma in International Financial Reporting Standards (IFRSs). These sorts of courses can be undertaken for two reasons: first, an accountant may want to add an additional qualification such as the diploma in IFRSs to her existing qualifications and be able to handle preparing financial statements to IFRSs; second, a professional accountant may have studied financial reporting under national standards (such as UK GAAP), and wish to gain technical knowledge in IFRSs because of their increasing worldwide use.

✓ **Association of Tax Technicians:** As you progress through your accountancy studies, you'll probably find that you become specialised in certain areas. For example, I specialise in accounting, financial reporting and auditing. However, some accountants decide they love tax and so go on to study for the Association of Tax Technicians (ATT) course. This course is purely focused on taxation and offers a good springboard onto more advanced taxation studies (see below). The ATT has a very good reputation and many students also find that studying for these exams is a brilliant way of gaining continuing professional development (CPD) credits, so you can get the best of both worlds (bonus!).

✓ **Chartered Institute of Taxation:** Whilst we're on the theme of taxation, the Chartered Institute of Taxation (CIOT) is the major taxation body in the UK and is very influential in the taxation profession. Many of its members come from a practice background and have studied for chartered or chartered certified qualifications before embarking on their CIOT qualification. This qualification is very prestigious in the tax profession, so if tax floats your boat, this qualification may be for you.

Keeping up to date with changes in IFRSs

Once you qualify as an accountant, the story doesn't end there! Accounting standards change quite frequently (especially IFRSs), so keeping up to date with changes is important. All of the professional accountancy bodies make it mandatory for the professional accountant to undertake regular *continuing professional development* (CPD). Fortunately, this need not be arduous or boring. Professional bodies tend to leave how to keep abreast of changes in things like IFRSs or UK GAAP up to you and you can do so in a number of ways, such as reading technical articles, attending seminars, doing research and even looking at websites such as my own at www.stevecollings.co.uk or www.accountingweb.co.uk.

Do you have what it takes?

Are you wondering whether financial accounting would be a good fit for you? Good accountants tend to have the following characteristics and personality traits, which are vital to enjoying the job:

✔ **The desire to work independently:** You must be able to work independently to succeed as a financial accountant. Even auditors who work in teams divide the tasks up and work independently on different pieces of the accountancy jigsaw, bringing everything together at the end.

✔ **A love for research, detail and logic:** Accountants do a tremendous amount of research and use this research to make decisions. Attention to detail is very important. Accountancy also uses a lot of what I refer to as *circular logic*: 'If this is true, then do that' but 'If that is true, do this'. Accountants need to be logical thinkers to work their way through tax legislation and accounting standards.

✔ **Great communication skills:** As a financial accountant, you must explain your decisions and results to other employees, clients and outside users. Communication skills, both oral and written, are very important. The people with whom you communicate will have different backgrounds, and many of them may have zero knowledge of accountancy, so you need to be able to explain your work clearly.

✔ **Decent computer skills:** Reasonable computer software skills and the ability to learn software programs are also a must. The good news is that, after you understand one accountancy software package, picking up how other accountancy software works is usually quite easy. Some employers use *bespoke* software (which is written for their own exclusive use), so specific training is required. Even if they don't use bespoke software, most employers realise that new employees need to be trained to use the company's preferred off-the-shelf software package (*off-the-shelf* means you buy it from a shop rather than have an accountancy software package tailored to your specific needs).

✔ **The willingness to listen and learn:** The ability to *learn* is crucial. Here's what I mean: if you're doing the accounts for a skiing shop, you don't need to be up to speed on every aspect of running the business – you don't even need to be able to ski! But to do a professional, competent job, you must know basic industry facts (for example, having a bit of knowledge on the average markup on a pair of skis and ski jackets). Without the basic knowledge of the way a company does its business, you won't know if your facts and figures make sense.

The key is to make sure that your CPD is relevant to your day-to-day working life and that you can apply what you've learnt to your working life as well. You must record your CPD activities so that you can demonstrate what you've actually learnt to the relevant professional body at the end of each year.

Considering Your Employment Opportunities

As an educated financial accountant with at least a couple of years' experience under your belt, your career options are pretty wide-ranging. Over the years, I've been everything from a bookkeeper to an accountancy author. I've worked in various companies such as a plant hire company and a security company. I now work as the technical partner at an accountancy firm in Manchester as well as write books and lecture to fellow professionals. One thing I can say about being a financial accountant is that it's never boring!

Working for a practice or setting up in practice

Many accountants start their career working in practice and then moving on to another branch of the accountancy tree, such as working for a company as, say, a financial controller or director. I was different in that respect: I started off working for different companies and then eventually found my niche in practice. Many accountants bite the bullet and set up their own accountancy practice, but doing so takes guts and sheer determination. Many of those who do set up on their own do succeed, however. To quote Audrey Hepburn: 'Nothing is impossible, the word itself says I'm possible.'

But not everyone seeks the flexibility of self-employment. If you want the challenge of working for many clients (which is the nature of public practice) but desire the stability of working for an employer, you may prefer to focus on jobs at an accountancy firm. These firms range in size from the Big Four (KPMG, Ernst & Young, PricewaterhouseCoopers and Deloitte) to regional accountancy firms, such as Grant Thornton and a plethora of others.

Here are a few examples of the work you can do as an accountant in practice:

- **Financial statement preparation:** Many small and medium-sized businesses require help preparing their financial statements. An accountant is contracted to do a *compilation*, which consists of using client source documents (such as bank statements, cleared cheques and invoices) to show revenue, expenses, costs, gains and losses on the income statement (profit and loss account), balance sheet and statement of cash flows (cash flow statement).

  Most financial accountants who prepare financial statements also do the year-end tax returns for the same companies. Being a chartered or a chartered certified accountant is not a requirement to prepare compilations. However, good people skills and patience are required. (In my experience, compilation work requires quite a bit of client handholding.)

✔ **Forensic accounting:** The word *forensic* means that this type of accounting relates to legal proceedings or testimony. The forensic accountant may be hired by a company that plans to pursue fraud charges against an employee, a lawyer in a divorce case who suspects a spouse is hiding assets or anyone else involved in litigation. The accountant gathers facts, considers the circumstances and applies relevant legislation to come to an opinion about what a business or individual has done. Then, he may be asked to stand as an expert witness in court during the legal proceedings.

✔ **Assurance services:** You must be an accountant qualified with one of the Consultative Committee of Accountancy Bodies (CCAB; such as ICAEW, ACCA, CIPFA, ICAS and Chartered Accountants Ireland) to work in this field, which includes all types of auditing services. For example, all business owners and managers want to know how well their businesses are doing. That's where you come in. Because you're an outsider, you can take a step back and cast a fresh, independent eye on the way a company is doing business. You can give company management a firm foundation upon which to base any needed changes.

A subset of assurance is *attestation* services, meaning the accountant issues written documents expressing his conclusion about the reliability of a written assertion that's the responsibility of another party. The number of topics you may focus on during an attestation engagement is pretty much limitless. For example, you may conduct a *breakeven point analysis*, which requires figuring out how much revenue the client has to bring in to cover expenses.

Practice accountants also conduct audits, which means they gather and judge evidence to issue an opinion on the truth and fairness of a company's financial statements. This means they have to assess the effectiveness of a company's *internal controls*: policies and procedures set in place to provide guidelines on how employees should do their jobs.

Working for a company

Not every accountant has multiple business clients. Someone who does accounts work for a single company is called a *private* or *industry accountant*. Quite a few private/industry accountancy jobs are available. Depending on the size of the business, the job can be tailored to a specific task or cover the whole thing from start to finish – from recording accounting transactions to preparing financial statements.

Here are a few examples of the types of private accounting jobs available to financial accountants. Being a fully-qualified accountant may not be a requirement but can certainly be helpful:

✔ **Financial director:** A *financial director* is the chief accounting officer of a business entity and is responsible for both financial and managerial accounting functions. In a small business, a financial director may carry out every function from bookkeeping to preparing the financial statements.

In a larger company, the financial director oversees all other accounting departments and is responsible for reporting the results of financial operations to the managers of the company and to the board of directors. A professional accountancy qualification isn't necessary for this role, nor is an upper-level degree in accounting, but both are certainly assets for people in this position.

✔ **Departmental accountant:** In this position, you can handle a variety of financial accounting tasks; you could handle purchase ledger or credit control, account for company assets or handle stock exchange issues. Departmental accountants also take care of cash payments and receipts.

This position can be managerial because this person is responsible for such tasks as the monthly completion of the financial statements and consolidation of domestic and international subsidiaries, co-ordination and support of annual and interim audits, and tax compliance. Departmental accountants interact frequently with senior management and play a critical supporting role in business processes, customer quotes and proposals, and management analyses pertaining to the effectiveness and efficiency of business operations.

✔ **Bookkeeper:** A bookkeeper is a para-professional who works in accountancy. No specific education, experience or licensing is required for this designation. Many bookkeepers learn accountancy by doing; they start at a business in the purchase or sales ledger department and then fill in the gaps in their accounting knowledge by perhaps doing a bookkeeping or accountancy course at college.

Bookkeepers record the daily transactions in the accounting cycle, and they carry out routine tasks and calculations such as paying bills and bank statement reconciliation. In small businesses, the bookkeeper also may double as the receptionist and secretary. Depending on their knowledge base, bookkeepers can sometimes prepare the initial financial statements, which are then reviewed and adjusted by an independent accountant hired by the business.

Working in public finance

Not-for-profit organisations are those lacking a profit motive. Your two biggies are not-for-profit agencies and governmental agencies. Here is a quick look at the accountancy work in each:

✔ **Not-for-profit accountants** work for organisations that are run for the public benefit – not because of any profit motive. In fact, not-for-profit organisations render goods and services to the community regardless of whether the costs they incur to provide the goods or services will ever be recouped from the recipients. These types of organisations include some schools, religious organisations and charities.

✔ **Public sector accountants** work for regional and central government. Their job is similar to that of the not-for-profit accountant in that no profit motive exists. The motive comes from providing services to a community, city or nation or working for public organisations such as a hospital or schools. Public sector accountants prepare financial statements that are open to the general public. The financial statements must show accountability to citizens while pursuing the goals of efficiency and effectiveness.

Another good financial accounting job is working on government audits for your local or central government. Consider HM Revenue and Customs (HMRC).

HMRC inspectors examine business and individual tax returns to assure compliance with tax legislation. HMRC also employs technical accountants whose job is to check that a company, partnership or individual has correctly applied accounting standards and the requirements of the Companies Act 2006. Technical accountants work alongside tax inspectors and may flag up instances of non-compliance with UK GAAP or company law.

Looking at the Future of Financial Accounting

The world of accountancy has dominated the headlines during the recent recession and the dubious accounting treatments that took place at various banking institutions. Demand for highly skilled accountants is still high, but competition is stiff; 50 people applying for one accountancy vacancy in practice isn't uncommon. To be successful in your application, you need to stand out from the crowd; you've got to be prepared for hard work and be dedicated. While accountants can earn mega bucks, that comes at a price: the price tag is the amount of graft that you have to put in to be a successful accountant. Don't be under any illusions that as soon as you make partner or become a financial director life is a bed of roses – the decisions you make (or don't make) could end the company's or the firm's life!

Wondering about the money? Many qualified accountants can earn in excess of £100,000; some a lot less. Because the job market is saturated with high level accountants seeking alternative employment, salary levels have fallen considerably over the last five years. Trainee accountants in practice can earn around £10,000 to £15,000 depending on the job involved. Practice trainees tend to earn less than their industry counterparts because of the costs incurred by the company in putting a trainee through their training. Equity partners in an accountancy practice tend to earn their salaries and then take a share of the profit made by the practice at the end of the year; if the practice has a good year, their earnings can thus be significant. Many recruitment agencies publish average salary expectations across the UK, so if you're unsure of how much a trainee or a qualified accountant can expect in your area, check out one of the main recruitment agency's salary guides to give you an indication. If the pay sounds good to you, keep reading. Next I explain how changes in the accounting profession and the business world in general will affect the work you do in the future.

Examining the evolution of financial accounting

In addition to the shift in student career paths, new business start-ups are on the rise as a result of redundancies in the corporate world. Gone are the days when you'd be assured of a job for life with a large company. The small business has now become the backbone of our economy. Small businesses need financial accountants to help with business start-up, financial statement preparation, budgeting and tax return preparation.

Additionally, accounting scandals in the past decade have resulted in a change in financial laws and regulations. Enhanced regulation has increased the demand for financial accountants and auditors. For more information about this topic, see Chapter 4. And as I discuss earlier in this chapter, financial misbehaviours have also opened up new, interesting accounting specialities such as forensic accounting. (See Chapter 21 for a quick rundown of ten common financial shenanigans.)

Factoring in the changing nature of business

The circumstances under which businesses operate have changed dramatically in the last couple of decades. The combination of the introduction of e-commerce in the late 1990s and technological advances that allow businesses to connect electronically with one another and with their customers has changed the way companies and individuals do business. The increasing number of e-commerce business start-ups has boosted the need for financial accountants who can audit *through the computer* (tracing transactions from their original input into a computer system to their eventual destination).

Associated with this need is the demand for accountants who understand how to account for e-business income and expenses.

I have good news for computer geeks who are also interested in accountancy! In the past, businesses produced paper trails that auditors, investors and other interested parties could follow to discover various information when examining the financial statements. But these days, those trails are increasingly electronic. Electronic data can be manipulated when a company's internal controls are lacking, and the info is more difficult to track down than a piece of paper in a filing cabinet. So financial accountants who are savvy in computer forensics are – and will continue to be – in high demand. An example of computer forensics is knowing how to retrieve password-protected data from a CD or memory stick.

Thanks to technological advances, more small businesses are doing business globally. Thus, financial accountants and auditors with knowledge of International Financial Reporting Standards (IFRSs) and of standards on ethics and auditing used by other countries are in great demand. As the number of multinational companies increases, interest is also growing in IFRSs that use principles-based accounting for transactions such as working out the fair value of assets and liabilities.

Of course, no one has a crystal ball. But how the world of accountancy operates today indicates that, if you're interested in making a career in financial accounting, you should have great employment prospects – especially if you keep your technology skills up to date.

Chapter 3

Introducing the Primary Financial Statements

*T*his chapter provides a brief overview of the three key financial statements: the balance sheet (known internationally as the *statement of financial position*), income statement/statement of profit or loss (sometimes called the *profit and loss account*) and statement of cash flows (often coined the *cash flow statement*). (Later in the book, I go into much more detail about each one.) If you're going to be an accountant, you have to get to know financial statements inside out. To get you moving in the right direction, I show you the purpose of each financial statement and which accounts show up on each one. I also give you an overview of how accounts on one financial statement interact with accounts on another.

You find out about the three balance sheet components: assets (things a company owns), liabilities (stuff a company owes) and equity (the bit that's left over that belongs to shareholders). I also discuss the various sections on the income statement, including the difference between revenue from the company's operations (sometimes known as 'sales' or 'turnover') and other gains and losses that a company may incur over its lifetime. You learn why a statement of cash flows is so crucially important to users of financial statements that are prepared using the accruals method of accounting (accounting for things as and when they arise rather than when they are paid or received). And finally, I introduce the three sections of the statement of cash flows – operating, investing and financing – and explain what types of information you record in each. You'll also get to see how the statement of cash flows differs significantly in the UK in relation to its international counterpart.

The *official* definitions of assets, liabilities and equity are much more complex that something a company owns or owes – I'm just giving you an insight as to what they are in the section above. Why not check out *IFRS For Dummies* (Wiley) written by me if you want an insight into the official definitions. Financial statements and financial accounting may never become the love of your life, but if you decide to pursue a career in accountancy, you have to enjoy spending time with them at least a little, because they're crucial in the work you will do.

Understanding How Healthy a Business Actually is

You may have heard accountancy referred to as the 'language of business'. That's because financial statements are the end result of the accounting process, and these written reports are used by many different people and entities (collectively referred to as 'stakeholders') to make their own important investment and business decisions.

As I explain in Chapter 1, *financial accounting* is the process of classifying and recording everything that takes place during the normal course of a company's business. The results of these events are put on the appropriate financial statement and reported to the external users of the financial statements. External users include investors, creditors, banks and regulatory authorities such as HM Revenue and Customs (HMRC) and Companies House.

External users of the financial statements differ from internal users in that the external user is generally less savvy than the internal user. When I say *less savvy*, I'm not referring to this person's educational qualifications; an external user may very well hold a PhD from Oxford University! What I mean is that the external user will often have less knowledge about the company's operations. The external user usually has no idea what's going on within the company because this person isn't privy to the day-to-day operations.

In contrast, the internal users of the financial statements are employees, directors and other forms of management – all the guys and gals who work at the company.

The facts and figures shown in the financial statements give the people and other third parties using them a bird's-eye view of how well the business is performing. For example, by looking at a company's balance sheet, you can see how much money the business owes to trade and other creditors and what resources it has to pay that debt. The income statement shows how much money the company is making, both before and after business expenses are deducted. Finally, the statement of cash flows shows how well the company is generating and spending its cash. A company can bring in a boat-load of dosh, but if it's spending that cash in an unwise manner, or not getting in what it's owed, it's not a healthy business.

This chapter only gives a brief overview of each primary financial statement. While you prepare each statement using the same accounting facts (see Chapter 5), each one presents those facts in a slightly different way. I provide more detailed information about the three financial statements in other sections of this book: flick over to Part III for balance sheet info, Chapter 10 for the lowdown on the income statement and Chapter 11 for a discussion of counting pounds and pence on the statement of cash flows.

Reporting Assets and Liabilities in the Balance Sheet

The balance sheet (or *statement of financial position* as it is known internationally) shows how healthy a business is on the specific date of the balance sheet (the specific date is usually a month-, quarter- or year-end date). Therefore, it reflects the business's financial position at a specific point in time. Most textbooks use the clichéd expression that the balance sheet is a 'snapshot' of the company's financial position at a given point in time. This expression means that when you look at the balance sheet as at 30 June 2013, you know the company's financial position as at that date.

Accountancy is based upon the *double-entry system*: for every action, there must be an equal reaction. In accountancy lingo, these actions and reactions are called *debits* and *credits* (see Chapter 5). The net effect of these actions and reactions is zero, which results in the books balancing.

The proof of this balancing act is shown in the balance sheet when the three balance sheet components perfectly interact with each other. This interaction is called the *fundamental accounting equation* and takes place when

Assets = Liabilities + Equity

When a company reports under International Financial Reporting Standards (IFRSs), the above equation changes slightly to:

Assets = Equity + Liabilities

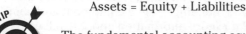

The fundamental accounting equation is also referred to as the *accounting equation* or the *balance sheet equation*.

Not sure what assets, liabilities and equity are? Fear not – you find out about each later in this section. But first, I kick off by explaining the classification of the balance sheet.

Understanding the structure of a balance sheet

A balance sheet groups similar accounts together. For example, all current assets (see Chapter 7) such as cash and trade debtors/receivables show up in one grouping, and all current liabilities (see Chapter 8) such as trade creditors/payables and other short-term debt show up in another grouping. This grouping is done for the ease of the balance sheet user so that it's easy to see how healthy a business is. If this grouping did not take place, the balance sheet would be a complete nightmare to interpret.

Also, people who aren't accounting geeks (poor them!) may not even know which accounts are short term versus *long term* (by 'long term', I mean they fall due after more than one year from the accounting period-/year-end). By classifying accounts on the balance sheets, the financial accountant gives the user information that is easy to use and more comparable.

Studying the balance sheet components

Three sections appear on the balance sheet: assets, liabilities and equity. Standing on their own, they contain valuable information about a company. However, a user has to see all three interacting together on the balance sheet to form a reliable opinion about the company.

Assets

Assets are resources a company owns. Examples of assets are fixed assets (sometimes known as 'non-current' assets), stock/inventory, trade debtors/receivables, prepayments, sundry assets and cash. I discuss each of these assets in detail in other chapters in this book (starting with Chapter 7), but here's a brief description of each to get you started:

- **Fixed assets:** The company's property, plant and equipment are all fixed assets. This category includes assets with anticipated long lives, such as the company-owned car, land, buildings, office equipment and computers. See Chapters 7 and 12 for more information about fixed assets. These sorts of assets are known as *tangible* fixed assets (*tangible* means you can physically touch them). Fixed assets can also be *intangible* (in other words they're invisible) such as computer software and goodwill.

✔ **Stock/inventory:** For a retail business that sells to the general public – like a clothes shop or a supermarket – any goods available for sale are included in its stock (sometimes called 'inventory'). For a *manufacturing* company – a business that makes the items retailers sell – stock also includes the raw materials used to make those items. See Chapters 7 and 13 for more information about inventory.

✔ **Trade debtors/receivables:** This account shows all the money that customers owe to a business for completed sales transactions. For example, Company A sells goods to Company B with the agreement that B pays for the goods within 30 business days. Business A includes the amount of the transaction in its trade debtors figure.

✔ **Prepayments:** *Prepayments* are expenses that the business pays for in advance, such as rent, insurance, annual subscriptions or advances to employees.

✔ **Other debtors/receivables:** Any other resources owned by the company go into this catch-all category. Rent deposits are a good example of other assets. Say the company rents an office building, and as part of the lease it pays a £1,000 deposit to the landlord. That £1,000 deposit appears in the 'Sundry assets' section of the balance sheet until the property owner reimburses the business at the end of the lease.

✔ **Cash:** Cash includes accounts such as the company's bank account, which the business uses to receive customer payments and pay business expenses, as well as the company's cash in hand balance which it uses for petty cash expenses.

Petty cash refers to money the company keeps handy for insignificant daily expenses. For example, the business runs out of milk in the staff canteen and sends an employee to the shop down the road to buy some more.

Liabilities

Liabilities are amounts that a company owes to third parties. For example, money can be owed to an unrelated third party, such as a bank, or to employees for wages earned but not yet paid. Some examples of liabilities are trade creditors/payables, payroll liabilities payable and bank loans. I discuss each of these liabilities in detail in Chapter 8. For now, here's a brief description of each:

✔ **Trade creditors/payables:** This is a current liability (in other words, a liability that will fall due to be paid within 12 months) reflecting the amount of money the company owes to its suppliers. This category is the flip side of trade debtors/receivables because a trade receivable on one company's balance sheet appears as a trade payable on the other company's balance sheet.

✔ **Payroll liabilities:** Most companies *accrue* payroll and related payroll taxes (such as pay as you earn (PAYE) and national insurance contributions (NICs)); the word 'accrue' means a company owes its employees money but has not yet paid them. This process is easy to understand if you think about the way you've been paid by an employer in the past. Most companies will pay their employees in arrears, which means you may have to work, say, a week and then get paid for that week's work in the next week.

In addition to recording unpaid wages in this account, the company also has to add in any PAYE and NICs that will be deducted from the employee's wages.

✔ **Bank loans due within one year:** Bank loans payable that are due in full less than 12 months after the balance sheet date are short term ('short term' also means 'current') – or could be the short-term portion of a long-term bank loan. A good example of this is a *working capital loan*, which is where a bank gives a company a loan with the expectation that the loan will be paid back from the collection of monies from the borrower's trade receivables.

✔ **Long-term bank loans:** If a short-term bank loan has to be paid back within 12 months after the balance sheet date, you've probably guessed that a long-term loan is paid back after that 12-month period! A good example of a long-term loan is a mortgage. *Mortgages* are used to finance the purchase of property (see Chapter 12).

Equity

Equity shows the owners' (the shareholders') total investment in the business. As such, equity shows the difference between assets and liabilities. It's also known as *net assets* or *net worth*. Examples of equity are retained earnings (accumulated profits a company has made over the years) and paid-up share capital (shares in a company that have been paid for by the shareholders). I discuss both equity accounts in detail in Chapter 9. For now, here's a brief description of each:

✔ **Retained earnings:** This account shows the result of income and dividend transactions (dividends are sums of money paid to shareholders out of profits that have been taxed as a return on their investment). For example, the business opens on 1 January 2013 with a 31 December 2013 year-end. In the year to 31 December 2013 it has made a net profit of £50,000 (wow!) but has also paid £10,000 in dividends to shareholders. The retained earnings for the year ended 31 December 2013 are £40,000 (£50,000 – £10,000).

Retained earnings accumulate year after year – hence the word 'retained'. So if in 2014 the same business makes £20,000 and pays no dividends, the retained earnings as at 31 December 2014 are £60,000 (£40,000 + £20,000).

✔ **Paid-up share capital:** This element of equity reflects the shares the company has issued to its shareholders and which the shareholders have paid for (hence the words *paid up*). A company will sell shares at *par value*, which is the face value of the shares; so, for example, if Sue decides to buy 100 £1 shares in Breary's Bricks Limited, she will pay £100 for the shares.

Sometimes, however, it may be that the company wants to raise money by issuing more shares for more than par value. What happens in this situation is that a company will have an increase in its share capital figure, but will also have a 'Share premium' account to take the excess over par value. Let me take you through how this works with an example.

Sue decides to subscribe to £100 worth of £1 shares (£1 is the par value) in Breary's Bricks Limited on 1 January 2013. The balance sheet of Breary's Bricks Limited as at that date will be as follows:

Current Assets
Cash at bank   £100
Equity
Share capital   £100

On 30 June 2013, Breary's Bricks decides it needs to raise finance so it issues a further 100 shares at a value of £1.50 per share. Here you can see that the par value is £1, but the company has issued further shares for £1.50 (in other words, at a price higher than par value). The share capital figure will increase by the par value, but the excess is posted to a 'Share premium' account. So this is the effect on Breary's Bricks' balance sheet following the additional share issue:

Current Assets
Cash at bank (Cash balance of £100 + additional 100 shares × £1.50)   £250
Equity
Share capital (100 shares at £1)   £200
Share premium (100 shares at £0.50)   £50

Seeing an example of a balance sheet

A balance sheet groups together similar accounts so the financial statement user has an easier time reading it. In Chapter 7, I show you a full-blown balance sheet that is structured in accordance with generally accepted accounting practice (GAAP; see Chapter 4). In Figure 3-1, I give you a very abbreviated version of what a balance sheet looks like.

Lucas Lighting Limited
Balance Sheet as at
31st March 2013

	£
Assets	
Property, plant and equipment	175,000
Current assets	14,125
	189,125
Liabilities	
Current liabilities	2,300
Long-term liabilities	90,525
Total liabilities	92,825
Equity	
Paid-up share capital	6,000
Retained earnings	90,300
Total equity	96,300
Total liabilities and equity	189,125

Figure 3-1: An abbreviated balance sheet.

Posting Profit or Loss: The Income Statement/Profit and Loss Account

Next up in your exciting walkthrough of the three financial statements is (drum roll, please) . . . the *income statement* (more commonly known as the 'profit and loss account'), which shows income, expenses, gains and losses. It's also known as a *statement of profit or loss* (or P&L) – mostly among non-accountants, particularly small business owners. As the true financial accountant that you are (or soon will be!), you use the terms *income statement*, *statement of profit or loss* or *profit and loss account* depending on what generally accepted accounting practice (GAAP) you are working with.

Here, I provide only a brief introduction to the income statement. For the complete lowdown on the income statement, the accounts it contains and how to prepare one, have a nosey at Chapter 10.

Studying the income statement components

The income statement shows financial results for the accounting period it represents. It lets the user know how the business is doing in the short term. And please bear in mind that the company's performance is not just a question of whether it made or lost money during the financial period. The issue at hand is more a matter of the relationship among the different accounts in the income statement.

For example, maybe you see that a company's *gross profit*, which is the difference between sales and cost of sales, is £500,000. (Not sure what cost of sales is? Don't panic – you find out in the next section of this chapter!) Based on the amount of gross sales or historical trends, you expect gross profit to be £700,000. Well, your scorecard is coming in £200,000 short – not good. And if you're a member of company management or the business owner, you need to find out why.

Historical trends, which I discuss in Chapter 14, refer to a company's performance measured in many different ways tracked over a period of time – usually in years rather than in months.

Perhaps you're thinking, 'Hang on – what about the equity section of the balance sheet? Doesn't that provide a scorecard too?' Well, look back to the definition of retained earnings I give earlier in this chapter: *retained earnings* is the accumulated total of net income or loss from the first day the company is in business all the way to the date on the balance sheet (less dividends and other items that I discuss in Chapter 9). Retained earnings does provide valuable information, but because it's an accumulation of income that you can't definitely tie to any specific financial period, and because it can potentially be reduced by other accounting transactions such as dividends, it doesn't really provide a scorecard like the income statement can.

Textbooks on financial accounting will focus on the main areas of an income statement such as revenue, cost of sales, operating expenses and other gains and losses. In this section, I give you just the basics on each. For a more comprehensive explanation of all the income statement accounts, make sure you read Chapter 10.

To kick off, let's talk about everyone's favourite topic: revenue!

Revenue

Revenue is the inflow of assets, such as cash or trade receivables, that the company brings in by selling a product or providing a service to its customers. In other words, revenue is the amount of money the company is due to bring in doing whatever it's in the business of doing.

The revenue account shows up on the income statement as *revenue* or *turnover*. Both names mean the same thing: revenue before reporting any deductions from revenue. Deductions from revenue can be *sales discounts*, which reflect any discount a business gives to a good customer who pays early, or *sales returns*, which reflect all products customers return to the company after the sale is complete.

Cost of sales

Cost of sales reflects all costs directly associated with any product a company makes or sells, whether the company is a retailer or a manufacturing company.

If a company is a *retailer* (it buys products from a manufacturer and sells them to the general public), the cost of sales is calculated by working out how much it cost to buy the items the company holds for resale. Keep in mind that to accurately calculate this amount, you have to understand how to value *closing stock/inventory*, which is the inventory remaining on the shelves at the end of the financial period, an issue I discuss in Chapter 13.

Because a manufacturer makes products, its cost of sales consists of raw material costs plus the labour costs directly related to making any products that the manufacturer offers for sale to the retailer. Cost of sales also includes factory overheads (such as electricity), which consists of all other costs incurred while making the products.

A service company, such as an accountancy firm or a solicitors' practice, will not have any cost of sales because it does not sell a tangible product.

Operating expenses

Operating expenses are expenses a company incurs that relate to its activity and aren't directly tied to cost of sales. Two key categories of operating expenses exist:

- **Distribution costs:** Any expenses a company incurs to sell its goods or services to customers. Some examples are salaries and commissions paid to sales staff, and advertising expenses.

- **Administrative expenses:** All expenses a company incurs to keep up the normal business activities. Some examples are office supplies, payroll costs, office rents and utilities, and legal and professional costs (such as accountancy fees and lawyers' bills).

Other income and expense

You classify all other income the company brings in peripherally as *miscellaneous income* or *other income*; either description is fine. This category includes interest or dividends paid on investments or any gain realised when the company sells a non-current asset. For example, the company purchases new computers and sells the old ones; the amount the company makes from the sale of the old ones is included in this category.

Other expenses are expenses the company incurs that aren't associated with normal operations. Here are two types of expenses you typically see:

- ✔ **Interest expense:** The cost of using borrowed funds for business operations, expansion and cash flow (such as a bank loan).

- ✔ **Loss on disposal of a fixed (non-current) asset:** If the company loses money on the sale of an asset, you report the loss in this section of the income statement.

Seeing an example of an income statement

I show you a full-blown income statement prepared in accordance with generally accepted accounting practice (GAAP – see Chapter 4) in Chapter 10. In Figure 3-2, I give you a very abbreviated version of what an income statement looks like.

Gabriella Gardening Limited
Income Statement for the year-ended
31st March 2013

	£
Revenue	45,000
Cost of sales	20,000
Gross profit	25,000
Operating expenses	10,000
Operating profit	15,000
Other gains and losses	5,000
Net profit	20,000

Figure 3-2: A simple income statement.

Showing Us the Money: The Statement of Cash Flows

This section offers an overview of the statement of cash flows (sometimes called the 'cash flow statement', particularly in the UK). You prepare the statement of cash flows using certain components of both the income statement and the balance sheet. The purpose of the statement of cash flows is to show how the company has generated cash and how the company has spent this cash. This information is used by investors and potential creditors to gauge whether the business should have sufficient cash flow to pay dividends or repay loans.

The statement of cash flows is very important for financial accounting because generally accepted accounting practice (see Chapter 4) requires you to use the accrual method of accounting. This means that you record revenue when it is earned and realisable (regardless of when money changes hands), and you record expenses when they are incurred (regardless of when they are paid). On the flip side, when using the cash basis of accounting, a transaction isn't acknowledged until money changes hands. The cash basis of accounting is not widely used. The statement of cash flows gives the financial statement user a basis for understanding how non-cash transactions showing up on the balance sheet and income statement affect the amount of cash the company has at its disposal.

Seeing how companies raise and spend cash

If I could choose only one of the three primary financial statements to evaluate a company's ability to pay dividends and meet short-term obligations (both of which indicate a healthy business), I would pick the statement of cash flows. That's because even though the income statement shows eventual sources and uses of cash, the statement of cash flows gives you a better idea of exactly how a business is paying its bills.

As a general rule, a business presents itself in a more positive position if its costs are being covered by cash it brings in from the day-to-day running of the business rather than from borrowed funds. As a potential investor or lender, I want to see that the cash the company brings in through operations exceeds any cash brought in by selling assets or borrowing money. This is because selling assets and borrowing money can never be construed as continuing events the way bringing in cash from selling goods or services can be.

Financial accounting, which is done on the accruals basis (see Chapter 6), does not show the cash ins and outs of business operations. The statement of cash flows gives the user of the financial statements a better idea of cash payments and receipts during the year in two ways:

- By eliminating the effects of trade receivables and payables.
- By showing cash brought in by means other than the operations of the business and cash paid out for items outside the scope of the company's operations – for example, for the purchase of fixed (non-current) assets.

Taking a look at each section of the statement of cash flows

A statement of cash flows has three sections: operating, investing and financing. Each section addresses cash inflows and cash outflows that the business experiences under completely different circumstances:

- ✔ **Operating:** This section shows items reflecting in the income statement. The three big differences between the cash and accruals bases of accounting (see Chapter 6) are *trade receivables*, which is money owed to the company by its customers, *trade payables*, which is money the company owes to its suppliers, and *inventory*, which are goods held by the business for resale to customers.

- ✔ **Investing:** This section usually shows the sale and purchase of long-term assets such as property, plant and equipment and long-term investments. The purchase of long-term assets is reflected on the balance sheet (see Chapter 7). The sale of long-term assets is reflected both on the balance sheet and in the income statement (see Chapter 10). It is reflected on the balance sheet as a reduction of the amount of assets the company owns, and in the income statement as a gain or loss from disposing of the asset.

- ✔ **Financing:** The financing section shows the cash effects of long-term liability items (paying or taking out loans beyond a period of 12 months from the balance sheet date) and equity items (the sale of shares and payment of dividends to shareholders).

The above method of preparing the statement of cash flows is given in IAS 7 *Statement of Cash Flows*. In the UK, FRS 1 *Cash Flow Statement* requires a more detailed approach to preparing the cash flow statement. I take a look at this approach in the section 'Looking at the differences between a UK cash flow statement and an IFRS statement of cash flows'.

Seeing a statement of cash flows

I show you a full-blown statement of cash flows prepared in accordance with generally accepted accounting practice (GAAP – see Chapter 4) in Chapter 11. In Figure 3-3, I give you a very abbreviated version of what a statement of cash flows looks like.

Alicia Architraves Limited
Statement of cash flows for the year-ended
31st March 2013

	£
Cash flows from operating activities	5,000
Cash flows from investing activities	(10,000)
Cash flows from financing activities	(200)
Increase (decrease) in cash	(5,200)
Opening cash balance at 1 April 2012	5,672
Closing cash balance at 31 March 2013	472

Figure 3-3:
A very basic
statement of
cash flows.

You can prepare a statement of cash flows in two different ways: the direct method and the indirect method. I show you how to prepare a statement of cash flows using each method in Chapter 11. For now, here's what to remember:

✔ The direct method reports major classes of gross cash receipts and payments.

✔ The indirect method starts with net profit (or 'operating profit') from the income statement and adjusts for non-cash items reflecting in the income statement such as depreciation, which is allocating the cost of non-current assets (things like cars, property and machinery) over their useful life. (See Chapter 12 for more info about depreciation.)

Looking at the differences between a UK cash flow statement and an IFRS one

In the earlier section 'Taking a look at each section of the statement of cash flows' I tell you that a cash flow statement prepared to UK GAAP under FRS 1 *Cash Flow Statement* requires more detailed approach. This is because FRS 1 requires cash flows to be classified under nine headings, rather than IAS 7's three headings. These headings are:

✔ Operating activities

✔ Dividends from joint ventures and associates

✔ Returns on investment and servicing of finance

✔ Taxation

✔ Capital expenditure and financial investments

✔ Acquisitions and disposals

✔ Equity dividends paid

✔ Management of liquid resources

✔ Financing

When the new UK GAAP comes into play for accounting periods commencing on or after 1 January 2015, the format of the cash flow statement will be the same as in IFRS (operating activities, investing activities and financing activities).

Chapter 4

Acronym Alert! Setting the Standards for Financial Accounting

. . . .

In This Chapter

▶ Taking a quick glance at accountancy history

▶ Introducing the accountant's code of conduct (set by the IESBA)

▶ Meeting the public accounting oversight agencies (such as the FRC)

▶ Reviewing recent changes at the standard-setting house

▶ Finding out about generally accepted accounting practice (GAAP)

. . . .

*I*f you're not into following rules, financial accounting may not be the best career choice for you. You may want to consider performing arts instead, or perhaps politics.

But if you're the kind of person who thrives in a structured work environment, you've come to the right profession. The work of an accountant is carefully guided by standards, rules and regulations that I introduce in this chapter.

After a whirlwind tour through the history of accountancy, I present an overview of the code of professional conduct, which is set by the International Ethics Standards Board for Accountants (IESBA) and is adopted by many professional bodies in the UK and other countries. These standards give you a roadmap to follow when you're trying to figure out how to interact with your clients or employer and how to handle various situations arising during day-to-day business operations.

Next, you meet the financial accounting standard-setting bodies and find out why *publicly owned* companies (those whose shares are freely traded on a public stock exchange) abide by different standards to privately owned companies.

Throughout this book, I refer to the acronym GAAP, which stands for *generally accepted accounting practice*. In this chapter, I explain that GAAP defines for financial accountants the acceptable practices in the preparation of financial statements in the UK as well as in other countries. Many countries currently use their own national standards, but lately we're seeing an increase in the adoption of International Financial Reporting Standards (IFRSs), which is why this book frequently refers to IFRSs. So now I kick off the chapter with a look at the history behind the world of accountancy.

Walking through the Origins of Number Crunching

Accountancy has evolved considerably over the years. No sooner has an accounting standard been issued than it's amended to take account of emerging issues or even replaced with something else! This constant change is to make sure that financial statements prepared by financial accountants convey all the information needed for *external stakeholders* (anyone who's interested in the financial affairs of the company, such as potential investors, tax authorities, bankers and shareholders). If you've already studied for an accountancy qualification, you've probably become aware that accountancy dates back to prehistoric times. If not, here are just a few number-crunching historic facts that place accountancy in the context of world history:

- Cavemen traded beads and other trinkets to acquire food and other basic necessities. These trades required some equitable method of measuring what trinkets were exchanged for how much food, for example, thus providing the origins of the concept of keeping track of – or *accounting* for – items.

- Later in history, formal accounting records were kept to make sure subjects were paying the required amount of taxes to the Holy Roman and other empires.

- The Industrial Revolution in the eighteenth and nineteenth centuries ushered in the mass production of goods through the use of machinery rather than craftsmen working with their hands. Mass production required a more sophisticated approach to recording the movement of goods, services and money, ramping up the activities and professionalism of the accountancy sector. It also resulted in the separation of ownership from management.

- Accountants plied their trade in a mostly unmonitored environment until the US stock market crash of 1929. This event had a huge effect on the UK, resulting in more than 2.5 million people being unemployed. Following this crash a series of principles were adopted within the accountancy profession governing how financial statements should be prepared.

- Fast-forward to the present and this series of principles has expanded into hundreds of principles covering every accountancy topic imaginable, from how financial statements are prepared to accounting for different types of businesses.

Advice for the befuddled financial accounting student

Most financial accounting students are relatively new to the wonderful world of accountancy and business-related lectures. If you're an accountancy novice, my best advice to you is to forget all your preconceived notions of accounting – especially as they tie into what you feel is logical. I've often seen students pulling their hair out because the way UK GAAP or IFRSs work doesn't make sense to them. Sometimes, financial accountants handle transactions in a certain way simply because *that's the way it's done*. After you go through the work of regulatory agencies in this chapter, I hope you come to realise that for the novice, at least, you need to have a good overview of the regulatory system and just go with the flow.

You may feel exasperated at times with the long-windedness of the accountant's job. You may also wonder who the head nit-pickers are and from where they derive their authority. Well, read on! This chapter answers both questions and gives you an insight into why the job of a financial accountant is like it is.

Understanding the Role of the Professional Bodies

Financial accountants absolutely *must* maintain the highest level of ethical behaviour and operate using a code of conduct. This means that financial accountants must always act in an ethical manner and do the right thing – regardless of whether doing the right thing at that particular moment is the best choice for the accountant personally.

Why is the accountant's ethical behaviour so crucial? The reports that financial accountants prepare are used by individuals to make important investment decisions that can have a huge future effect on the users' hard-earned dosh. The users of the financial reports must be given accurate, comparable financial statements so they can make educated decisions about how to invest their money. Professional financial accountants are in a significant position of trust, and a recent survey in the UK showed that the majority of small business owners held their accountant in far greater esteem than their bank manager.

In the UK, anyone can call themselves an accountant. You don't have to be professionally qualified to operate as an accountant and many accountants are *qualified by experience*, which means they've worked in the job for so long that they're on the same level as a professionally-qualified accountant who's worked in the profession for the same length of time. However, many accountants belong to a professional body, and the UK has several of them:

the Institute of Chartered Accountants in England and Wales (ICAEW), the Association of Chartered Certified Accountants (ACCA), the Association of Accounting Technicians (AAT) and the Chartered Institute of Management Accountants (CIMA), to name but a few. Whilst being a member of a professional body isn't obligatory for working as an accountant in the UK, it is mandatory for an auditor to be a member of one of the Consultative Committee of Accountancy Bodies (CCAB) because audit is a regulated profession in the UK. Check out CCAB's website (www.ccab.org.uk) to identify the relevant bodies.

So what exactly do the professional bodies do? Well, essentially, they influence the accountancy profession by being involved in advising standard-setters and other regulatory bodies as to how accounting standards, tax legislation and company law should work. They also impose ethical rules on their members and regulate them by making sure they undertake continuing professional development (CPD), which means keeping abreast of changes and developments within the profession. They also monitor accountancy practices to ensure work of a high standard. Professional bodies, therefore, reassure the public that an accountant is properly regulated, required to work to certain standards and technically capable of doing the job . An accountancy practice undertakes a variety of work for the general public. Below are definitions of three key terms you'll encounter in relation to an accountancy practice:

- ✔ The purpose of financial statement *auditing* is to gather enough evidence about a company's transactions and events to be able to issue an opinion on whether the financial statements are free of material (significant) misstatements.

- ✔ A financial accountant provides an *attestation* service when she issues a report on a subject that's the responsibility of another person or business. For example, a company can hire you to calculate the rate of return on the company's investments (see Chapter 14), making sure your figures match the company's report on the same topic.

- ✔ *Private* companies are close companies (meaning privately owned). Their shares aren't traded on any open-to-the-public stock exchange. For example, if you start a company, you aren't required to sell any of your shares unless you want to. In contrast, a *publicly traded* company's shares are available for purchase in stock exchanges such as the London Stock Exchange.

Getting to grips with the Financial Reporting Council

The Financial Reporting Council's Codes and Standards Division (FRC) is the body responsible for issuing accounting and auditing standards in the UK. The FRC issues the standards and procedures that financial accountants must follow when preparing financial statements and performing audit services for companies. It also sets quality control standards to use when conducting *peer reviews*, which occur when one accountancy firm evaluates the operations of another accountancy firm. Most UK GAAP standards are derived from their international equivalents, which are set by the International Accounting Standards Board (IASB) and the International Auditing and Assurance Standards Board (IAASB).

The FRC has 16 members on its Board , most of whom work for (or have worked for) public accountancy firms (such as KPMG LLP), or otherwise work in the field of accounting for major listed companies or in an academic capacity.

Curious about these mysterious FRC standards? They're called *Financial Reporting Standards* (FRSs), *Statements of Standard Accounting Practice* (SSAPs), *Urgent Issues Task Force Abstracts* (UITFs) and the *Financial Reporting Standard for Smaller Entities* (FRSSE). For auditors, they need to refer to the *International Standards on Auditing (UK and Ireland)*. Phew – that's a lot to go through! To add to the confusion, the UK also uses IFRSs (but that's mainly confined to the bigger companies that are listed on a stock exchange).

Many changes are planned to come into effect during 2015. Then, all the FRSs/SSAPs and UITFs will be scrapped and a new standard – the Financial Reporting Standard applicable in the UK and Ireland – will be introduced. This reporting standard will apply to companies that aren't 'small' – in other words, they don't have sales of more than £6.5 million and fixed and current assets amounting to £3.26 million, and have no more than an average number of 50 employees (to be classed as 'small', a company has to meet two out of those three criteria for two consecutive years). The FRC has stated that small companies will have to revisit the FRSSE and align it with the new UK GAAP, but for now the situation will remain as it is.

A lot of information about the accounting and auditing standards and procedures is available free of charge on the FRC website at `www.frc.org.uk`. From the home page, select 'Accountants' or 'Auditors', followed by 'Codes and Standards'. You need these standards for compilation assignments or audits, for example.

A *compilation* occurs when a financial accountant prepares financial statements for a company using only data given to him by company management. A *review* occurs when the financial accountant gives limited assurance that nothing has come to the accountant's attention that suggest the financial statements contain material misstatements.

Taking a look at the International Accounting Standards Board (IASB)

International Financial Reporting Standards (IFRSs) are set by the IASB. Currently, the IASB currently has 15 full-time members who are all responsible for the development and publication of IFRSs. They're also responsible for approving interpretations of IFRSs by the IFRS Interpretations Committee (previously known as the International Financial Reporting Interpretations Committee, IFRIC). The IASB works closely with lots of outsiders around the world, such as banks, analysts, the accountancy professions, business leaders and many others.

The IFRS Interpretations Committee is the body that interprets IFRSs and is comprised of 14 voting members who are appointed by trustees and work in a variety of professional backgrounds in different countries. Their job is to review widespread accounting issues that have arisen around the world in the context of IFRSs and provide authoritative guidance.

Perusing the Code of Ethics for Professional Accountants

The Code of Ethics for Professional Accountants of the International Ethics Standards Board of Accountants (IESBA) contains five principles of professional conduct by which its members must abide: integrity, objectivity, professional competence and due care, confidentiality and professional behaviour.

Here's a brief explanation of each of the five principles:

- ✔ **Integrity:** This characteristic means you're honest when dealing with others. In the world of financial accounting, integrity means that you serve the company for whom you are preparing the financial statements to the best of your ability, keeping in mind that this may not be the same thing as completely agreeing with the way the company wants its financial statements prepared. You can't be concerned that management will be mad at you or fire you if you disagree with them.

- ✔ **Objectivity:** When you're objective, you're neutral and unbiased in all decision-making processes. You base your opinions only on facts and not on any preconceived notions you may have. You interpret rules and policies, such as generally accepted accounting practice (GAAP), in a truthful and sincere manner – staying true to both the form and spirit of the particular principle or regulatory issue.

Professional accountants who provide auditing and other attestation services must be independent in both mind and appearance. Being *independent* means you have no special relationship to or financial interest in the company that would cause you to disregard evidence and facts when evaluating them. For example, preparing the financial statements for a business owned by a close relative can justifiably cause those viewing your report to doubt its veracity or your objectivity.

✓ **Professional competence and due care:** In a nutshell, this principle means you have the technical skills, ability and experience to perform the work at hand and crucially you keep updating your knowledge. You must be both competent and practise diligence. In addition, due care means you plan and supervise adequately any professional activity for which you're responsible

✓ **Confidentiality:** Professional accountants have a duty to ensure that confidentiality is observed at all times. A professional accountant cannot disclose information to any third party without proper and specific authority, unless a legal or professional right or duty to disclose exists (if the client is involved in illegal acts, for example). Professional accountants also cannot use confidential information acquired during their work for their personal advantage or to the advantage of third parties.

✓ **Professional behaviour:** Professional accountants must comply with relevant laws and regulations and avoid all action that would discredit the profession. Professional accountants must be seen to be behaving in a professional manner at all times, including the professional accountant's marketing or advertising.

Following Regulatory Issues

In addition to the various professional bodies such as ACCA, ICAEW, CIMA, CIPFA, AAT and so on, other organisations give financial accountants official guidance on how to prepare financial statements. Public and private companies have different agencies monitoring them and keeping them on the right track.

In this section, I discuss the London Stock Exchange, which was founded in 1801. It was charged with regulating the stock market and preventing corporate abuses relating to the offering and sale of shares and securities and corporate reporting. Also in this section, I explain how accountancy firms are regulated in the UK and by whom and some of the consequences that can occur when an accountancy practice fails to work to the required standards expected of a professional firm.

Introducing the London Stock Exchange

The London Stock Exchange was opened by Elizabeth I in 1571 as the *Royal Exchange*. Over the centuries it's experienced some turbulent events, the most dramatic of which was probably the 'big bang' of the early 1980s. The big bang refers to the major modernisation of the stock exchange during which the distinction between *jobbers* (a jobber is someone who makes sure brokers have someone to buy or sell shares from or to for a client) and *brokers* (a broker is someone who carries out transactions for the investors who hire them) was abolished and the exchange's operations were computerised. Fixed commission charges were also abolished during the big bang.

The London Stock Exchange's main role is to allow companies who are listed on it to raise finance, increase their profile and obtain a market valuation through a variety of routes.

A *premium listing* is a prestigious listing which can only be obtained by companies that meet the strict criteria of the UK 'super-equivalent' listing rules, which are higher than the EU minimum requirements. A company that obtains a premium listing is expected to meet the UK's highest standards of regulation and corporate governance.

A *standard listing* allows companies to access the Main Market by meeting EU-harmonised rules rather than the UK's 'super-equivalent' requirements.

The London Stock Exchange has a choice of markets, which enables companies in the UK and international companies to access one of the world's deepest pools of investment capital through the:

- **Main Market:** This is the Exchange's flagship market for larger, more established companies.
- **Alternative Investment Market (AIM):** This is the world's leading growth market for the smaller, more ambitious company.
- **Professional Securities Market:** This is the Exchange's regulated market for listed debt and depositary receipts.
- **Specialist Fund Market:** This market is specifically designed for issuers of specialist funds.

Most successful companies eventually have to make the decision to list on a stock exchange (the company is *floated*). It's fair to say that a stock market listing increases the company's external and internal profile and enhances how it's viewed by stakeholders, potential investors and shareholders.

A word of warning: the decision to float is a major one and cannot be taken on a whim. Detailed management consultation and the advice of professionals is necessary to ensure the decision is right not only for the company, but also for those who may be directly affected by the decision to float.

The *London Stock Exchange Admission and Disclosure Standards*, published by the London Stock Exchange, sets out the rules and responsibilities relating to a company that's admitted to trade on it. It also outlines disclosure obligations for those companies seeking admission, or already admitted to trade on the Exchange. To download this document, visit www.londonstock exchange.com and click on 'For Companies and Advisers'.

As a financial accountant, your exposure to the London Stock Exchange will be limited unless you work for a company whose shares are publicly traded or you work for an accountancy firm conducting financial statement audits for publicly traded companies.

Monitoring accountancy firms in the UK

The Big 4 accountancy firms (PricewaterhouseCoopers, Deloitte, Ernst & Young and KPMG) are all monitored by the Codes and Standards Division of the Financial Reporting Council (FRC). By *monitored*, I mean that the FRC regularly checks out the Big 4 to make sure they're abiding by standards (such as UK GAAP and IFRSs, as well as auditing standards), regulations and legislation. The FRC also monitors the mid-sized firms to make sure they're applying the rules as they should.

Smaller firms are monitored by their professional body on a periodic basis. Usually this can be anything from a three- to six-year cycle, depending on the findings of the professional body. If an accountancy practice is found to be complying with the applicable standards, regulations and legislation, it will usually not be inspected for another six years. Some professional bodies' policies and procedures may involve shorter or longer timescales for re-inspection, however.

If the firm is found to be falling short of the mark, however, the professional body's procedures may mean that additional visits are required to make sure that any recommendations and improvements are actually undertaken. Sometimes the professional body will also require file reviews to be undertaken by external file reviewers. These may not be connected with the professional body but must send a copy of their report to it so that it can see if the accountancy firm is improving its work.

Some professional bodies make it a mandatory requirement for member firms to send the results of at least one file review to the professional body on an annual basis so that the professional body can see if standards are being maintained even though no inspection has taken place. In any event, having at least one file review per year (even if your professional body doesn't make it a mandatory requirement) is a good idea because it either provides reassurance that you're doing things right or flags up areas where the practice needs to improve.

In some serious cases, if an inspection reveals substantial failings the punishments become more severe. The firm can be fined huge sums of money for failing to apply the required standards and in some particularly serious cases the professional body may even revoke the firm's practising certificates!

Professional bodies will inspect the firm's work and look at its internal procedures, such as staff recruitment policies, staff induction, anti-money laundering regulations administration, bookkeeping and accountancy processes, staff training and CPD, as well as other practice management issues. The professional bodies do this to make sure that the member firm is applying the standards expected of a professional accountancy firm. This is a vital tool, and one which benefits accountancy firms, because being a member of a professional body assures the public that you're mandated to comply with certain professional standards.

Recognising Big Brother: The Financial Reporting Council

In the preceding section, I mention the Financial Reporting Council (FRC). The FRC is an independent regulator, which focuses its attention on promoting high levels of audit quality, corporate reporting and governance.

One of the FRC's jobs is to review accounts that have been approved for large private companies, companies listed on the Alternative Investment Market (AIM) and companies listed on the mainstream stock exchange (PLCs). Each year the Conduct Committee reviews many accounts for companies. It has the power to request a company to make changes to its accounts where it finds errors or omissions, or where information is deemed to be inadequate. In rare cases, the FRC also has the power to obtain a court order to require a company's financial statements to be amended.

The FRC's Conduct Committee prepares annual reports each year which detail its findings and also provides the names of those accountancy firms that have been subjected to review. These reports are publicly available and can be downloaded at www.frc.org.uk (click on 'Our Work' and then select 'Annual activity reports').

Getting to know the Financial Reporting Council (FRC)

The Financial Reporting Council (FRC) has recently undergone a massive programme of change, which received Parliamentary approval in June 2012. According to the FRC, these changes were necessary both to enhance its independence from those it regulates and enable it to issue a more proportionate range of sanctions. At the time of writing, the chair of the FRC is Baroness Hogg.

The FRC is comprised of the Codes and Standards Division and the Conduct Division. The *Codes and Standards Division* is supported by three councils that advise on accounting, auditing, and assurance and actuarial matters. These councils are currently chaired by a former PricewaterhouseCoopers (PwC) partner, an ex-Ernst & Young chairman and a member of the pension regulator and FSA employee, respectively. The *Conduct Division* covers all supervisory and disciplinary matters, including the review of financial reports and inspection of the compliance of large firms with auditing standards.

Understanding generally accepted accounting practice (GAAP) in the UK

GAAP defines for financial accountants the acceptable practices in the preparation of financial statements in the UK. The importance of the information I provide in Parts III, IV and V of this book directly ties back to GAAP. Specifically, GAAPs tell financial accountants exactly how financial data has to show up in the statement of profit or loss/income statement (profit and loss account), statement of financial position (balance sheet) and statement of cash flows (cash flow statement).

For example, GAAP states that assets, liabilities and equity go on the balance sheet and not in the income statement. GAAP is also pretty picky as to how these accounts are arranged on the balance sheet (see Part III). In addition, GAAP gives specific rules for separating operating revenue (which is related to the business activity) from non-operating revenue (non-business-related revenue, such as profit from selling a company asset), which I explain in Chapter 7.

Like most things in life, there are exceptions to the rule that all businesses must follow GAAP. Some businesses can deviate from GAAP, and I cover a few of these instances in Chapter 22. Is GAAP the same for public and private companies? Well, in the UK, not necessarily. In the UK, companies listed on the Alternative Investment Market (AIM) and public limited companies (PLCs) must report under EU-adopted IFRSs. Other companies report under UK GAAP (unless they choose to report under EU-adopted IFRSs, which is very rare indeed because of the extensive disclosure requirements mandated by these standards). In the past, establishing and modifying GAAP was a collaborative effort by the Accounting Standards Board (ASB) in conjunction with the (now defunct) Urgent Issues Task Force (UITF), which used to issue urgent clarifications in cases where confusion surrounded an accounting standard. This work is now overseen by the FRC Codes and Standards Division, which is currently developing the new UK GAAP: the Financial Reporting Standard applicable in the UK and Republic of Ireland. This is due to take effect for accounting periods commencing on or after 1 January 2015; earlier adoption is permitted, however, if a company wishes to do so.

Changes in the FRC's structure won't impact your day-to-day working life in the world of accountancy as such, so don't panic!

Looking at IFRSs

In the preceding section, I mention that two financial reporting frameworks exist in the UK: UK GAAP and EU-adopted IFRSs. Listed companies (PLCs) in the UK had to adopt EU-IFRSs in 2005, and AIM-listed companies had to do so in 2007. So, why do we have two frameworks?

Well, those responsible for standard-setting in the UK have always intended to move to an international-based framework eventually, which is why many of the standards in current UK GAAP are, more or less, aligned to IFRSs. In 2009, the UK's (now defunct) Accounting Standards Board admitted that UK GAAP, in its current form, had become overly complex and voluminous. To be honest, I think many of us working with UK GAAP on a day-to-day basis would whole-heartedly agree with that conclusion!

IFRSs date back as far as the early 1970s and more than 120 countries around the globe are reported to be allowing, or mandating, the use of these standards. 'Why?' I hear you ask.

Well, many countries adopt IFRSs (for example, the UK has done so in relation to AIM and PLCs) because they want consistency in financial reporting and believe that following IFRSs grants access to more sources of capital because investors, creditors, financial analysts and other users of the financial statements welcome standards that require high-quality, transparent and comparable information. Without common standards, comparing financial information prepared by companies located in different parts of the world is inherently difficult, particularly in an increasingly global economy.

Will IFRSs eventually take over? That's certainly the long-term plan of the IASB – but only time will tell!

Part II
Looking at Some Accounting Basics

Breary Brick Co. Ltd
Trial Balance

Account No.	Account Name	Debit £	Credit £
0001	Delivery van	35,000.00	
0002	Delivery van depreciation		5,000.00
1001	Inventory	27,488.50	
1002	Trade receivables	13,194.56	
1003	Petty cash	50.00	
1004	Bank account	17,113.25	
1100	Trade payables		2,500.00
1101	VAT		265.31
1102	Credit card account		1,645.22
1103	PAYE and National Insurance payable		2,211.00
1104	Bank loan payable		5,411.00
1105	Directors current account		1,000.00
1200	Ordinary shares		100.00
1300	Profit and loss reserves		3,996.00
4000	Sales		135,117.62
5000	Purchases	41,091.55	
6000	Gross wages	10,001.22	
6005	Employers National Insurance	4,189.65	
7000	Light and heat	3,266.98	
7100	Insurance	2,150.44	
7200	Rent	2,000.00	
8000	Accountancy	1,700.00	
		157,246.15	157,246.15

Go to www.dummies.com/extras/financialaccounting for online bonus content.

In this part . . .

✔ Grasp the basic methodology of financial accounting.

✔ Understand how bookkeeping works.

✔ Learn how to tell the difference between the cash-based method of preparing financial statements and the accruals-based method

✔ Be clear on the principal accountancy concepts.

✔ Go to www.dummies.com/extras/financial accounting for online bonus content, including an extra Part of Tens chapter: 'Ten Differences Between Some National Standards and IFRS'.

Chapter 5

Doing the Books: The Process behind Financial Accounting

- -

- -

*I*n this chapter, I discuss the nuts and bolts of collecting, sifting through and entering accounting info into business accounting software. Accountants call the process of recording accounting transactions *bookkeeping*.

Some bookkeeping tasks involve basic data entry done by clerks. Others, like preparing journal entries, are mostly done by junior accountants or book-keepers. 'What are *journal entries*?' I hear you ask. Well, they're the accountant's way to enter transactions into the accounting system. (For example, the accountant records any bank charges shown on the company's bank statement.) I discuss journal entries in detail later in this chapter.

Will you need to deal with journal entries during your accounting career? That depends. If you work for a small company in a one- or two-person finance department, you could very well be the *financial controller* (the big chief in charge of the company's purse strings) and be doing the journal entries yourself. If, instead, you work for a large firm of accountants that provides external auditing services to clients, the chances are you won't ever initiate journal entries yourself. However, you'll most certainly review journal entries while auditing the company's financial statements. And you may propose journal entries for your client to process if you find errors.

No matter where your accounting career takes you, you need to know what bookkeeping involves, and I'm here to help!

Shedding Some Light on Bookkeeping

Most people who aren't familiar with accounting think in stereotypes when the word 'bookkeeping' comes up. They conjure up images of someone who looks like Bob Cratchit from *A Christmas Carol* – a beleaguered clerk bent over a list of accounts doing the boring, mundane task of writing up the books and making sure they balance. In the broadest sense possible, this image does relate to modern financial accounting. Bookkeeping involves recording daily transactions in the accounting cycle, such as entering customer invoices and paying supplier bills. *Bookkeepers* (the name for the employees doing the 'keeping') may also carry out routine tasks and calculations such as running payroll and doing the *bank reconciliation*: making sure the cash in the company's bank account equals the cash reflected by the cashbook.

Depending on the depth of their knowledge, bookkeepers may also prepare the company's initial financial statements, which are then reviewed and adjusted by the external accountants. So a bookkeeper can be a jack-of-all-trades. But bookkeepers are not *usually* qualified accountants (such as Chartered or Chartered Certified accountants).

A bookkeeper may not have any specific education, experience or licensing related to accounting. Many bookkeepers learn accounting by doing: starting at a business in the purchase ledger department or credit control department and then perhaps filling in the gaps in their accounting knowledge by undertaking an accounting-related course (such as a bookkeeping course).

Analysing the Effect of Business Transactions

In this section, I walk you through the basics of bookkeeping, including the rule of debits and credits (debits and credits are sometimes referred to as the *double-entry* principle, which is discussed below) and why proper bookkeeping keeps the financial statements in balance. You also discover the five steps for entering transactions into the accounting records.

Modern financial accounting is a *double-entry* system: double entry means that for every entry into the company accounting records, an opposite and equal entry is necessary. In other words, debits must always equal credits. (Financial accounting has quite a bit in common with Newton's third law of motion – the one about every action having an equal and opposite reaction.) Technology can certainly help you here: no accounting software package worth its salt will let you enter a single-sided transaction into the books.

Seeing how the fundamental accounting equation works

The *fundamental accounting equation* (also known as the *accounting equation* or the *balance sheet equation*) proves that all transactions are equal and opposite. It demands that

Assets = Liabilities + Owners' equity

A truncated version of this equation states

Net assets = Owners' equity

This version of the equation just moves liabilities over to the other side of the equal sign; *net assets* are all assets minus all liabilities. Before I go any further, I need to clarify what is meant by assets, liabilities and owners' equity:

- ✔ **Assets** are things a company owns (and controls). Chapter 7 discusses all the typical types of business assets. Some examples are cash, equipment and cars.

- ✔ **Liabilities** are debts the company owes to others. See Chapter 8 for the complete lowdown on liabilities. The main sorts of liabilities you encounter in your financial accounting class or at work as a financial accountant are trade creditors (sometimes called 'trade payables') and loans.

- ✔ **Owners' equity** is what the owner puts into the business when he/she sets it up and also what's left over in the business at the end of the day – a company's assets minus its debts. Many financial accounting textbooks call owners' equity 'shareholders' funds', but it all amounts to the same thing. Chapter 8 discusses the different components of owners' equity.

Here's a simple example of the fundamental accounting equation at work; assume the numbers represent a company's assets, liabilities and owners' equity in thousands, millions or perhaps even billions of pounds:

Assets = Liabilities + Owners' equity

100 = 40 + 60

Or

Net assets = Owners' equity

60 = 60

Getting familiar with accounts

As an accountant within a business, you summarise accounting transactions into accounts that you use to create financial reports. Each and every account your company uses is annotated in a list called the *chart of accounts*. The business uses that chart of accounts to record transactions in its general ledger (sometimes called the 'nominal' ledger). The *general ledger* is a record of all financial transactions within the company during a particular accounting period. You find out everything you need to know about the general ledger at the end of this chapter.

The chart of accounts is not a financial report. It's merely a list of all accounts you've previously set up to handle the company transactions.

When you're 'doing the books', as the saying goes, you record your normal business transactions using accounts you set up in the chart of accounts. Each account in the chart of accounts has a unique account number. Regardless of what accounting software package your company uses, the numbering sequence is pretty much set in stone to ensure consistency among companies and among their financial reports.

The number of accounts you can set up in the chart of accounts is virtually unlimited, so you can customise it to fit your business perfectly. Here's an example of a numbering sequence that could be used in a company's charts of accounts:

Number Sequence	Account Type
1000 to 1999	Assets
2000 to 2999	Liabilities
3000 to 3999	Equity
4000 to 4999	Income
5000 to 5999	Cost of sales
6000 to 7999	Operating, general and administrative expenses
8000 to 9999	Non-business-related items of income and expense

Instead of using a four-digit numbering sequence, some software programs use a three-digit numbering sequence. For example, instead of 1000 to 1999 for assets, some software programs may use 100 to 199 but the actual structure of a chart of accounts is pretty much standard.

In the previous section, I define assets, liabilities and equity. And the income accounts (numbers 4000 to 4999) are pretty easy to understand; they represent any money the business takes in for the products or services it sells.

Here's a brief explanation of the accounts in the 5000–9999 numbering sequence:

- ✔ **Cost of sales:** Cost of sales is the cost of the product that a company sells. The company can either make the product that it sells or buy it from someone else and then resell it. I talk much more about cost of sales in Chapters 10 and 13.

- ✔ **Operating, general and administrative expenses:** These accounts reflect all expenses a business incurs while performing its activities that do *not* directly relate to making or selling a product – in other words, any expense that's not a cost of sales. Some examples are telephone and postage expenses. You can find out more about these types of expenses in Chapter 10.

- ✔ **Non-business-related items of income and expense:** A company may bring money in or spend money that generally accepted accounting practice (GAAP) classify as *non-business-related*. For example, a business treats interest it earns on investments as non-business income. If a company sells a non-current (fixed) asset (a long-term asset that it owned such as a car or a building) at a loss, that's an example of a non-business expense. Chapter 10 has more info about this topic as well.

Keep in mind that, if a company is in the business of lending money, interest earned on these loans *is* considered business income. Likewise, a car dealership must report losses on sales of vehicles as business expenses.

Defining debits and credits

Now that you understand the basics of accounts and the chart of accounts, it's time to learn about *journal entries*, which you use to enter financial information into the company's accounting software.

Preparing journal entries is a major area of concern for first-year accounting students, and small business owners. The logistics of presenting the journal entry don't cause the concern; instead, the worry is how to figure out which account is debited and which is credited (the double-entry principles).

Here's one of the immutable laws of accounting: assets and expenses are *always* debited to add to them and credited to subtract from them. Liability, revenue and equity accounts are just the opposite: these accounts are *always* credited to add to them and debited to subtract from them. Always, always, always – no exception to this rule exists – ever!

A common confusion is to mix up debits and credits where a bank account is concerned. Think about your own personal bank account. When your bank account is in *credit* it means you have money in the account (known as being *in the black*). On the flip side when your bank account is in *debit* it means you're overdrawn (known as being in the *red* - boo!). Be careful not to mix these types of debits and credits up. A bank account in *credit* means the bank owes you the money in the account whereas you owe the bank account if your account is in debit. When you're doing the bookkeeping, if you *debit* the bank account in the accounting records, you're putting money *in* the account. When you *credit* the bank accounting records you're paying money *out*. This is because you're recording the transactions from the point of view of the company and not the bank.

Seeing how debits and credits work

Before you enter a transaction into an accounting system, you have to consider the *transaction methodology*, a five-step process for deciding the correctness of whatever entry you're preparing. After you get into the financial accounting rhythm, following this process becomes as natural as breathing. Here are your five considerations:

- **What's going on?** This question addresses the need for the entry into the books. For example, did the company buy a new piece of business equipment or sell something to a customer?

- **Which accounts does this event affect?** Is the account an asset, a liability, an owners' equity, a revenue or an expense? Assets would definitely be affected by the purchase of business equipment, and revenue would be affected by a customer sale.

- **How are the accounts affected – by a debit or credit?** Looking back to your rules of debits and credits, buying assets adds to the account so it's a debit. Making a sale adds to a revenue account so it's a credit.

- **Do all debits for an entry equal all credits for the same entry?** Think about the fundamental accounting equation, which I discuss earlier in this chapter. For every debit there has to be an equal credit (double entry).

- **Does the entry make sense?** Do the actions you take match the facts and circumstances of the business event? For example, although the net effect on the books is the same, you can't credit an expense account to record revenue.

In the next section, I look at the different types of journals available to you to record transactions. I also give you plenty of examples of journal entries so you can see the concept brought to life.

Getting to Grips with Journals

Journals are a lot like the diary you may have kept as a child (or maybe still keep!). They're a day-to-day recording of events. But journals record business transactions taking place within a company's accounts department. Accountants call journals the *books of prime entry* because no transactions get into the accounting records without being entered into a journal first.

A business can have many different types of journals. In this section you find out about the most common ones your financial accounting class discusses, which are tailored to handle cash, accruals or special transactions. Want to find out more? I discuss cash journals first.

Using journals to record cash transactions

All transactions affecting cash go into the cash receipts or cash payments journal.

Cash receipts journal

Let's talk about the most popular cash journal first: the cash receipts journal. After all, everyone loves to receive a bit of dosh!

When accountants use the word *cash*, it doesn't just mean paper money and coinage; it includes cheques, credit card transactions and electronic money (such as BACS or CHAPS transfers). In accounting, *cash* is a generic term for any payment method that is assumed to be automatic. When you sign a cheque and send it off to one of your suppliers, part of your implicit understanding is that the funds are immediately available so the cheque clears. Ditto paying with a credit card, which represents an immediate satisfaction of your debt with the supplier. (Never mind the fact that a three-day lag usually occurs between the time the payment is processed and when the money hits the supplier's bank account.)

Here are examples of some cash events that require posting to the cash receipts journal:

- **Customer sales made for paper money and coinage:** Many types of businesses still have booming cash sales involving the exchange of paper money and coins. Some examples are supermarkets, retail shops and some service providers such as hair salons.

- **Customers making payments on their accounts:** I talk about *accounts receivable* (commonly referred to as 'debtors'), which is money customers owe a business, in the 'Recording credit transactions' section later in this chapter. For now, just remember that any payment a customer makes for goods or services previously billed goes in the cash receipts journal.

- **Interest or dividend income:** When a bank or investment pays a business for the use of its money in the form of interest or dividends, the payment is considered a cash receipt.

   As a technical matter, many businesses record interest income reflecting on their monthly bank statement in the general journal, which I discuss a little later in this section.

- **Asset sales:** Selling a business asset like a car or office furniture can also result in a cash transaction. An example could be where a company is refurbishing its finance director's with deluxe new leather chairs so it's selling off all the old chairs to someone else who pays cash for them.

Keep in mind that this list isn't exhaustive; these are just a few of the many instances that can necessitate recording a transaction in the cash receipts journal.

Various types of cash receipts receive different treatment in a company's profit and loss account (or income statement). For example, cash sales are treated one way, and interest income and dividends are treated another way. I give you the details in Chapter 10.

The cash receipts journal normally has two columns for debits and four columns for credits:

- **Debit columns:** Because all transactions in the cash receipts journal involve the receipt of cash, one of the debit columns is always for cash. The other is for *sales discounts*, which reflects any discount the business gives to a good customer who pays early. For example, a customer's invoice is due within 30 days, but if the customer pays early, it gets a 2 per cent discount. *Trade discounts* are another type of discount which customers are often given when they make bulk purchases of products.

- **Credit columns:** To balance the debits, a cash receipts journal contains four credit columns:

   - Sales

   - Trade receivables (or trade debtors)

   - *Output tax*, which is the amount of value added tax (VAT) the business collects on the transaction (and doesn't apply to every transaction)

   - *Miscellaneous*, which is a catch-all column where you record all other cash receipts like interest and dividends

Not all sales are subject to VAT. HM Revenue and Customs determines what types of transactions are VATable and which aren't. For example, certain items of food and drink are zero-rated (VAT is charged at 0 per cent), as are lottery tickets. Cars, by contrast, are charged VAT at the standard rate (currently 20 per cent). Check out HMRCs website at www.hmrc.gov.uk for more on what is and what's not VATable.

In addition to the debit and credit columns, a cash receipts journal also contains at least two other columns that don't have anything to do with debits or credits:

✔ The date the transaction occurs

✔ The name of the account affected by the transaction

Depending on the company or accounting system, additional columns may be used as well.

Figure 5-1 shows an example of a portion of a cash receipts journal.

Cash Receipts Journal

	Date	Account	Receipt total Debit	VAT Credit	Sales Credit	Trade Receivables Credit	Sales Discount Debit	Misc Credit
Figure 5-1: A partial cash receipts journal.	15.1.13	Interest received	32.50					32.50
	16.1.13	ABC Company Ltd	5,100.00			5,100.00		
	23.1.13	Joe Bloggs	120.00	20.00	100.00			

Cash payments journal

On the flip side, any payment the business makes using a form of cash gets recorded in the cash payments journal. Here are a few examples of transactions you see in a cash payments journal:

✔ **Retail purchases:** When a *retailer*, a company selling goods to the public (see Chapter 10), pays cash for the goods it buys for resale, the transaction goes in the cash payments journal.

✔ **Payments the company is making on outstanding accounts:** This includes all cash payments a company makes to pay for goods or services it obtained from another business and didn't pay for when the original transaction took place. You can find more on this topic in the 'Recording credit transactions' section later in this chapter.

✔ **Payments for operating expenses:** These transactions include cheques or bank transfers a business uses to pay utility or telephone bills.

The cash payments journal normally has two columns for debits and two for credits:

✔ **Credit columns:** Because all transactions in the cash payments journal involve the payment of cash, one of your credit columns is for cash. The other is for *discounts received*, which are reductions in the amount a company has to pay the supplier for any purchases on account. For example, a business offers customers a certain discount amount if they pay their bills within a certain number of days (sometimes referred to as a 'settlement' discount).

> ✔ **Debit columns:** To balance these credits, the debit columns in a cash payments journal are trade payables (or trade creditors) and *miscellaneous* (a catch-all column where you record all other cash payments for transactions, such as the payment of operating expenses).

A cash payments journal also contains at least three other columns that don't have anything to do with double-entry principles:

> ✔ The date the transaction occurs
>
> ✔ The name of the account affected by the transaction
>
> ✔ The name of the company that supplied the goods/services (which means who the payment is made to)

Depending on the company or accounting system used, more columns could be used as well. Figure 5-2 shows an example of a partial cash disbursements journal.

Cash Payments Journal

Figure 5-2: A partial cash payments journal.

Date	Cheque no.	Payee	Payment total Credit	VAT Debit	Accounts Payable Debit	Settlement Discount Credit	Stationery Expenses Debit
1.3.13	125	Toner cartridges	300.00	50.00			250.00
1.4.13	126	Supplier A	412.00	68.67	343.33		
1.5.13	127	Overseas supplier B	5,000.00	–	4,900.00	100.00	

Recording credit transactions

Credit transactions take place whenever cash doesn't change hands immediately. For example, a customer makes a purchase with a promise to pay within 30 days. These transactions are accounted for under the 'accruals' method of accounting (which means transactions are recognised in the accounts when they arise, not when they are paid or settled) (see Chapter 6).

For trainee accountants or those new to the world of accountancy dealing with all the different types of credit transactions can seem rather daunting but don't worry, I walk you through all of the ones you'll see in your financial accounting textbook and give you a complete explanation of each. And, before you finish this section of the book, I'll outline some typical credit transactions.

Following is information about the two main types of credit journals. The first applies when goods/services are sold to customers on credit – the *sales journal*. The second applies when goods/services are received on credit from a supplier – the *purchases journal*. I discuss other accrual-type journals in the upcoming section 'Finding out about other journals'.

Sales journal

The sales journal records all sales that a business makes to customers *on credit* (or 'on account'), which means no money changes hands between the company and its customer at the time of the sale. A sales journal affects two different accounts: trade receivables (sometimes called 'trade debtors') and sales. In the sales journal, trade receivables and sales are always affected by the same amount. The sales journal is often referred to as the *sales day book*.

Figure 5-3 presents an example of a sales journal.

Figure 5-3: A partial sales journal.

Sales Journal

Date	Invoice Ref	Customer	Debit Accounts Receivable Credit Sales/Revenue
15.2.13	3254	Customer A	3,000.00
17.2.13	3255	Customer B	521.23
21.2.13	3256	Customer C	785.25

When you record credit sales in your sales journal, you follow up by posting the transactions to each customer's listing in the trade receivable ledger. (See the 'Bringing It All Together in the Ledger' section of this chapter.)

Use the sales journal only for recording credit sales. Sales returns, which reflect all products the customers return to the company after the sales are done, do not get recorded in the sales journal. Instead, you record them in the general journal, which I discuss later in this section.

Purchases journal

Any time a business buys using credit (*on account*), it records the transaction in its purchases journal. The purchases journal is also known as the *purchases day book*. The purchases journal typically has a column for date, number and amount. It also has the following columns:

- ✔ **Trade payables:** Because the company is purchasing on account, the current liability account called 'trade payables/trade creditors' is always affected.

- ✔ **Terms:** This column shows any discount terms the company may have with the supplier. For example, *2/10, n/30* means the company gets a 2 per cent discount if it pays within 10 days; otherwise, the full amount is due in 30 days. (The *n* in this abbreviation stands for 'net'.)

✔ **Name:** The company records the name of the supplier from whom the purchase is made.

✔ **Account:** This column shows to which financial statement account(s) the purchase is posted to. In the example shown in Figure 5-4, two accounts exist: trade payable (T/P) and purchases. Because no other accounts (such as VAT) are affected, T/P and purchases are for the same amount. If the company is charged VAT, a column would be added to report this amount as well.

Purchases Journal

Figure 5-4:
A partial
purchases
journal.

Date	Reference Number	Supplier	Credit Trade Payables Debit Purchases
4.3.13	1993	Supplier A	125.63
8.3.13	2357	Supplier B	2,587.00
1.4.13	1485	Supplier C	5,000.00

Finding out about other journals

The discussion of journals wouldn't be complete without a brief rundown of other types of journals you'll stumble upon in your dealings with financial accounting, as well as the general journal. I cover both issues in this section.

Special journals

Here are three additional journals you'll encounter:

✔ **Payroll journal:** This journal records all payroll transactions such as gross wages, pay as you earn (PAYE) tax and other deductions (such as national insurance paid by the employee) leading to *net pay*, which is the amount paid to the employee.

✔ **Purchases return and allowances journal:** This journal shows all subtractions from gross purchases because of products a company returns to the supplier or discounts given to the company by the supplier.

✔ **Sales returns and allowances journal:** This journal shows all subtractions from gross sales because of products customers return or discounts given to the customers.

This list isn't exhaustive; some companies may have other journals, and some smaller companies may not use all of these. However, if you understand the basic methodology of all the journals I discuss in this chapter, you'll be well prepared for your financial accounting lectures and any work you have to do as a financial accountant.

Sometimes a bookkeeper may not fully understand a transaction or may need to undertake some additional investigation work. For example, there may be an amount of money paid into the bank account by BACS for which there is no meaningful reference on the bank statement. The bookkeeper cannot just ignore this deposit into the bank account because her bank reconciliation will not balance. While she investigates this amount of money, she can post the amount into a *suspense account*. A suspense account is a temporary account which holds transactions that need to be investigated further. At the accounting period end, the suspense account must be cleared out to nil.

General journal

The *general journal* is a 'catch all' type of journal where transactions that don't appropriately belong in any other journal get posted. Many companies record interest income and dividends in the general journal.

This journal is also used for adjusting and closing journal entries:

- **Adjusting journal entries:** One key reason you'd adjust journal entries is to make sure the books are recording transactions under the accruals basis of accounting. For example, on 30 April 2013 employees have earned but not yet been paid £5,000 in gross wages (the next payroll run is on 2 May 2013). So, to make sure that your company's revenue and expenses are matched, you post an adjusting journal entry debiting 'payroll costs' in the profit and loss account for £5,000 and crediting 'wages payable' in the balance sheet as a liability for £5,000.

  You also adjust journal entries to *reclassify* transactions when the way in which a transaction was originally recorded is correct but circumstances change after the fact and the transaction needs to be adjusted. For example, your company buys £1,000 of supplies on 1 April 2013, and the transaction is originally posted as stock. On 30 April 2013, a stock take is carried out (see Chapter 13). Only £800 of the stock remains, so you have to debit your 'purchases expense' account in the profit and loss account for £200 and credit 'stock' in the balance sheet also with £200.

- **Closing journal entries:** You use this type of entry to clear out all *profit and loss accounts*, which reflect all the revenue and expenses for a certain time period. You then transfer the net amounts to the balance sheet as 'profit and loss account reserves' (sometimes called 'retained earnings'). You take this step to set the profit and loss account figures to zero so you know exactly how much revenue and expense are recorded during a certain time period. (See Chapter 10 for information about the profit and loss account.) Four closing journal entries are necessary:

  - You debit all revenue accounts and miscellaneous income accounts.

- You credit all cost of sales and expenses accounts with the same amounts as they have been originally debited with.

- You post the difference between the debits and credits in steps 1 and 2 – which is the net profit for the period – to profit and loss account reserves in the equity section of the balance sheet (sometimes called 'retained earnings').

  Here's an example. If in step 1 you debit income by £5,000 (to reduce income to zero) and in step 2 you credit expenses with £3,000 (to reduce expenses to zero), you now have a balance left over of £2,000, which is profit (income is more than expense by £2,000). This remaining credit is posted to profit and loss account reserves (retained earnings). And crediting retained earnings is a good thing!

- Finally, if the owners have paid themselves any dividends during the period, you credit the dividend account reducing it to zero and debit retained earnings.

In all honesty the chances are you'll never have to prepare the first three closing entries yourself because all accounting software systems do this task for you automatically. However, you do need to understand what goes on with the debits and credits when the books close.

You clear out only profit and loss accounts with closing journal entries. Balance sheet accounts are permanent accounts. Until you cease using the account (for example, you close a bank account), no balance sheet accounts are zeroed out at the year- or period-end. Part III of this book provides lots more info about balance sheet accounts.

Seeing examples of common journal entries

It's time for you to review a few journal entries so the concepts I discuss earlier in the chapter really come to life. First, keep in mind the general format of a journal entry, which is shown in Figure 5-5:

Date	Account Name and Narrative	Debit £	Credit £
1.4.13	Bank account	100	
1.4.13	Interest received		100

Figure 5-5: The standard journal entry format.

Being interest received on bank current account

> ✔ The date of the entry is recorded in the left-hand column.
>
> ✔ The account debited or credited is in the middle column.
>
> ✔ The amounts are shown in the right-hand column.

Proper journal entries always list debits first and credits afterwards.

Journal entries can have more than one debit and one credit. And the number of accounts debited and credited don't have to be the same. For example, you can have five accounts debited and one account credited. However, the final monetary amount of the debits and credits has to match.

Let's prepare the journal entry for service income, which records cash and accrued income. You provide a service to your client, Mr Jones, on 15 May 2013, giving him invoice number 200 in the amount of £700 for services rendered. Before he leaves your office, he pays you £200 in cash with a promise to pay the remaining balance of £500 next week. The journal entry to record this transaction is shown in Figure 5-6.

Figure 5-6: | 15.5.13 | Cash | 200.00 | |
Recording | | Trade receivables | 500.00 | |
service | | Service income | | 700.00 |
income. | | *To record invoice number 200* | | |

Under the accruals method of accounting (see Chapter 6), both the cash receipts and the promise to pay the remaining balance have to be reported at the time the transaction takes place because the service has been rendered and the income has been earned.

Every journal entry should have a brief explanation (called a 'narrative'). It doesn't have to be extremely detailed but should be long enough that you or anyone else reviewing the journal entry can understand why you made the journal entry. The description for the journal entry in Figure 5-6 ('To record invoice number 200') is brief but completely understandable.

Let's do one more journal entry before moving onto the last section in this chapter. Say you borrow £5,000 from your bank on 1 July 2013. The terms of the loan are that you have to pay £200 worth of interest on 31 July 2013, and pay the loan back in full plus another £200 in interest on 30 August 2013. Figure 5-7 shows how your journal entries look from start to finish.

| 1.12.12 | Bank account | 5,000.00 | |
| | Loan account | | 5,000.00 |

Being working capital loan received

| 31.1.13 | Interest expense | 200.00 | |
| | Bank account | | 200.00 |

Being interest payment on loan

Figure 5-7:
Journalising
a loan
transaction.

31.1.13	Loan account	5,000.00	
	Interest expense	200.00	
	Bank account		5,200.00

Being redemption of loan and payment of interest

Bringing It All Together in the Ledger

At this point you may be thinking, 'Okay, the journals are the books of prime entry, but what happens then? How do entries into these journals turn into the financial statements?' That's the subject of this section. The accounts and amounts debited or credited affect the company's ledgers, which I define next.

Realising what a ledger is

A *ledger* records transactions taking place in a company during a particular accounting period. Picture a big book. Every page of the book has a title that corresponds with an account from the chart of accounts. For instance, page 1 may be titled '1001 Cash at Bank'. On this page, you'd list the total of the monies you paid into your company bank account, as well as the total of all the withdrawals from the bank account for a given period – say, for a month.

A business has one big ledger: the general ledger. The *general ledger* lists all transactions taking place in all the accounts during the accounting period. You may also see subsidiary ledgers (often referred to as 'memorandum accounts') that list in detail transactions happening only in specific accounting circumstances. For example, the *payroll subsidiary ledger* lists all payroll transactions. The *trade receivables subsidiary ledger* lists all customers owing your company money and the amount of their current outstanding balance.

Walking through the basic accounting period

In most businesses, the accounting period is based on a calendar month. Using January as an example, during that month's accounting period, employees in various accounts departments are hard at work entering daily transactions into journals and ledgers as the accounting events unfold from 1 January through to 31 January. For example, the business receives an invoice from a stock supplier for purchases made on 12 January, and the invoice will be paid when the supplier statement arrives showing all purchases the company makes during January. (See Chapter 8 for more information about purchases and payables.) A clerk in the purchase ledger department enters this invoice into the purchases journal, increasing stock and trade payables. Both actions affect the balance sheet (see Part III of this book). However, by doing a stock take (see Chapter 13), accountants at the company reclassify some of this purchase to cost of sales — a profit and loss account — via a journal entry.

Also, during each accounting period the cost of using any non-current (fixed) assets such as property, plant and equipment (see Chapter 7) has to be reclassified from the balance sheet to the profit and loss account. This step is done by preparing a journal entry to account for depreciation expense (see Chapter 12). And, of course, the business has to record all types of revenue and any other business- and non-business-related expenses in the appropriate journal.

While a company enters accounting transactions in journals contemporaneously during the accounting period, preparation of the financial statements takes place after all entries to the journals post to the ledgers and the accounting period ends. How quickly the financial statements are prepared varies by company. However, keep in mind that some journal entries can't be made until after the business bank statement arrives, which varies by bank.

Posting transactions to the ledgers

When you *post to the ledgers*, you simply take accounts and numbers from transactions you enter in the journals and record them in the correct ledger. If a subsidiary ledger is the first point of recording, the transaction eventually flows through the subsidiary ledger to the general ledger. For example, a customer sale on credit first gets posted to the sales journal and then is reported in the trade receivables subsidiary ledger under the customer's name.

Then, that amount flows from the trade receivables subsidiary ledger to the trade receivables listing in the general ledger, combining with all other customers owing the business money to show a grand total of trade receivables. Following on with the same transaction, the combined total of all the transactions in the sales journal also posts to the sales day book in the general ledger.

Until modern accounting software arrived, posting to the ledgers was a laborious process requiring the use of ledger paper with about 14 columns. Luckily, this practice has largely become a thing of the past because over-the-counter accounting software packages have become so cheap and easy to use.

With most accounting software programs, no formal procedure to post to the ledgers exists. Every time you enter a transaction in a journal, it automatically posts to the correct ledger. However, bespoke accounting software may require the user to actively select the posting command.

Viewing an example of a general ledger

While the theory of a general ledger is the same in every instance, general ledgers from one company to another using different types of accounting software will look slightly different. Figure 5-8 shows a very simple partial general ledger for a small services company. It starts with a revenue account, 'consultancy fees', and ends with an operating expense account, 'bank charge'.

The debit, credit and balance columns in Figure 5-8 should be self-explanatory. Here's what some of the other columns mean:

- ✔ **Type:** The original nature of the transaction.

- ✔ **Date:** The day the transaction took place.

- ✔ **No.:** The identifying number from the journal of original entry. For example, 1008 is the company cheque number used to pay James Fine.

- ✔ **Name:** Whatever name you put in the journal of original entry.

- ✔ **Memo:** Any explanation for the transaction that you put in the original entry.

Breary Brick Co.
General Ledger

	Type	Date	Ref	Name	Memo	Debit	Credit	Balance
4050-Consulting								0.00
Fees	Receipt	1.1.13	7		Calderwood job	0.00	55,000.00	55,000.00
	Receipt	26.3.13	2		John's office colours	0.00	500.00	55,500.00
	Receipt	31.3.13	3		Walk-in job	0.00	100.00	55,600.00
	Invoice	1.4.13	1	Byrne		0.00	1,725.00	57,325.00
	Invoice	7.4.13	5	Leavitt	Monthly storage fee	0.00	75.00	57,400.00
	Invoice	30.4.13	3	Woodward	Renovation	0.00	4,207.50	61,607.50
Total 4050-Consulting Fees						0.00	61,607.50	61,607.50
5300-Wages								
	Payment	31.3.13	1008	Isabelle Byrne	Gross wages	800.00	0.00	800.00
	Payment	30.4.13	1009	Megan Breary	Gross wages	200.00	0.00	200.00
Total 5300-Labour						1,000.00	0.00	1,000.00
5400-Subcontract Labour	Payment	31.3.13	1010	Lisa Weaver	Consultancy	1,500.00	0.00	1,500.00
Total 5400-Subcontract Labour						1,500.00	0.00	1,500.00
5500-Bank Charges				Direct				
	Payment	31.3.13		debit	March bank charges	15.00	0.00	15.00
Total 5500-Bank Charges						15.00	0.00	15.00

Figure 5-8:
A partial general ledger.

Recognising the purpose of the trial balance

The *trial balance* is a listing of all the accounts in the general ledger and the balance they hold as at the date of the report. The purpose of the trial balance is to make sure all debits equal credits. Accountants also use it as a front-line tool to review the accuracy of the financial statements.

For example, you run the trial balance, quickly scan it and see that an expense account carries a balance that seems too high based on your professional judgement and knowledge of the company. You check the general ledger and see that a rent payment to the business landlord for £5,000 was posted to postage and stationery expense by mistake. Figure 5-9 shows an example of a partial trial balance.

Accounting software should not allow a user to enter a transaction that's out of balance, so technically the trial balance should always be in balance. Should the accounting system allow an out-of-balance transaction to occur, the software has a serious flaw and shouldn't be used.

Breary Brick Co. Ltd
Trial Balance

Account No.	Account Name	Debit £	Credit £
0001	Delivery van	35,000.00	
0002	Delivery van depreciation		5,000.00
1001	Inventory	27,488.50	
1002	Trade receivables	13,194.56	
1003	Petty cash	50.00	
1004	Bank account	17,113.25	
1100	Trade payables		2,500.00
1101	VAT		265.31
1102	Credit card account		1,645.22
1103	PAYE and National Insurance payable		2,211.00
1104	Bank loan payable		5,411.00
1105	Directors current account		1,000.00
1200	Ordinary shares		100.00
1300	Profit and loss reserves		3,996.00
4000	Sales		135,117.62
5000	Purchases	41,091.55	
6000	Gross wages	10,001.22	
6005	Employers National Insurance	4,189.65	
7000	Light and heat	3,266.98	
7100	Insurance	2,150.44	
7200	Rent	2,000.00	
8000	Accountancy	1,700.00	
		157,246.15	157,246.15

Figure 5-9:
A partial trial balance.

Chapter 6

Taking a Butcher's at Accounting Methods Under UK GAAP and IFRS

....

In This Chapter

▶ Getting to grips with the cash and accruals methods of accounting

▶ Walking through other types of accounting besides financial

▶ Discovering the conceptual framework

....

*W*hile most student accountants take financial accounting only because it's a core requirement for an undergraduate and graduate business degree, many students actually become extremely passionate about the subject. If you're also coming round to the way of thinking that accounting isn't that bad, this chapter gives you some information about other types of accounting besides financial that you may be interested in. And the good news is that the basic accounting facts you learn in your studies apply to just about any accounting speciality.

Before I discuss other types of accounting, I explain the difference between the cash and accruals methods of accounting. Accountancy courses are primarily concerned with the accruals method because it's required under generally accepted accounting practice (GAAP, which I explain in Chapter 4). However, to truly understand the accruals method you have to understand how it differs from the cash method.

In addition, you get an introduction to the International Accounting Standards Board's (IASB) *Conceptual Framework*. (If you aren't familiar with the IASB, check out Chapter 4.) I walk you through these concepts, tying them into material you encounter in Parts III and IV of this book and throughout your financial accounting class. The UK has its own *Statement of Principles* that was originally issued by the UK's Accounting Standards Board (ASB), which is now the Financial Reporting Council. In a nutshell, the *Statement of Principles* and the *Conceptual Framework* both do the same thing!

Distinguishing between Key Accounting Methods

This book is about financial accounting, which means the company operates on the accruals method of accounting according to GAAP. (If you struggle with the accruals method and GAAP, don't worry – I cover both in the upcoming 'The accruals basis' section.)

However, another method of accounting exists besides the accruals basis: the cash method. This section gives you an expanded version of what you'll potentially come across when this method is appropriate.

Going through this information is important for a few different reasons. First, to really understand a topic, you often have to understand why it differs from the alternatives. Second, if after finishing your accountancy studies you find you have an affinity for the whole debiting and crediting extravaganza, you'll need to know what other accounting specialities are available. Finally, to be a well-rounded financial accountant, you have to have at least a basic understanding of the other methods and types of accounting – not only to know the differences, but also to be able to explain to individuals who might not be as savvy on accountancy about the different methods and the method that is appropriate in a given situation. In addition, financial accountants may well have to refer to management accounting records used in the production of internal management accounts in order to produce the financial accounts.

The cash basis

Using the cash basis of accounting couldn't be easier. You record income when the company is paid, and you record expenses when they're paid – not when they're incurred. However, the ease of using the cash method is more than offset by the fact that the cash basis fails to match revenue to the expenses the company incurs to earn that revenue. Because of this failure, cash basis financial statements usually do not present as accurate a picture of how the business is performing as the accruals basis of preparing financial statements does. Certainly in the UK, financial statements have to be prepared that give a *true and fair view*. Financial statements prepared using the cash basis would hardly give a true and fair view if the company buys and sells goods on credit because the company's trade receivables and trade payables wouldn't be included.

Leslie's Lilos Limited has revenue of £40,000 and expenses totalling £15,000 which are directly associated with revenue (known as *cost of sales*) in April. £20,000 of the revenue was received in cash, and the rest is on account. Leslie's Lilos paid cash for the entire £15,000 of expenses.

An 'earned and realisable' example

If you're at all confused about how a transaction becomes earned and realisable, here's an example to bring the concept into focus:

A florist customer's wedding is taking place in a couple of days, and the customer has just given the florist a personal cheque paying in full for the reception table arrangements. Is this income earned? No, the florist has not earned the revenue from the wedding job until all floral arrangements are present and accounted for on the reception tables.

At face value, because the florist has a cheque in his hands, you may be tempted to say that this revenue is realisable even though the flowers haven't been delivered yet. But hang fire: a couple of days after the wedding, the florist finds out the customer's cheque has bounced because the customer has closed the account on which the cheque was drawn. The florist calls the customer's mobile, but it's disconnected. He subsequently finds out that the customer has also moved, leaving no forwarding address.

Is the revenue from this job now earned and realisable? Earned, yes – the florist delivered on his end of the contract. Realisable, no, because the florist has no realistic expectation of ever being paid. Under the accruals method of accounting, this transaction is not recorded as revenue. (And under the cash method of accounting, it's not recognised because money did not change hands.)

Using the cash method, Leslie's Lilos net income for April is £5,000 (£20,000 cash revenue less £15,000 cash expenses). But that £5,000 of net income grossly under-represents the volume of activity the company had during the month. The figures could be just as wildly inaccurate if the company didn't pay any of its expenses and had cash sales of £30,000 – or for any other scenario involving using cash changing hands as a criteria for recording net income.

Some small businesses use the cash method because they have little activity in the way of trade debtors/receivables or trade creditors/payables. But the vast majority of businesses use the accruals basis, which I explain next.

The accruals basis

Using the accruals method of accounting, you record revenue when it's earned and realisable (by *realisable*, I mean turned into cash), and you record expenses when they're incurred regardless of whether they have been paid. Wondering what the criteria are for revenue to be *earned* and *realisable*? The earned criterion is satisfied when the supplier satisfactorily fulfills its contractual obligations with the customer. *Realisable* means that there is an actual expectation of collecting the money for the job from the customer.

The accruals method takes cash out of the equation, because money changing hands doesn't determine whether you recognise a transaction. As a result, a company using the accruals method will have a *trade receivable*, which shows how much money customers owe to the business, and a *trade payable*, which shows all the money a company owes to its suppliers.

The statement of cash flows, which I discuss briefly at the end of this chapter and explain in detail in Chapter 11, is the financial accountant's bridge between the cash and accruals methods of accounting. That's because the statement of cash flows shows how a company has generated cash and what it has spent that cash on – an aspect missing from the accruals method. Therefore, it gives the users of the financial statements a chance to look beyond the accruals-based numbers.

Sorting through Standards for Other Types of Accounting

While many chartered and chartered certified accountants work in financial accounting, other fields also exist in which accountants can pursue employment. In this section I discuss four accounting fields: management accounting, not-for-profit, governmental and international. (For an insight on life as an accountant, be sure to check out Chapter 2.) The basic accounting concepts you learn in your financial accounting studies remain the same in these fields, but some important differences exist between these four and financial accounting.

For example, if you work in an accounting field other than financial accounting, you have to follow standards different from (or in addition to) those I discuss in Chapter 4. Other organisations besides the financial accounting standard-setters give official guidance on how to prepare financial statements and reports. For example, in the UK instead of following GAAP, charitable organisations will follow the Statement of Recommended Practice (SoRP) on charity accounting.

But wait, I don't want to get ahead of myself! Read on, because in the next few sections, I give you the lowdown on these four types of accounting and note who provides guidance to accountants in these fields.

Management accounting

Management accountants provide economic and financial information for the internal users of financial statements, such as a company's directors, management and human resources department. For example, human resources personnel use managerial accounting reports to make sure they have the right mix of employees to keep the business running smoothly. Additionally, management accounting reports measure quality, performance and how close each department or business unit comes to meeting its goals. They also measure managerial effectiveness and efficiency – a topic I touch on in Chapter 1.

In order to be useful, management reports are issued frequently – sometimes daily. There's no messing around! Other times, accounts staff prepare and distribute the reports the day after a reporting period ends. Management accounts are rarely spot on to the exact penny, but are reliable enough for management and other interested parties to make informed decisions.

Because these reports are only used internally, no regulatory bodies or other external authority tells the management accountant how she should do her job. However, accountants are all bound by ethical standards issued by their professional bodies and even if the management accountant is not professionally qualified, she'll still have to undertake her job to the best of her ability.

Not-for-profit accounting

As I explain in Chapter 2, not-for-profit businesses are run for the benefit of the public good – not because of any profit motive. These types of organisations include hospitals, schools, religious organisations and charitable agencies.

Obtaining 'not-for-profit' status can sometimes mean meeting certain strict criteria. For example, a charity must be able to demonstrate its purpose and its objectives and is generally not able to pay its trustees for their services. In the UK, many not-for-profit companies operate as a *company limited by guarantee*, which means that the company does not have shares or shareholders but still has the benefit of corporate status. Since the introduction of the Companies Act 2006, the number of *Community Interest Companies* (CICs) has increased. These are companies that are limited by guarantee, or companies limited by shares (a company *limited by shares* means the company issues shares to shareholders and in the event of the company being wound up the shareholders liability is only limited to the amount they have invested), but with special conditions applied to make sure that the companies' profits and assets are used for the benefit of the public.

The not-for-profit accountant's job has two additional components (in addition to the typical accounting duties): preparing budgets and preparing the financial information for grant applications. Budgets are crucial because the organisation needs to be able to predict what amount of money has to be obtained through grants, donations and fundraising efforts in order to serve the organisation's purpose.

One difference in keeping the books for profit-seeking versus not-for-profit organisations is that not-for-profits use *fund accounting*, which groups transactions together into funds or accounts that share a similar purpose. This way, the organisation has a better idea of what resources it has available for each specific function.

If not-for-profit accounting interests you, check out *Nonprofit Bookkeeping & Accounting For Dummies* by Sharon Farris (Wiley) for much more information about this field.

Government accounting

At the city or county level, the cash comes in from sources such as council taxes; funding from the central government such as for schools and roads; interdepartmental government transfers; fines; value added tax; licences and permits; and issuances of bonds. Funds are then dished out to cover costs.

Government accountants also prepare financial statements that are open to the general public. The financial statements must show accountability to the general public while pursuing the goals of efficiency and effectiveness. The financial statements are also used by external users (see Chapter 1) to decide whether to invest in government bonds; see Chapter 8.

In the UK, government accountants are mainly qualified with the Chartered Institute of Public Financial Accountants (CIPFA). CIPFA is the only professional accountancy body dedicated to public finance.

International accounting (IFRS)

International accountants work for multinational businesses performing financial and management accounting, preparation of corporate tax returns and auditing. (Remember that *auditing* is the process of investigating financial information prepared by someone else to see if it is fairly stated.) They should be familiar with the legal regulations and standards of the countries with which their employer conducts business.

International accountants have to deal with foreign currency translations, such as how many UK pounds equal how many euros (EUR) and then incorporate this translation into the company's financial statements in its presentation currency (the currency in which the financial statements are prepared).

An important organisation for international accountants is the International Accounting Standards Board (IASB; www.ifrs.org). The IASB is active in making its accounting standards (International Financial Reporting Standards) global and many countries have adopted the use of IFRSs as their financial reporting framework. This process is referred to as *harmonisation*, and the purpose is to develop a single set of global accounting standards that will provide high-quality, transparent and comparable financial statement reporting.

If you want more information on IFRSs, consider getting a copy of *IFRS For Dummies* written by me? It offers a great down-to-earth rundown of how IFRSs are applied in both the real world and in studies.

Many professional courses on accountancy will examine IFRSs because of their global domination, so if you're pondering over the thought of becoming an accountant, the chances are you won't escape IFRSs!

Considering the Conceptual Framework and Other Principles

Accountancy dates back to the Stone Age as a way of working out the supply and demand of commerce. Long before we had shops and cash registers, people had to have some way of making sure an adequate trade of good for good or good for service existed. Also, accountancy was put to use as far back as the Holy Roman Empire (and probably even earlier) to make sure that all subjects to the empire were paying their share of taxes. Note I didn't say their *fair* share of taxes, which is always a lively subject for debate!

As I say in Chapter 4, standard-setting wasn't prevalent in the olden days and it wasn't until the early 1970s that the (then) International Accounting Standards Committee started to issue accounting standards. In the UK, things started a little later when the (then) Accounting Standards Board started to issue standards in 1982.

The International Accounting Standards Board (IASB) organises its conceptual framework in what it calls the *Conceptual Framework for Financial*

Reporting. Now, in the UK, we also have the *Statement of Principles*, which more or less does the same thing. For the sake of consistency, however, I talk here about the IASB's version as UK GAAP is set to be replaced in 2015 with an international-based GAAP. The *Conceptual Framework for Financial Reporting* was issued in 2010 and was a revised version of the previous *Framework Document*.

The purpose of the *Conceptual Framework* is to provide the IASB with a theoretical and conceptual framework for issuing new, and amending existing, IFRSs and IASs. Its purpose is to:

- ✔ Assist in the development of future IFRSs, as well as assist the IASB when it reviews existing standards by setting out the underlying concepts.

- ✔ Promote harmonisation of accounting regulation and standards by reducing the number of permitted alternative accounting treatments.

- ✔ Assist other standard-setters in setting their own national standards.

- ✔ Assist auditors to form an opinion as to whether (or not) financial statements have been prepared in accordance with IFRSs.

- ✔ Assist users in interpreting financial information contained in a set of IFRS financial statements.

- ✔ Allow those interested in the work of the standard-setting process at the IASB to have an insight into the IASB's approach to standard setting.

The following four concepts – objectives, characteristics, elements and financial statement measurement – augment the information any textbook provides and give you a handy introduction to the financial accounting information I address in the next two parts of this book.

Here, I provide just the condensed version of the four concepts. But I also cite the chapters you can go to for more detailed information on each. Ready to get started? First let's talk about what financial accounting is attempting to accomplish.

The objective of financial reporting

What is the purpose of financial accounting? It's the process of classifying and recording all accounting events taking place during the normal course of a company's business. These events include earning revenue, paying bills, bringing in gains and incurring losses.

The results of all these events are arranged into the correct financial statement (the balance sheet, income statement and/or statement of cash flows) and reported to the external users of the financial statements (often called the *stakeholders*). External users include investors, creditors, banks and regulatory agencies such as HM Revenue and Customs (HMRC) and the London Stock Exchange. Want to know more? I discuss this topic in Chapter 1.

Characteristics of financial statement information

Besides organising accounting events into financial statements, how do financial accountants serve the needs of the external users? Well, just like adding salt instead of sugar to a cake mix is going to make your end result seriously out of whack, adding the wrong ingredients to your financial statements is going to give your users the equivalent of an inedible cake.

What sorts of characteristics must be present so you can make sure the financial statements totally serve the needs of your users? Well, the IASB's *Conceptual Framework* splits the characteristics into two bits: fundamental qualitative characteristics and enhancing qualitative characteristics. These characteristics are then broken down into sub-components, as follows:

- **Fundamental qualitative characteristics:** Financial information is:

  - **Relevant:** The information is capable of making a difference in the decisions made by users.

  - **Faithful in its presentation:** The information is complete, neutral and free from error.

- **Enhancing qualitative characteristics:** Financial information is enhanced when it's:

  - **Comparable:** Financial statements should be prepared so that the user can compare the information with another entity in the same industry/service sector or compare financial information from one accounting period to the next.

  - **Verifiable:** financial information should be verifiable, that is, information should be available to back up the financial statements.

  - **Timely:** Financial information should be prepared on a timely basis because the longer it takes to prepare financial statements after the accounting period has ended, the less meaningful it is. However, on the flip side, it might be that a certain amount of time must pass so as to assess seasonal fluctuations or obtain some other information that might not be available until some time after the accounting period has ended.

- **Understandable:** The information in the financial statement has to be understandable to people not privy to the internal operations of the business. Of course, being understandable is a relative concept. However, basically this characteristic means the financial information must be laid out in a fashion so that users with a reasonable understanding of the business world (and a willingness to do research on specific topics as needed) can understand the important issues in the financial statements.

The *Conceptual Framework* also includes materiality as a sub-section of relevance. An item is *material* if the financial information's omission or misstatement may cause the user of the financial statements to arrive at the wrong conclusion.

Where materiality is concerned, be especially careful. Sometimes (particularly in auditing), you can calculate materiality using a variety of methods. Something that may be immaterial in numerical terms may become material in nature – for example, if it turned a profit into a loss.

Elements of the financial statements

Financial statements have to be prepared in such a way that the user can understand what's going on in the business. It would be pretty pointless if this was not the case as financial statement information would be all over the place – not to mention against the law in most jurisdictions. Accountancy courses will introduce the concept of the *elements* of the financial statements. The elements of the financial statements are laid down in the *Conceptual Framework* and underpin the financial statements. See Chapter 1 for an introduction to the elements of the financial statements.

Financial statement measurements

Communicating with parties interested in the business via the financial statements requires the measurement of all accounting transactions. *Measurement* refers to the fact that every accounting event has to have a cost or a value in order to be recognised in the financial statements. You may be confused about the difference between cost and value. Well, you're not alone. This issue can be thorny even among seasoned financial accountants.

Depending on their nature, accounting transactions may be recorded in different ways. If a transaction is recorded at *historic cost*, it shows how much the company paid in cash or how much the company was owed, or was paid, during the transaction. *Net realisable value* (NRV) can also be used, which is the amount of cash a business anticipates receiving from an asset in the normal course of business – after factoring in any related costs. You find all sorts of good information about historic cost and NRV in Chapter 7.

Part III
Bonding with the Balance Sheet

Total Assets			75,245.00
Total Equity			16,278.88
Liabilities & Equity			
	Liabilities		
		Current liabilities	
		2010 Trade payables	34,202.62
		2210 Short-term loan obligations	1,365.50
		2215 Salaries control account	145.00
		2220 Corporation tax	668.00
		2225 Deferred income	500.00
		2230 PAYE & National insurance	2,000.00
		2240 Accruals	85.00
		Total current liabilities	38,966.12
		Non-current liabilities	
		2710 Loan	20,000.00
		Total non-current liabilities	20,000.00
		Total liabilities	58,966.12
Total Liabilities and Equity			75,245.00

Go to www.dummies.com/extras/financialaccounting for online bonus content.

In this part . . .

- ✔ Learn the importance of tangible and intangible assets.

- ✔ Understand how to account for long- and short-term liabilities.

- ✔ Come to grips with the importance of equity.

- ✔ Get a feel for different sorts of share.

- ✔ Go to www.dummies.com/extras/financial accounting for online bonus content, including an extra Part of Tens chapter: 'Ten Differences Between Some National Standards and IFRS'.

Chapter 7

Looking at Assets

*P*art III of this book is all about the financial statement called the *balance sheet* (internationally known as the *statement of financial position*), which reports a company's assets (the things a company owns and *controls*. *Control* means the company can control access to the benefits such assets bring to the business, for example revenues), liabilities (the amounts a company owes) and equity (the bit left over that belongs to the shareholders). In Chapter 8, I walk you through the liabilities part of the balance sheet, and Chapter 9 is all about the equity part of the balance sheet. This chapter gets the party started by focusing on assets.

Assets are resources a company owns – stuff like property, plant, equipment and cash. Businesses have many different types of assets, which are classified as either *current* or *non-current*. Current assets (such as stock/inventory, trade debtors/receivables, bank and cash accounts) are *liquid*, which means they either are cash or can quickly be turned into cash. You'll often see current assets listed on the balance sheet in the *order of liquidity*; this means that they're listed from the least to the most liquid starting with inventory, which then gets sold and turns into a receivable, which then pays the company so turns into cash.

Non-current (sometimes referred to as *fixed*) assets are not liquid; converting them to cash may take time. Examples of non-current assets often include *tangible* assets (assets you can touch) such as a company's cars, computers, office buildings or factories. But not every non-current asset is tangible. For example, consider a company's patents and trademarks, as well as investments that a business makes in other companies – these are all *intangible* assets (intangible assets are those assets that don't have a physical form; in other words, you can't kick them!). And a mysterious asset called *goodwill* also exists, which comes into play only during business combinations (a topic I discuss in Chapter 17); that, too, is an intangible asset.

Some types of leased equipment are considered assets too, which may seem strange because the company doesn't own them outright. I devote Chapter 19 to accounting for leases.

Current? Non-current? Tangible? Intangible? The topic of assets may seem a little overwhelming at first because so many kinds of assets exist. But in this chapter, I give you a straightforward, easy-to-understand lowdown on the different types of assets a company might own. By the end of it, things might not seem as daunting as you first thought!

Homing in on the Historic Cost Convention

Before I start identifying and explaining typical business assets, I want to explain how the values of most assets are normally shown on the balance sheet. Regardless of their *market value* (sometimes called *fair value*), which is what a knowledgeable, willing person will pay for the asset in an arm's length deal (by *arm's length*, I mean unbiased and uninfluenced), most assets go on the balance sheet at their original historic cost.

Here's an example to explain what I mean.

Woodward's Windows Limited buys a building for £200,000 in 1999. In 2012, the market value of that building is £400,000, but the value of the building stays on the balance sheet at £200,000. This value is also known as the building's *book value*. If the asset is subject to depreciation (writing off the cost of the building over its estimated useful life, a topic I cover in Chapter 12), the historic cost (£200,000) minus the depreciation is known as the asset's *net book value*.

One caveat: you record *short-term investments* – investments (financial instruments) that the company buys to sell in the short term – at their market value under UK GAAP's fair value accounting rules (referred to sometimes as *alternative accounting rules*). I discuss this topic in the 'Short-term investments' section later in this chapter. The same thing applies in IFRS, where you see the phrase '*at fair value through profit or loss*'.

Keeping Track of Non-Current (Long-Term) Assets

You classify an asset as *noncurrent* or *long term* if the asset will mature or be used in the business for more than 12 months after the date of the balance sheet. For example, a loan that the company expects to receive after the 12-month cutoff date (the cutoff date being the date of the balance sheet) is classified as non-current. Natural resources such as coal, oil and timber are also non-current assets. So are mineral deposits, like gold and diamonds.

In this section, I focus on the most common types of non-current assets you'll encounter both in your accountancy studies and in the real world. I start with tangible assets (those you can kick) and then discuss intangibles (those you can't kick).

Meeting the tangibles: Property, plant, and equipment (PP&E)

In this section, I introduce you to a company's tangible assets. *Tangible* assets, also called *fixed* assets, include 'property, plant, and equipment' (PP&E) – a category that includes land, buildings, equipment, furniture, and fixtures and fittings.

I devote an entire chapter to an account directly related to PP&E – that of depreciation. *Depreciation* is the method of writing off the cost of an item of PPE over its estimated useful life to the income statement (or profit and loss account) (see Chapter 10). To get the complete lowdown on depreciation, check out Chapter 12.

Land

Land is the earth on which the company's office buildings or manufacturing facilities sit. The cost of the land plus any improvements the company has made to the land to use it for business operations reflect on the balance sheet at historic cost.

Three types of costs relate to the purchase of land:

- **Purchase price:** The price paid for the land.
- **Incremental costs:** Legal fees incurred when the buyer purchases it from the seller.

✔ **Land improvements:** Expenses the company incurs to get the land ready for use, which include the cost of clearing the land if necessary to build the manufacturing plant or adding alleyways and fences to an existing property. In addition, an initial estimate of the costs of dismantling, removing and restoring the site to its original condition are also costs that relate to the purchase of land.

Because it's not considered to be 'used up' in the way that other PP&E is, land is never depreciated (written off to the income statement over its estimated useful life). Land also has an indefinite life, so that's another reason why it isn't depreciated.

Buildings

This category covers the company-owned structures in which the company conducts its business operations. It includes office buildings, manufacturing facilities, warehouses and off-site storage facilities.

Unlike land, buildings are depreciable (see Chapter 12). Also, if you're studying accountancy that examines UK generally accepted accounting practice (GAAP) and you're preparing a balance sheet, make sure you list land and buildings separately because doing so is a GAAP requirement.

In real-life accountancy, financial accountants use valuations for the land element and the buildings element to include on the balance sheet for land and buildings. Or, if the business purchases a piece of raw land and constructs its own building, calculating the cost of each is simple because you have the purchase agreement for the land and all related expenses to construct the building already separated out for you. You won't have to undertake any complex calculations – feel free to breathe a deep sigh of relief!

Equipment

This category is quite broad, encompassing any equipment a company uses to make the products it sells to customers. For example, a manufacturing company such as a bakery includes all the mixers, ovens and packaging machines it uses to turn the yeast and flour into loaves of bread ready to ship to the supermarkets.

A retailer, such as a department store, (which doesn't make any products) includes in this category any office computer equipment it owns, plus forklifts or ladders to move its stock/inventory around. Retail shops also usually categorise their cash registers as equipment.

Furniture and fixtures

Last up in our parade of PP&E are furniture and fixtures, which include desks, chairs and filing cabinets. Next time you're in the office, take a look around; chances are that any new items of furniture are capitalised in the company's balance sheet as furniture and fixtures.

A retailer such as a clothes shop has fixtures to present clothes for sale like floor or wall display racks. Mannequins are also considered fixtures and, depending on their quality, can be quite sizeable in terms of monetary amounts on the balance sheet.

If the company leases any of its PP&E, the leased items may not be considered company property and therefore don't show up in the PP&E section of the balance sheet. Real care must be taken here because, if the lease has characteristics of ownership of the asset, you *do* record the leased asset on the balance sheet. Leasing presents all sorts of difficulties and so I devote an entire chapter (Chapter 19) to this subject.

Investigating intangible assets

The big difference between tangible and intangible assets is that *intangible assets* (usually) don't have a physical presence. When you really scratch the surface of this subject, you'll probably find intangibles a lot more interesting than desks and filing cabinets!

Differentiating the two types of intangibles

Two types of intangible assets exist. The first type, which is the most common, includes intangible assets with long lives such as leasehold improvements, patents, copyrights and trademarks:

- ✔ **Leasehold improvements:** When a company leases its business location and then makes alterations to the building to suit its business activities, but which cannot be removed once the lease comes to an end, such alterations are known as *leasehold improvements*.

  Leasehold improvements are intangible assets, but sometimes they represent tangible improvements to a leased property, such as turning a large building into individual offices to rent out. In this situation, the balance sheet will lump them with PP&E rather than with the non-physical intangibles such as patents. Confused? Check out Figure 7-1 at the end of this chapter to see what I mean.

- ✔ **Patents:** Patents provide licensing for inventions or other unique processes and designs. Items that can be protected by patents can be anything from a new drug to a new designer clothing logo.

- ✔ **Copyrights:** Securing a copyright means that someone can't use the company's printed work (such as books or articles) or recorded work (such as music or films) without permission. Any original piece of work is automatically copyrighted.

- ✔ **Trademarks:** These are unique signs, symbols or names the company can use to create a brand or image. When a company has a trademarked name or symbol, no other company can use it. (There's only one McDonald's, for example.)

The second category of intangibles is *goodwill*. Goodwill arises when one business purchases another business (or a share in another business) for a price greater than the *fair value* (the price knowledgeable, willing parties will pay in an arm's length transaction) of the net assets acquired in the sale. (*Net assets* are total assets less total liabilities.)

Alexander Business Attire Limited buys Alicia's Funky Fashions Ltd for £250,000. The fair value of Alicia's Funky Fashions net assets is £175,000. Alexander Business Attire acquires £75,000 (£250,000 – £175,000) of goodwill in the transaction. You can find out much more about the somewhat complex topic of business combinations and goodwill in Chapter 17.

Writing intangibles off using amortisation

Amortisation is similar to depreciation (see Chapter 12) but is applied to intangible assets and is used to move the cost of intangible assets from the balance sheet to the income statement over the intangible asset's useful economic life. Most intangibles are amortised on a straight-line basis using their expected useful life. For example, in UK GAAP, FRS 10 *Goodwill and Intangible Assets* allows goodwill to be amortised (written off) over its expected useful life and this useful life is capped at 20 years (if a company wants to write it off over more than 20 years, it must have a justifiable reason for doing so).

If you're reporting under IFRS you must not, under any circumstances, amortise goodwill. This is because IFRS 3 *Business Combinations* specifically requires goodwill to be tested annually for *impairment* (checking to see if the amount of goodwill on the statement of financial position is actually over-stated). UK GAAP is also set for major changes very soon (at the time of writing, new UK GAAP is set for implementation for accounting periods commencing on or after 1 January 2015) and the 20 years capped life I mention above is set to be reduced to five years.

What about the balance sheet cost of intangibles? Leasehold improvements are easy: the amount is the actual cost for any improvements the company makes. The useful life for leasehold improvements is usually the term of the underlying lease. Patents, copyrights and trademarks the business buys are treated similarly: you have the cost of purchase as a basis for the amount you amortise.

Internally-generated intangible assets and internally-generated goodwill cannot be recorded on a balance sheet unless a readily ascertainable market value is available. In reality, hardly any intangible assets will have a readily ascertainable market value, and those that do will hardly ever be internally-generated. If you're ever a bit stuck on this subject, check out FRS 10 in UK GAAP; IFRS 3 for goodwill under international standards; and IAS 38 for intangible assets under international standards.

Learning about Current Assets

Current assets include cash and any asset that a company anticipates converting to cash within a 12-month period from the date of the balance sheet. On the balance sheet, you should list current assets in *order of liquidity* (starting from the hardest to turn into cash and ending with the easiest to turn into cash and cash itself). Because short-term investments are the least liquid, they show up on the balance sheet first. Other common current assets are stock/inventory, trade receivables, loans receivable, stock/inventory and prepaid expenses and cash (cash being the most liquid because it's already cash!). Here, I cover each type in turn.

Short-term investments

Short-term investments can be equity (stocks and shares) and debt (loan notes) investments that a company invests in to put any surplus cash to work making money. (I discuss investments and bonds in Chapter 8, and stocks and shares in Chapter 9.) Just to be clear: the company is not recording its *own* equity and debt as investments here. Instead, the company is recording stocks and shares in *other* companies it purchases as investments.

To be able to classify these investments as short term (in other words, *current*) on the balance sheet, the company must be planning to sell them within 12 months of the balance sheet date. Two types of short-term investments you'll probably come across are held-for-trading and available-for-sale investments. I explain both here and offer examples of how to handle them.

Held-for-trading investments

Held-for-trading investments are debt and equity instruments that a business purchases to sell in the short term to make a profit. You record held-for-trading investments on the balance sheet initially at cost. Then, as their value fluctuates, you record them at market value, with any unrealised gain or loss going to the income statement. *Unrealised* means the gain or loss is on paper only. You won't have realised gain or loss until you actually sell the instruments.

Judith Jumpers Limited buys 100 shares in Lisa's Lingerie Ltd for £1,000. To record this transaction, the balance sheet 'investments' account is increased by £1,000 and cash is decreased with the same amount.

Sadly, at the end of the month after purchase, these 100 shares are now worth only £900 (boo!). To adjust the current asset section of the balance sheet, you need to reduce 'investments' by the £100 drop in value. Then you also increase 'Loss on current asset investment' in the income statement (see Chapter 10) by £100.

Earlier in the chapter, in the 'Homing in on the Historic Cost Convention' section, I explain that historic cost is not used on the balance sheet when you're dealing with certain types of financial instruments (those that are carried on the balance sheet at market value under the alternative accounting rules). In the example above you can see that the value of Judith Jumper's investment on the balance sheet is reflected at less than historic cost. This is sometimes known as a *diminution in value*.

Available-for-sale investments

These instruments are debt and equity investments that a company opts not to classify as held-for-trading financial instruments. The difference is important because unrealised fluctuations in the value of available-for-sale financial instruments do *not* show up on the income statement as gain or loss. Instead, any changes go into 'other comprehensive income' or (in UK GAAP) via the 'statement of total recognised gains and losses' (see Chapter 9).

Here's an example of how to handle an available-for-sale transaction.

Byrne Enterprises Limited buys 2,000 shares in Breary Concrete Ltd for £5,000, and decides to classify the shares as available-for-sale. At the end of the month, the fair value of the shares is £6,000. Neil Byrne, the director, is jumping for joy as his company has an unrealised gain of £1,000!

To record this transaction, you increase the value of the investment on the balance sheet by £1,000 (from £5,000 to £6,000) and increase 'fair value reserve' in the equity section of the balance sheet by £1,000.

Beyond the scope of what you have to do for your accountancy studies, in real-life financial accounting, the recognition of unrealised gains and losses may have a deferred tax effect (see Chapter 18).

Inventory

If you're a student accountant, you need to get a grip on two different types of inventory. The first type consists of products that are bought from a manufacturer that are available for sale in shops and supermarkets. The second type of inventory are the stuff used by manufacturers to make products that are then sold onto a customer, which includes direct materials, work in progress and finished goods.

I devote an entire chapter to inventory – Chapter 13. Here, I just give you brief snippets and examples of inventory terminology.

Retail inventory

Accounting for retail inventory is easier than accounting for manufacturing inventory because a company, such as a retail outlet, has only one class of inventory to keep track of: goods the business purchases from various manufacturers for resale on to its customers.

Here's an example of how a retailer handles an inventory purchase. The buyer in charge of lawnmower inventory at a major home improvement store sees that her department is running low on a certain type of lawnmower. The buyer follows the purchasing process, and the end result is that the department receives a shipment of mowers from its supplier.

This transaction is a purchase (a cost), but it's not an expense until the store sells the mowers to customers. So the business records the entire shipment of mowers on the balance sheet as an addition to both inventory (see Chapter 13) and trade creditors/payables (see Chapter 8). I use *trade payables* instead of *cash* because the department store has payment terms with this supplier, and money has yet to change hands during this transaction (known as buying goods on *credit*).

Manufacturing inventory

Because a manufacturing company doesn't simply buy finished goods for resale to customers, its inventory is a bit more fiddly as it generally has three major components:

- ✔ **Raw materials inventory:** This inventory reflects all materials the company owns that it will use to make a certain product. For example, for the lawnmower manufacturer this includes the steel to form the body, leather or fabric for the seat, and all the other bits and pieces that make the mower work. In essence, any materials that you can directly trace back to making the mower are raw materials inventory.

- ✔ **Work-in-progress:** At any point in time during the manufacturing process, the company probably has items that are in the process of being made but aren't yet complete; these are called *work-in-progress*. For a lawnmower manufacturer, this will include any mowers that aren't completely put together and ready to give a lawn a haircut at the end of the accounting period. The company values its work-in-progress based on how complete each mower is in the manufacturing process.

- ✔ **Finished goods:** These are costs you associate with goods that are completely ready for sale to customers but haven't yet been sold. For the lawnmower manufacturer, this category consists of mowers not yet sold to retail home improvement shops.

Companies can use many different methods to place a value on closing inventory. I discuss everything you need to know on this topic in Chapter 13.

Trade receivables

Trade receivables (often referred to as *trade debtors*) is the amount of money that customers owe a business for goods they've purchased from the company or services the company has rendered to them. Just about all types of businesses can and probably do have a trade receivable.

For example, I prepare the financial statements for one of my clients. We review the financial statements together, and I give the client an invoice for £500. A couple of weeks later, my client sends me a cheque for payment in full. In that two-week period between when I drop off the financial statements and receive the payment, that £500 is on my books as a trade receivable.

Now, it's a sad fact of life that businesses extending credit to their customers almost always have some customers who just won't pay their bills. Under generally accepted accounting practice (GAAP; see Chapter 4), you have to make a provision for any amounts that may become bad debts. You may be asked to make a provision for bad debts (sometimes called an *allowance for doubtful debts*) in your accountancy studies and you'll also more than likely come across such provisions in your day-to-day work in accountancy. To make sure you're fully prepared, I want to show you how to account for bad debt.

GAAP requires that businesses extending credit to their customers estimate the amount of debts that won't be paid. Companies use a few different methods to do this calculation, usually based on their past experiences with bad debt.

For example, a company in business for five years has found during this period of time that 2 per cent of all credit sales will be uncollectible. If nothing in the current period causes the company to question the correctness of this percentage, it will use the percentage to estimate its uncollectible accounts in the current period. Generally, businesses often have a set percentage, based on the total amounts owed at the year-end to work out their provisions, for example 5 per cent of the total trade receivables.

Norah makes sales to customers on account during a year amounting to £50,000. Using the 2 per cent figure, the estimate for uncollectible debts is £1,000 (£50,000 × 0.02). The journal entry (see Chapter 5) to record this amount is made to debit 'bad debt expense', an income statement account (see Chapter 10), and to credit 'allowance for doubtful debts', a balance sheet contra account, for £1,000 each. In the next year if the estimate for uncollect-ible debts is £1,500, only the movement of £500 (£1,500 minus £1,000) will be recorded as debit 'bad debt expense' and credit 'allowance for doubtful debts'.

A *contra account* carries a balance opposite to the account's normal balance. Because the normal balance for an asset is a debit, the normal balance for a contra-asset account, such as 'allowance for doubtful debts', is a credit. 'Allowance for doubtful debts' is also known as a *provision for doubtful debts*, which is an offset against the main account. That's because, while the trade receivables account itself is carried at the actual amount that the customers owe, the allowance for doubtful debts contra-asset account serves to reduce trade receivables to the amount estimated to be collected, or what's called *net receivables*.

Until the company is reasonably sure that a customer on account won't cough up the cash, the journal entry is just an estimate not tied to any particu-lar customer. These types of provisions are usually called *general* bad debt provisions.

When you determine that a particular customer's account is uncollectible (maybe the business went bust), your next step is to remove the amount from both 'allowance for doubtful debts' and the customer trade receivable balance. After all, the situation's pretty clear cut – you know the customer won't be paying and these sorts of provisions are known as *specific* bad debt provisions.

A *specific* bad debt is one that directly relates to a customer, whereas *general* bad debt provisions do not relate to any specific customer. You can make a specific bad debt provision directly to the bad debt expense account without impacting your general provisions.

Newbury Supplies owes you £1,000. You send the company a letter stating that the account is now overdue and Royal Mail returns the letter as undeliverable, with no forwarding address. You are unable to locate Newbury Supplies. You must make a journal entry to debit 'allowance for doubtful debts' for £1,000 and credit 'trade receivables – Newbury Supplies' for £1,000.

Now, what if, out of the blue, the owner of Newbury Supplies sends you a cheque for the £1,000 after you've written off the balance owed? You would need to credit 'allowance for doubtful debts' in the income statement for £1,000 (because the original debit went there when the debt was first written off) and then debit the bank account with £1,000. The entry would not need to touch trade receivables.

Loans receivable

A *loan receivable* is a short-term debt that someone owes you, meaning it becomes due for payment within 12 months of the balance sheet date. A company will sometimes make a loan to a third party – for example, to one of its customers to help them out with short-term cash flow problems. Generally, a short-term loan has three major components:

- ✔ **Principal (sometimes called *capital*):** The amount owed to the company by the debtor.

- ✔ **Rate:** The calculation that will be used to determine the amount of interest the debtor pays on the principal. It's always stated as an annual rate even if the loan is for a period shorter than one year.

- ✔ **Time:** The period within which the debtor has to pay back the loan.

A loan receivable is shown in the current assets part of the balance sheet only for the debt you anticipate will be paid back within 12 months of the balance sheet date. Any portion of the loan receivable extending past that 12-month period gets put in the long-term assets section of the balance sheet.

Prepaid expenses

Prepaid expenses are expenses the business pays before they're due. Many companies pay a year's worth of business insurance at once. They may also pay rent and interest expense on loans in advance.

Stella pays an invoice for £1,200 that covers 12 months of car insurance for the company vehicle. You originally post this amount as an increase to prepaid expenses. Then, as each month passes, you move the portion of the insurance the company has used off the balance sheet into the income statement by debiting insurance expense for £100 (£1,200/12 months) and crediting prepaid expenses for the same amount.

Cash

Okay, before we start talking about cash, I want to emphasise that the definition of cash goes beyond actual notes and coinage. Any sort of account that's backed by cash is deemed to be a cash account. For example, when you go to the supermarket and pay the bill using your debit or credit card, that card payment is the same as cash. That's because when you enter your PIN, or sign for the transaction, you attest to the fact that there are funds in your bank account allowing this card payment to immediately clear – that is, funds can be withdrawn on demand.

Depending on the size of the business, it may organise and manage the way it brings in money and pays its bills in one or more types of cash accounts. A large service business may have a separate bank account for day-to-day transactions and a foreign currency bank account. Some companies have bank accounts for which they earn interest income (sometimes called *deposit accounts*).

You may be wondering why a company complicates its bookkeeping with different bank accounts to pay expenses and bring in dosh. In some cases, having different bank accounts creates a safer business environment. For example, having a dedicated purchase ledger bank account allows purchase ledger clerks to do their job (process cheques to pay suppliers and perform electronic transfers) while having access to a limited, defined amount of cash.

But when it comes to cash accounts, it's really the Wild West out there in the business world. Some small businesses may have several bank accounts – many more than they actually need – and some large businesses may only have one.

Accountancy textbooks often concern themselves with making sure you understand that cash accounts are included in the *current assets* section of the balance sheet. Don't worry, I provide a full-blown assets section of a balance sheet at the end of this chapter so you can see this concept at work. However, it's also important that you understand the business purpose for different types of bank accounts – so here they are, with brief descriptions:

- ✔ **General bank account:** A business usually earmarks a particular bank account, which it calls its *general* account, to handle business activities such as depositing cash and paying bills.

- ✔ **Payroll account:** Many mid-sized and large companies (and some small ones, too) have a bank account that's used only to pay employees. What the company does is work out the total amount of cheques or BACS transfers it needs to pay employees and transfers that amount from its general account to cover the payroll payments.

- ✔ **Merchant account:** If a business allows customers to pay by credit card, it probably has a dedicated merchant account into which the only deposits will be from its *merchant provider*: the company that helps it process customer credit cards. Normally, withdrawals from this account go to the general bank account to cover bill-paying withdrawals.

- ✔ **Petty cash account:** Most companies have a cash box to pay for small daily expenses such as milk and sundry office items. Petty cash is often maintained using the *imprest system*, which means it always carries the same balance. By this, I mean that anytime the cash box is checked, it should contain cash or receipts equalling the petty cash fund amount. So if the fund is £300, cash and receipts in the box have to equal £300.

✔ **Sweep account:** A sweep account is a way for the company to automatically earn investment income (interest). The way it works is that each evening, any extra cash in the company's general account is gathered up and transferred (swept) into investment (or deposit) accounts.

Money from many different companies is pooled into a bigger pot, thereby providing the advantage of a higher rate of return. Then as the company needs the money in order to clear cheques and withdrawals, the money is swept back into the general account.

Studying the Asset Section of the Balance Sheet

To wrap up this chapter, I show you in Figure 7-1 what the asset section of the balance sheet looks like. Liabilities and equity are each merely a line item in Figure 7-1. Check out Chapter 8 to see the liability section and Chapter 9 to see the equity section of a balance sheet fully developed.

ASSETS	
Non-current assets	£
Property, plant and equipment	52,655
Patents	830
Trademarks	500
	53,985
Current assets	
Short-term investments	1,600
Inventory	4,300
Trade receivables	6,800
Prepayments	500
Short-term loan	3,500
Cash	3,560
	20,260
Non-current assets	
Long-term loan	1,000
Total assests	75,245
Total equity and liabilities	75,245

Figure 7-1: The asset section of a balance sheet.

The company's property, plant and equipment (non-current assets) are listed first, net of depreciation charges (the method of writing off the cost of tangible non-current assets over their expected useful lives). Then any non-physical intangibles are shown – usually *net of amortisation*, which means that amortisation is subtracted before listing the values of the intangibles on the balance sheet (this net value is known as *net book value*).

Current assets are always shown after non-current (fixed) assets, in order of liquidity. If you're a student accountant, the only long-term current asset you're likely to come across is a loan that falls due after more than 12 months from the balance sheet date.

Chapter 8

Grappling with Liabilities

- -

In This Chapter

▶ Discovering how a company raises cash

▶ Identifying current liabilities

▶ Getting to grips with long-term debt

▶ Knowing when contingencies are reportable

▶ Accounting for bonds

- -

*P*art III of this book is all about the financial statement called the balance sheet (known internationally as the *statement of financial position*), which reports a company's assets and the claims against those assets. In Chapter 7, I walk you through the assets part of the accounting equation. This chapter is all about the claims, or debts, which in accounting lingo are called *liabilities*.

Nobody likes debt, but it's often an inevitable part of a company keeping its doors open for business. In this chapter, I cover both current and long-term debt. You find out what types of current liabilities help a business manage its day-to-day operations, and you learn about long-term debt obligations that businesses use to acquire assets. I cover basic long-term debt such as mortgages and loans, and I also discuss a method many companies use to raise finance – issuing bonds – focusing on the facets of this complicated topic. A third type of liability – contingent liabilities – also gets a mention in this chapter. These liabilities aren't always included in financial accounting reports, so I give you the lowdown on when and how to include them.

Seeing How Businesses Account for Liabilities

Liabilities are claims against the company by other businesses or its employees. Examples include:

- **Trade payables (often called trade creditors):** Money a company owes to its suppliers for services rendered and products it has purchased.

- **Deferred income:** Money received from clients that pay the business for goods or services they haven't yet received – like advance payments for subscriptions.

- **Salaries payable:** Salaries the company owes to employees.

Generally accepted accounting practice (GAAP, which I discuss in Chapter 4) dictates that when you prepare the liability section of the balance sheet, any claims against the company have to be broken down between *current* and *long-term* obligations. The dividing line between the two is the one-year mark: all liabilities that are due within one year of the date of the financial statements are considered current. All others are considered long term.

In Chapter 5, I introduce the fundamental accounting equation, which under UK GAAP is this:

Assets = Liabilities + Owners' equity

Based on the order of elements in this equation, liabilities show up on the balance sheet after total assets but before equity accounts. Current liabilities are shown first, followed by long-term liabilities. (Current and long-term assets receive similar treatment; see Chapter 7.)

The equation above is based on UK GAAP. However, financial statements prepared to IFRS GAAP require the liabilities section to be shown *after* equity, hence the equation under IFRSs becomes:

Assets = Owners' equity + Liabilities

Using the accruals method of accounting (which I explain in Chapter 6), all revenue must be matched with all expenses incurred during the production of that revenue. So if a company incurs costs but money doesn't change hands, a liability shows up on the balance sheet to reflect the amount that eventually has to be paid. For example, the company may buy goods from a supplier without actually paying for them yet (in other words, purchases the goods on credit); those goods appear in trade payables, which is a current liability.

Figure 8-1 shows a very simple liability section of the balance sheet, with all asset and equity accounts consolidated in a single line item each (the two shaded lines). Check out Chapter 3 for a more formal presentation of all sections of the balance sheet. Also, please note that I have chosen to show each account's chart of account number too. (See Chapter 5 for more information about the chart of accounts.) A formal balance sheet usually won't include this detail.

Total Assets	75,245.00
Total Equity	16,278.88
Liabilities & Equity	
Liabilities	
Current liabilities	
2010 Trade payables	34,202.62
2210 Short-term loan obligations	1,365.50
2215 Salaries control account	145.00
2220 Corporation tax	668.00
2225 Deferred income	500.00
2230 PAYE & National Insurance	2,000.00
2240 Accruals	85.00
Total current liabilities	38,966.12
Non-current liabilities	
2710 Loan	20,000.00
Total non-current liabilities	20,000.00
Total liabilities	58,966.12
Total Liabilities and Equity	75,245.00

Figure 8-1:
The liability section of a balance sheet.

Keeping Control of Current Liabilities

In this section, I cover just about every current liability, so by the end you'll be a whizz! To help you further, I even throw in some journal entries so you can see how the transactions get into the original books of entry (see Chapter 5).

But before you start, I want to make sure you understand why it's so important to separate out current from long-term liabilities. GAAP requires the separation so the user of the financial statements can easily glean the information necessary to work out a company's liquidity and solvency figures such as *working capital*, which is current assets minus current liabilities, or the *current ratio*, which is current assets divided by current liabilities. (A reminder: users of financial reports may be investors, banks or anyone else with an interest in the company's financial health; see Chapter 1.)

These financial ratios and tools (which I spell out in Chapter 14) give the user specific criteria for deciding how well the company is performing. For example, a bank thinking about making a loan to a business wants to gauge the expectation of being paid back on time. The viability of a company's working capital is a very important aspect here.

For this reason, it's rarely okay to net current assets with current liabilities under GAAP. To do so would eliminate the ability to use any sort of ratio analysis involving current asset or liability accounts. For example, if you purchase inventory on account, both the inventory and trade payables accounts increase.

Trade payables/creditors

Trade payables (commonly referred to as *trade creditors* in UK GAAP) includes money a company owes its suppliers for services and products that it's purchased in the normal course of business and anticipates paying back in the short term. For example, the company purchases inventory from a manufacturer or office supplies from a local stationery shop. The transaction originally goes in the *purchases journal*, which shows purchases on account, with a debit going to whatever cost or expense account is most applicable and a credit going to trade payables.

Per GAAP, trade payables are always assumed to be a current liability.

Note that the terms *trade payables* and *trade creditors* are often used synonymously. But technically, *trade payables* generally refer to suppliers from which a company buys business supplies and *direct materials*: items it uses to manufacture products for sale (see Chapter 10). Many suppliers selling on credit give a discount to customers who pay their trade payables early. For example, the terms of the purchase may require full payment in 30 days but a discount of 2 per cent if the customer pays the bill within 10 days. Figure 8-2 walks you through the debiting and crediting for £1,000 of inventory purchased on account with discount terms of 2 per cent if the bill is paid within 30 days and the subsequent payment.

Figure 8-2:
Inventory purchase on account and payment within discount period.

1. *To record the purchase made on 21 May 2013*

Debit inventory	1,000	
Credit trade payables		1,000

2. *To record the payment made on 1 June 2013*

Debit trade payables	1,000	
Credit cash at bank		980
Credit discounts received		20

Sundry creditors

Companies often have *sundry creditors* within their balance sheet, which are other types of liabilities that don't generally fall under the umbrella of trade payables, corporation tax and those sorts of things. Sundry creditors can include one-off transactions, such as small, infrequent supplies that aren't assigned an individual purchase ledger account.

Payroll and income taxes

The nature of the beast is that most companies *accrue* payroll and related payroll taxes (such as pay as you earn (PAYE) and national insurance contributions (NICs)), which means the company owes them but has not yet paid them. This concept is easy to understand if you think about the way you've been paid by your employer in the past.

Most companies have a built-in time lag between when employees earn their wages and when the employees are paid.

Stella's Stylish Shoes pays its employees on the 1st and 15th of every month with 15 days of wages in arrears. This means that when the employees get their pay packets on 15 July, the payments relate to work they did from 16 June to 30 June.

To match expenses to revenue when preparing financial statements for the one-month period ending 30 June, the gross wages earned but not yet paid as at 30 June have to be added to the balance sheet as a current liability.

Not only that, but you also have to account for any payroll taxes or national insurance contributions that will be deducted from the employee's wages when the wages are finally paid. Here are examples of employee payroll-related accruals that may be accrued for in a company's financial statements:

- ✔ **National insurance contributions (NICs):** These provide contributions towards a state pension. NICs are payable on a percentage basis on wages up to a certain amount. Employers also have to pay *employer NICs*, which are currently 13.8 per cent of an employee's salary.

- ✔ **Pay As You Earn (PAYE):** The company calculates this tax using the basic rate of income tax, which is currently 20 per cent. If you fall into the higher earnings tax bracket (set at £34,371 in 2012/13), you pay 40 per cent income tax. Bear in mind that the figure applied to higher earnings changes each tax year (the tax year starts on 6 April).

✔ **Health care or other insurance premiums:** An employer may pay only a portion of the health insurance premium for an employee and his family. The additional amount for health and other insurance, such as life insurance, is a deduction as well if the employee authorises it.

✔ **Pension deductions:** Many employers have pension plans that allow employees to make contributions into a pension scheme. In addition, many companies may also pay a contribution for their employees into their personal pension scheme as a 'perk'.

✔ **Employer benefits:** Additionally, the employer incurs as an expense any benefits that the company provides to employees (in the UK, this is known as *Class 1A National Insurance*). Employee benefits can include all sorts of different things, but the commonest are: company cars and vans; health care; and computers.

Class 1A NICs that an employer must currently pay are set at 13.8 per cent. This rate can be changed, however, so keep your eyes peeled. To check out rates and allowances, go to www.hmrc.org.uk.

So that you can better understand this class of current liabilities, here's a payroll scenario that's similar to what you'll come across in either your accountancy studies or the workplace.

Gabriella Gardening Limited has a year-end of 31 December 2012. On 29 December 2012, Emma, the company's payroll officer, ran the company's payroll. These wages will not be paid until 3 January 2013 and details of the payroll are as follows:

Gross pay		£50,000.00
PAYE		£17,000.00
Employee NICs	£3,500.00	
Pension deductions	£1,500.00	
Net wages		£28,000.00
Employer NICs	£6,900.00	

The question is, how does Emma record gross wages, tax and other deductions made from the employees' wages as short-term liabilities? Additionally, how does she record the related payroll tax expense? For the purposes of this scenario, you should assume that Gabriella Gardening has no employer benefit expense.

Wondering how to answer this question via journal entries? I show you how in Figure 8-3.

Figure 8-3:
Journal
entry to
record
accrued
payroll and
taxes.

To record accrued payroll

	£	£
Payroll expense	50,000.00	
Employers NIC expense	6,900.00	
PAYE (current liability)		17,000.00
Gross NICs (emploee + employer NIC as current liability)		10,400.00
Pension deductions (current liability)		1,500.00
Net wages account (current liability)		28,000.00
	56,900.00	56,900.00

When Emma finally makes the payments on 3 January 2013, she will credit the cash at bank account with £28,000 and debit the net wages account with £28,000. Doing so will clear the current liability. When she makes the payment to HM Revenue and Customs (HMRC) in respect of the PAYE and gross national insurance deductions, she'll also credit the bank account with £27,400, and debit the PAYE current liability account with £17,000 and the gross NICs current liability account with £10,400, which will clear out those liabilities. When the company makes the payment to the pension scheme for the employee contributions, Emma will credit the bank account with £1,500 and debit the pension deductions current liability account.

Deferred income

Another common short-term liability is that of *deferred income*. This current liability occurs when a company receives payment for goods or services rendered before it's actually provided the goods or services. Because the business has an obligation to fulfil its end of the contract, the deferred income is a current liability until the company completes its contractual obligations.

To record revenue, it has to be earned and realisable (*realisable* means the transaction will eventually turn to cash). However, in this situation, the revenue is not yet earned.

It's easier to bring this scenario to life using a typical illustration. Let's say you pay £120 for an annual subscription to a magazine, consisting of 12 issues. Until the magazine publisher sends the twelfth issue to you, your payment is not 100 per cent earned revenue for the publisher. This is because the publisher still 'owes' you one magazine.

The way this scenario works at the publisher's end is that it debits cash and credits unearned revenue for your payment of £120. Then each month after it sends you an issue, it records earning that portion by debiting unearned revenue and crediting gross sales for £10 (£120/12).

Other short-term liabilities

Other short-term liabilities include items such as loan payments that are payable within 12 months. Current liabilities can originate as short-term bank loans, or they can be the portion of a long-term debt that's due within the next 12 months. Another type of current liability you'll probably come across is *estimated warranty*, which reflects how much money a company may have to pay to repair or replace products sold to customers.

Here's more information on short-term bank loans, current maturities of long-term debt and estimated warranty expense:

- ✓ **Short-term bank loans:** When a company takes out a loan, it doesn't always have to be for an extensive period (such as a 30-year mortgage). In many cases, a company anticipates getting paid for a job it's performed and just needs a brief influx of cash to pay mandatory expenses such as payroll.

    A good example of this situation is a *working capital loan*, which a bank makes with the expectation that the loan will be paid back from collection of trade receivables. As long as the loan is due in full less than 12 months after the balance sheet date, you classify borrowed funds as current liabilities.

    It's important to examine short-term debt when determining the financial health of a company because it indicates whether a cash flow issue (see Chapter 11) could arise in the future. If the short-term debt is unreasonably high, the company may not have the excess money to make the loan payments.

    A company can also have a *revolving line of credit*, which is a loan with a pre-set limit on how much the company can withdraw at any one time, reflecting as current debt. This sort of current debt is much more flexible than a loan because the company borrows against it only when necessary.

- ✓ **Current maturities of long-term debt:** Say that a company has a mortgage on its land and building spanning 30 years, and it's in the third year of paying off the loan. To properly reflect this mortgage on the balance sheet, the principal amount (sometimes called the *capital amount*) the company owes in the next 12 months has to be shown as a current liability. The rest of the mortgage payable is a long-term liability, a subject I discuss in the next section.

    You can use an *amortisation schedule*, which shows how much of each mortgage payment goes to principal versus interest, to work out the current portion of the long-term debt.

✔ **Estimated warranty liability:** Warranties on products may be an assumed part of the purchase price or something the purchaser elects to buy – usually at the time of purchase. A good example is the warranty purchased for a computer from a PC shop. The computer comes with a six-month warranty from the manufacturer covering numerous performance and repair issues. Assume that if the computer breaks down within the six-month warranty period, the purchaser can send it back to be fixed, free of charge. The company has to calculate and record an estimate of how much it costs the company to fulfil the terms of the warranty.

A popular way to estimate warranty expense is to use a percentage of sales. This percentage is normally based on historical sales returns information. If in the past the company has incurred an actual warranty expense of 4 per cent, that same percentage should be the current year's estimate until the facts change. Below is an example of how to deal with warranty calculations.

Computers R Us makes computers. In the most recent month of operations, September, it sold £500,000 worth of computers. Historical warranty expense is 4 per cent of sales. So the estimated warranty liability is £20,000 (£500,000 multiplied by 4 per cent).

Also, during September, Computers R Us has actual expenses of £2,000 for labour and £3,000 (total of £5,000) for materials to fulfil warranty claims. Keep in mind that the £5,000 includes warranty costs not only for September purchases but also for purchases going back six months.

Ready to see how to get these transactions in the books by way of journal entry? Figure 8-4 gives you the lowdown on the entry to record the estimate and record actual warranty expense.

	Debit	Credit
Warranty Expense	20,000.00	
Warranty Liability		20,000.00

Figure 8-4: *To record estimated warranty expense for September*

Recording accrued and actual warranty expense.

	Debit	Credit
Warranty Liability	5,000.00	
Labour		2,000.00
Materials		3,000.00

To record actual warranty cost for September

Planning for Long-Term Obligations

If you've bought a car on finance, you're probably all too familiar with *long-term debt*: loans that won't be paid off by the end of the next 12-month period. Companies have long-term debt, too. While a company usually uses current debt as a vehicle to meet short-term obligations like payroll, it may incur long-term debt for the financing of company assets.

Managing long-term debt

If a company needs to raise cash and decides to do so by accumulating debt, the most common types are mortgages, loans, finance leases and financial instruments. Following is your financial accounting guide to the first three of these categories of long-term debt. Things like bonds are a much more complicated subject, and I devote the upcoming 'Accounting for Bond Issuances' section to them.

Any type of debt instrument between a lender and a borrower specifies *principal* (the amount borrowed), *rate* (how much interest the company pays to borrow the money) and *time* (the length of the loan). So any repayment of the debt is broken down between principal and interest according to the terms of the debt instrument.

Mortgages

Mortgages are used to finance the purchase of land and buildings (see Chapter 13). The property *collateralises* the mortgage, which means the property is held as security on the mortgage. If the company defaults on the mortgage, the bank/finance company seizes the property and sells it in an attempt to pay off the loan.

If you own a house/flat the chances are you purchased it by getting a mortgage from a bank. The paperwork involved in this transaction is quite significant, and it's a similar beast when a company purchases a property, with a whole host of documentation being transferred back and forth among the buyer, seller, lawyers and the bank itself.

Loan agreements

Loan agreements are formal written documents that spell out how money is being borrowed. In the earlier section 'Other short-term liabilities', I explain that the part of a loan that's going to be paid off within the 12 months following the financial report release is classified as short-term debt (a *current liability*). The remainder of the loan is considered a long-term debt (a *noncurrent liability*, or in UK GAAP lingo, *creditors falling due after one year*).

Financing asset purchases with debt versus equity

Companies raise money to purchase assets in one of two ways: debt or equity. *Debt* means the company borrows money with an obligation to pay the borrowed funds back. *Equity* means the company sells shares to investors.

What makes equity investing appealing is that the company is not under any obligation to buy back the shares from the investors. However, it also means that more voices are heard regarding how the business is run, especially in smaller companies – something that shareholders who also handle the day-to-day operations may not be all that eager to put up with.

Oddly enough, debt can end up making a company money. This situation is called *financial leverage*, and it takes place when the borrowed money is expected to earn a higher return than the cost of interest payable on the debt.

Additionally, interest expense on debt is tax deductible (which means the expense is allowed for tax purposes in working out the profit on which corporation tax is paid) while dividends payable to investors are not. Based on many factors, the company using debt to finance its asset purchases could also end up in a better position due to the decrease in taxes payable.

Here's an example: let's say you take out a student loan at 2 per cent interest to pay for your university accommodation. Your family wants to lend a helping hand and gives you a gift of £2,000 to put toward your living expenses. Because that gift frees up £2,000 of your student loan, you decide to invest this amount in a financial vehicle paying 3 per cent. You've just made 1 per cent using someone else's money. Woohoo!

Finance leases

Another type of long-term debt involves *finance leases*. A company doesn't always buy its fixed assets (see Chapter 7); sometimes it leases them. Doing so makes sense for any fixed asset that needs to be frequently replaced. For example, leasing computers makes sense for businesses that need to stay up to date with computer processing technology.

Finance leases have characteristics of ownership, which means the cost of the leased capital asset goes on the balance sheet as a depreciable asset. I offer a full discussion of accounting for leases in Chapter 19.

Anticipating contingent liabilities

A *contingent liability* is a liability that exists when a company has an existing circumstance as at the date of the financial statements that may cause a future loss depending on events that have not yet happened (and indeed may never happen). Here are two examples of common contingent liabilities:

✔ **Pending litigation:** This means the company is actively involved in a lawsuit that is not yet settled.

✔ **Guarantee of obligations:** This circumstance occurs when a business agrees to step in and satisfy the debt of another company if need be (the company agreeing to step in, if need be, is often referred to as the *guarantor*).

Contingent liabilities aren't provided for in the financial statements (see Chapter 15) because they don't satisfy the recognition and measurement criteria. Instead, such contingent liabilities are disclosed in the notes to the financial statements according to the dictates of IAS 37 *Provisions, Contingent Liabilities and Contingent Assets* (the UK's FRS 12 *Provisions, Contingent Liabilities and Contingent Assets* works in the same way as IAS 37). For the full lowdown on IFRSs, check out my other book, *IFRS For Dummies* (Wiley). Here are the three criteria that IAS 37 states must be met before a contingent liability becomes an actual liability:

✔ The company has a present obligation (legal or constructive) as a result of a past event(s).

A *legal obligation* results when a solicitor or court says that you're going to have to cough up some money, or give up another form of asset, to settle the liability. A *constructive obligation* is one that arises because of the company's actions, such as a pattern of past practice (for example, a long history of paying bonuses based on pre-tax profits using a specified formula), or because it creates a valid expectation in the minds of those parties (for example, announcing a programme of redundancies as the result of a division closing down or ceasing to trade).

✔ It's probable that an outflow of resources embodying economic benefits (in other words, cash or other assets) is required to settle the obligation.

✔ A reliable estimate of the obligation can be made.

If the contingency meets these three criteria for recognition of a liability, the journal entry involves a debit to a relevant expense account in the income statement (see Chapter 10) and a credit to a liability account.

Accounting for Bond Issuances

Well, I saved the best for last! I say that tongue-in-cheek because bonds (which are essentially *financial instruments*) are a somewhat thorny financial accounting issue. However, if you can get the gist of this section, you'll have no trouble dealing with this minefield in your work or in your accountancy studies.

Understanding the basics

Financial instruments are a way of raising finance. The way to look at a financial instrument is to consider that when a company raises finance, another third party is providing that finance. Financial instruments are basically things like loans, trade payables, shares and mortgages – anything the company uses as a means of finance. Many large companies issue bonds as a means of raising finance for things like capital expenditure, operations and acquiring other companies.

The person who purchases a bond receives interest payments during the bond's term (or for as long as she holds the bond) at the bond's stated interest rate. When the bond *matures* (the term of the bond expires), the company pays the bondholder back the bond's face value.

A bond is either a source of financing or an investment, depending on which side of the transaction you're looking at. The company issuing the bond incurs the long-term liability. The person or company acquiring the bond uses it as an investment; for a business, this investment is an asset (see Chapter 7).

A company can issue bonds to sell at:

- ✔ **Face value (also known as *par value*):** The principal amount printed on the bond

- ✔ A **discount:** Less than face value

- ✔ A **premium:** More than face value

Usually face value is set in denominations of £1,000. In the sections that follow, I explain what it means to the accountant when the company sells at face value, at a premium or at a discount.

The rate of interest that investors actually earn is known as the *coupon rate*. If the bond sells for a premium, the bond's coupon rate is generally lower than the rate stated on the bond. For example, if the face rate of the bond is 10 per cent and the coupon rate is 9 per cent, the bond sells at a premium. That's because the investor receives higher interest income on this bond than can be expected when factoring in the conditions of the current bond market; the investor is willing to pay more than face value for the bond.

On the flip side, if a bond sells at a discount, its coupon rate of interest is higher than the rate stated on the bond. For example, if the face rate of the bond is 10 per cent and the coupon rate is 11 per cent, the bond sells at a discount. In this case, the investor is making less interest income than can be expected when factoring in the conditions of the current bond market. So, to offset that disadvantage, the investor pays less than face value for the bond.

Accounting for bonds sold at face value

The easiest type of bond transaction to account for is when the company sells bonds at face value. The journal entry to record bonds a company issues at face value is to debit cash and credit bonds payable. So if the company issues bonds for £100,000 with a five-year term, at 10 per cent, the journal entry to record the bonds is to debit cash with £100,000 and credit bonds payable on the balance sheet for £100,000.

Addressing interest payments

Assume that the terms of a bond call for interest to be paid *half-yearly*, which means every six months. Suppose the bonds I introduce in the previous section are issued on 1 July 2012 and the first interest payment is not due until 31 December 2012. The interest expense is principal (£100,000) multiplied by rate (10 per cent) multiplied by the time fraction (1/2 year). So your journal entry on 31 December 2012 is to debit bond interest expense in the profit and loss account (income statement) with £5,000 and credit cash with £5,000.

Getting and amortising a premium

When a bond is issued at a *premium*, its market value is more than its face value. To make the concept come alive for you, I'll walk through a fairly simplistic example that will help you see how to handle the journals when a bond is issued at a premium.

> Alex Co PLC issues bonds with a face value of £500,000 at 102 per cent of face value. The term is ten years, and the rate is 10 per cent.

The journal entry to record this transaction is to debit cash for £510,000 (£500,000 times 102/100 (or 1.02)). You have two accounts to credit: 'bonds payable' for the face value of £500,000 and 'premium on bonds payable' for £10,000, which is the difference between face value and cash received at issuance.

The premium of £10,000 has to be amortised over the length of time the bonds are outstanding. *Amortisation* (writing off the premium over time) means that every year, over the life of the bond, you write off a portion of the premium. The term of these bonds is ten years, so using the *straight-line method* (which means you write off the same amount each period), the amount you have to amortise each year is £1,000 (£10,000 premium divided by the ten-year term).

Finally, to record the interest payable on these bonds for each year, you credit 'bond interest payable' for £50,000 (calculated by multiplying the face value of £500,000 times the rate of 10 per cent). You also debit 'premium on bond payable' for £1,000 (see the calculation in the previous paragraph) and 'interest expense' in the profit and loss for the £49,000 difference.

GAAP prefers the effective interest rate method when accounting for bonds issued at a discount or premium. However, using the straight-line method is okay when the results of the straight-line versus effective interest method are materially the same.

Reporting a bond discount

Okay, now let's go through an example of a *bond discount*, which means the bonds are issued at less than face value. Here's the situation:

> Alex Co PLC issues £500,000 face value bonds at 97 per cent of face value. The term is ten years.

The journal entry to record this transaction is to debit cash for £485,000 (£500,000 times 97/100 or 0.97) and debit 'discount on bonds payable' for £15,000, which is the difference between face of £500,000 and cash received of £485,000. You also have to credit 'bonds payable' for the face value amount of £500,000. The term on these bonds is ten years, so using the straight-line method, the amount amortised for bond discount each year is £1,500 (£15,000 discount divided by the ten-year term).

Then, to record interest payable on these bonds for each year, you credit 'bond interest payable' for £50,000 (calculated by multiplying the face value of £500,000 times the rate of 10 per cent) and credit 'discount on bonds payable' for £1,500. You then debit 'interest expense' in the profit and loss for £51,500.

In a nutshell, you're effectively amortising the discount to interest expense in the income statement over the life of the bond.

Redeeming and converting bonds

All good things must come to an end. At the end of the ten years, Alex Co PLC has to *redeem the bonds* (pay back the investors). At that point, bonds payable and all the other bond accounts (like bond premium or discount) have to be reduced to zero and the investors paid back for the amount of their investment in the bonds.

If the bonds are redeemed at full term (maturity), your regular amortisation journal entries should have already zeroed out the discount or premium on bonds payable.

Also, if the bonds are redeemed at full term, the bonds' value on the balance sheet should be equal to the face value amount, so it's an easy journal entry just debiting bonds payable and crediting cash. For Alex Co's bonds, the debit and credit amount is £500,000.

If a bond is *callable* – meaning the issuer pays off the bonds before the maturity date – any unamortised bond premium or discount must be *written off* (reduced to zero) as part of the transaction. This action may trigger a gain or loss on the transaction.

Convertible bonds (debt) can be converted into ordinary shares at the option of the owner of the bonds. The conversion feature makes convertible bonds more attractive to potential investors because it's possible to reap the benefits of the following circumstances:

✔ If the amount of dividends regularly being paid to shareholders is higher than the interest earned on the bonds, the investor gets increased cash by converting his bonds to shares.

✔ The investor also benefits if the value of the company's ordinary shares increases over the value of the bonds.

Chapter 9

Examining the Equity Section

*P*art III of this book is all about the financial statement called the *balance sheet* (internationally referred to as the *statement of financial position*), which reports a company's assets (the things a company owns), its liabilities (the stuff it owes) and owners' equity. In Chapter 7, I walk you through the assets part of the equation. Chapter 8 is all about the liabilities part of the balance sheet.

This chapter gets into the nitty-gritty of how the owners' interest in the business shows up on the balance sheet. *Equity* is the combined total of each and every owner's investment in the business. Another term for equity is *net assets* or *net worth*, which is the difference between assets and liabilities.

Depending on how a business is organised, its owners' equity can appear in a few different types of accounts on the balance sheet. The main types of business structures are sole traders, limited companies and partnerships. One other type of business structure exists in the UK: the limited liability partnership (LLP). LLPs are a bit of a halfway house between a partnership and a limited company but LLPs are protected by limited liability in company law (unlike a traditional partnership). Because most people are familiar with limited companies, I give that type of business entity the most attention in this chapter. But I also share all you need to know about sole traders and partnerships so you can handle the different types of accounting for these business structures. A company's *equity* may consist of different types of shares and additional paid-up capital (the term *additional capital* is known as *share premium*). In this chapter I explain the differences among ordinary and preference shares and treasury shares. You also find out about dividends and how your clients need to handle them. Plus, I touch on some other sorts of transactions which involve equity, including bonus share issues and rights issues.

Wait, I'm not finished! You also receive a tutorial on *retained earnings*: the total profit brought in by the business since it started that's not been paid out as dividends. Finally, you bring all this information together by walking through the equity section of a sample balance sheet for a limited company. Ready, then? Here we go.

Distinguishing between Different Types of Business Entities

Forming a business can be as easy as one, two, three or extremely complicated, depending on the type of business entity being created. Likewise, the owners' equity section of the balance sheet can range from bare-boned to quite elaborate – again, depending on the type of business entity.

Following are the ABCs of the three types of business entities and their unique components of equity. First, I give you a brief overview of sole traders and partnerships, which are very common throughout the world of financial accounting. Then I launch into a discussion of all you need to know about the most common type of business entity you'll come across, not only in your accountancy studies, but also in your day-to-day working life: the limited company.

Sole trader

Like the name implies, a *sole trader* has one and only one individual owner. This owner can't collectively own the business with anyone else – even with a spouse or another relative or friend. While only one owner can exist, the sole trader can hire as many employees as it needs, or even have family members working freelance for the business.

Forming a sole trader entity couldn't be easier. Most jurisdictions don't require formal documentation to be filed at regulatory authorities for a sole trader (but be careful – HM Revenue and Customs (HMRC) will need to be informed when a sole trader business starts and there will be a fine if they don't get informed in a speedy fashion). Instead, as soon as the company makes its first sale or incurs its first business expense, it's officially in business as a sole trader business.

The sole trader has two unique equity accounts: *capital introduced* (or *capital* account) and *drawings*. The capital introduced account shows cash and other contributions (such as equipment) that the owner makes to the business out of his own private funds. The drawings account shows money and other assets the owner takes from the business for personal use.

Figure 9-1 shows the owner's equity section of the sole proprietorship for Kai's Kayaks owned by Kai Bury. Not too complicated, right?

Kai's Kayaks
Capital Account as at
31 December 2012

Captial account brought forward 1 January 2012	20,000
Net profit for the year ended 31 December 2012	7,000
	27,000
Less drawings	(15,000)
Capital account as at 31 December 2012	12,000

Figure 9-1:
A statement of owner's equity for a sole trader.

Partnership

A partnership must have at least two partners holding any percentage of interest in a company. For example, one partner can have a 99 per cent interest and the other can have a 1 per cent interest, or each partner can have a 50 per cent interest. The division doesn't matter as long as the combined interest adds up to 100 per cent. Keep in mind that a partnership is not limited to two partners; there can be as many partners as the partnership wants to have and in some cases a partnership can involve as many as 100 individuals.

When a partnership is formed, the partnership agreement will set out how the partnership is to be comprised and how it will operate. This partnership agreement can be drawn up by the partners themselves, but many partnership agreements are drawn up by a solicitor. In the UK (and indeed in most other countries), certain conditions may govern a partnership:

- ✔ With *general partnerships*, all partners are personally liable for any legal action taken against the partnership and for any debts the partnership owes.

- ✔ In recent years, *limited liability partnerships* are increasingly in evidence. If you're a partner in a limited liability partnership, your liability for partnership debt is limited to your investment in the partnership (for more on limited liability partnerships, see the next section 'Limited liability partnership').

Partnerships mimic sole traders in that the equity section on the balance sheet has capital and a drawings account. Figure 9-2 shows the partner equity section of the Double-Trouble Partnership, whose partners, Sue and Mark Double, each own 50 per cent of the business.

Double-Trouble Partnership
Statement of Partners' Equity
as at 31 December 2012

	Capital Account: Mark Double	Capital Account: Sue Double	Total Capital
	£	£	£
Opening balance at 1 January 2012	10,000	7,000	17,000
Profit for the year to 31 December 2012	12,000	12,000	24,000
	22,000	19,000	41,000
Partners' drawings to 31 December 2012	(10,000)	(2,000)	(12,000)
Closing balance at 31 December 2012	12,000	17,000	29,000

Figure 9-2:
A statement of partners' equity.

The amount of drawings and income distributions a partner is allowed to take can differ from that person's partnership interest. So even though you have two equal partners, that doesn't mean they have to take the same amount of drawings. Hence the differences in opening and closing partners' capital accounts between partners in Figure 9-2.

Limited liability partnership

In the preceding section I mention a limited liability partnership (LLP). An LLP is a sort of half-way house between a limited company and a traditional partnership. However, in the UK, an LLP has the same protection as that of a limited company (as described in the following section) in that its members are protected against the LLP's debts only to the amount of money they've invested. The fundamental difference is that, in the UK, LLPs have to file their accounts with Companies House (so they're on public record) and file *annual returns*, which include details of the LLP's registered office, members and designated members together with other statutory information. The financial statements of an LLP also look different to those of the traditional partnership because they have to prepare accounts under a specific Statement of Recommended Practice (SoRP) for Accounting by Limited Liability Partnerships.

Further information on the SoRP for Accounting by Limited Liability Partnerships is available on the Internet.

Limited companies

If a business wants to operate as a company, it has to prepare and file a memorandum and articles of association with the Registrar of Companies (or Companies House). The memorandum and articles of association cover the basics about the company such as its name and address, the shares it issues (including the type and how many shares). If you want more info on memorandum and articles of association then visit the Companies House website at `www.companieshouse.org.uk`.

The type of information a particular jurisdiction requires for the creation of a company is a matter of law in that particular country and can be found by speaking to a *formation agent* (someone who prepares the necessary documentation to set up a company) or an accountant. Chapter 15 has more information about forming a company (also referred to as *incorporation*).

The balance sheet section called 'equity' or 'capital and reserves' or 'shareholders' funds' represents the claim shareholders of the company have to the company's net assets. Four common components to shareholders' equity exist: paid-up share capital, share premium, treasury stock and retained earnings. *Paid-up share capital* and *share premium* involve transactions dealing with share issues. *Retained earnings* shows profit and dividend transactions. In the sections that follow, I give a run through of each of these components, starting with paid-up share capital and the share premium account, then retained earnings and finishing with treasury stock.

Sifting Through Share Capital

Paid-up share capital represents money the shareholders in a company invest in the business (contributed capital). It consists of purchases for preference shares (but see the first bullet point below for an important point on these), ordinary shares and premium paid on share capital. Here's a definition of each:

- ✔ **Preference shares:** Now you have to be very, very careful with preference shares because they only show in the equity section of the balance sheet if (and only if) they do not entitle the holder of the preference shares to cash (either by way of redemption of the shares or by way of dividends (note: dividends paid on preference shares are *interest charges in the paying company's financial statements*). Where preference shares do not contain such redemption features, and are rightly classified as equity, they're at the top of the pecking order. What this means is if a company sells its assets and closes its doors, preference shareholders get back the money they invested in the company plus any *dividends* owed to them (money paid to the shareholders based on their proportionate ownership of the shares) before the ordinary shareholders get their share of the pie. (For more information on dividends, see the 'Paying dividends' section later in this chapter.)

Following the rules for issuing shares

Previously in the UK, the concept of *authorised* share capital existed, which referred to the upper limit on the number of shares that a company could issue. Although the Companies Act 2006 no longer recognises authorised share capital, that's not to say that other jurisdictions follow the same principles. It may well be the case that your particular country still has 'caps' on the number of shares that can be issued, so it's best to check this out with your accountants or auditors if you're unsure.

A company's shares can be both *issued* and *outstanding* at any point in time. Here's how these terms are defined:

- ✔ *Issued:* A share is issued when the company sells it to an investor (the shareholder) and receives cash or some other benefit in return.

- ✔ *Outstanding:* After a share is issued, it's classified as outstanding for as long as it's in the hands of the shareholder. The company can buy back outstanding shares of shares, resulting in treasury stock. I fully explain treasury stock, which is issued but not outstanding, in the 'Buying back shares' section of this chapter.

In almost all cases, preference shares will entitle the holder of those shares to cash – either by way of redemption at some point in the future, or by way of periodic interest payments (dividends). Where this is the case, the preference shares aren't shown in equity, but are instead shown as a liability (see Chapter 8 for more on liabilities). However, some countries that report under their own national accounting standards do still recognise preference shares in the equity section of the balance sheet, but for those companies reporting under UK GAAP and IFRSs, this is not the case.

- ✔ **Ordinary shares:** Ordinary shares are shares that aren't preference shares and don't carry automatic rights to dividends. Ordinary shares represent residual ownership in a company and a share allows the owner of that share to vote in matters put forward to the shareholders for approval in shareholders' meetings. Ordinary shareholders are entitled to receive dividends, if any are available *after* dividends to the preference shareholders are paid.

Ordinary shareholders elect the board of directors that oversees the business. The board of directors will then elect the management and senior management who will oversee the day-to-day operations of the business. In order to be a real company, at least one ordinary share has to be issued. After all, somebody has to be in charge of the business!

- ✔ **Share premium account:** This account represents the excess of what shareholders pay to buy the shares over the par value of the shares. *Par value* is what a share is worth (its *face value*). Wondering how par value is determined? Whoever was in charge of originally forming the company decided on the amount of par value. Most of the time, par value is an insignificant amount selected at random (usually £1 but it can be £100 or even 1 pence).

Cahill Cars' ordinary shares are worth £10 per share. Liza comes along and buys 20 shares for £15 a share. The addition to Cahill Cars' ordinary shares is £200 (20 shares at £10 par value). Additional paid-in capital (the *premium*) is £100, which is calculated by multiplying those 20 shares by the excess Liza paid for the shares over their par value (20 shares times £5).

Recording Retained Earnings

The *retained earnings* account (sometimes called *profit and loss reserves*) on the balance sheet shows the company's total net profit or loss from the first day it was in business to the date of the balance sheet. (See Chapter 10 for information on how to calculate net profit or loss.) While paid-up share capital is money contributed by the shareholders, retained earnings is *earned* capital.

Keep in mind that retained earnings are reduced by *dividends*: earnings paid to shareholders based upon the number of shares they own. I discuss dividends in the next section.

Judith's Jumpers opens its doors on 1 January 2013. On 2 January 2013, retained earnings is £0 because the company didn't previously exist. From 2 January 2013 to 31 December 2013, Judith's Jumpers has a net profit, after tax, of £20,000 and pays out £5,000 in dividends to the shareholders.

On 1 January 2014, the retained earnings amount is £15,000 (£20,000 – £5,000). Then, to work out the retained earnings figure as at 1 January 2015, you start with £15,000 and add or subtract the amount of profit/loss after tax the company made or lost during 2014 (and subtract any dividends paid).

Spotting Reductions in Shareholders' Funds

During your accountancy studies, or your day-to-day working life, you'll come across two situations that reduce shareholders' funds (equity) other than when a company makes a net loss. These situations are when a company pays dividends to its shareholders or when the company buys back outstanding shares (treasury stock). Although both transactions reduce equity, they're completely different types of accounts. While you may be scratching your head wondering what treasury stock is all about, you may be somewhat familiar with dividends. Don't worry! I thoroughly explain both in this section.

The two important dates in the life of a dividend

The company's board of directors is in charge of deciding how much of a dividend to issue, and when. However, the board can't just wake up one morning and decide that today's the day to distribute some cash in the form of a dividend! The dividend cycle consists of two events:

1. **Declaring the dividend:** This is the date on which the board of directors authorises the dividend. After a dividend is declared, the company has a legal responsibility to pay it.

   The company records this legal responsibility by making a resolution in the board meeting and then reducing retained earnings and increasing a short-term liability: dividends payable. The amount by which retained earnings are reduced and the liability increased is the dividend per share multiplied by all shares outstanding. So if the company has 5,000 shares outstanding and declares a dividend of £2 per share, the amount is £10,000 (£2 × 5,000 shares).

2. **Paying the dividend:** The date on which the dividend is declared (see step 1 above) is not necessarily the date on which the dividend is paid. This is vitally important because tax legislation (as is the case in the UK) often says that any tax due on a dividend is payable when it's *receivable* and this date can be different to when it becomes *payable*. Paying cash dividends reduces both cash and dividends payable. For example, if the total dividends paid were £10,000, you debit dividends payable and credit cash for £10,000 each. Now, in the UK, for the purposes of tax if the dividend was declared on 31 March 2013, but not actually paid until 7 April 2013 (in the next tax year), the dividend would have to be put on the shareholder's self-assessment income tax return in the tax year ending 5 April 2013! This is because the dividend was receivable in the tax year to 5 April 2013. Boo!

Corrections of accounting errors made in prior periods and discovered in the current period also reduce equity. To make sure I have all bases covered, I discuss this topic in Chapter 20.

Paying dividends

Dividends are distributions of company earnings to the shareholders. They're made in the form of cash (yeah!). An important point to emphasise where dividends are concerned is that they're *always* paid out of *after-tax* profits.

Dividends are *not* an expense of doing business. They're a balance sheet transaction only, serving to reduce both cash (in the case of cash dividends) and retained earnings. This is why they're always paid out of post-tax profit (or paid out of retained earnings).

Dividends are paid to shareholders in the form of cash or an electronic bank transfer (usually the latter nowadays), based upon how many shares in the company they own. For a company to be able to pay dividends, two conditions must be met:

- ✔ The company has positive retained earnings.
- ✔ The company has enough ready cash to pay the dividends.

Neil owns 1,500 ordinary shares in Leslie's Lilos. Leslie's Lilos has both a surplus of cash and positive retained earnings so the board of directors decides to pay a cash dividend of £12 per share. Neil's dividend is £18,000 (1,500 shares times £12).

The reduction to retained earnings for a cash dividend is very straightforward: you reduce retained earnings by the amount of the dividend.

Buying back shares

The term treasury stock sounds both very complicated and like something that the government would issue. However, *treasury stock* refers to shares that have previously been sold to investors and then bought back by the issuing company.

You record treasury stock on the balance sheet as a contra shareholders' equity account. *Contra accounts* carry a balance opposite to the normal account balance. Because equity accounts normally have a credit balance, a contra equity account weighs in with a debit balance.

Under generally accepted accounting practice (GAAP), it's not appropriate to record any sort of gain or loss on treasury stock transactions.

One reason a company may buy back shares of its own stock is to prevent a hostile takeover. The fewer shares trading in the open market, the smaller the chance that a controlling stake in the company could be purchased by another company.

Getting to grips with share splits

One other type of share transaction that doesn't reduce retained earnings is a share split. A *share split* increases the number of shares outstanding by issuing more shares to current shareholders proportionally by the amount they already own. Share splits are typically done when a company believes the trading price of its shares is too high; the split reduces the price per share.

Heaton Enterprises' shares are trading for £100, and the company thinks this high price affects the average investor's desire to purchase the shares. To get the price of the shares down to £25 per share, the company would issue a 4-for-1 split. Every outstanding share would now be equal to four shares.

Seeing Increases in Shareholders' Funds

A shareholder's funds can increase in one of two ways: via a bonus issue or a rights issue. These issues are offered by a company as a means of either holding on to existing cash or raising more cash. I explain each issue in turn below.

Boning up on bonus issues

A bonus issue takes place when a company issues further shares to the shareholders in proportion to their existing shares (for example, a company may give a shareholder one additional share for every five shares she holds). The bonus issue is given to the shareholder free of charge. 'Why on earth would a company give shares away for free?' I hear you ask.

Well, a bonus issue means that the shareholder receives additional shares at no extra cost to her and companies usually do this as an alternative to paying dividends. Dividends are usually paid in cash, or cash equivalents (see the earlier section 'Paying dividends'), so from the company's point of view, making a bonus issue instead of paying dividends will preserve cash.

A company will also undertake a bonus issue if it's under-capitalised, which means that it hasn't got a lot of shares in issue. When a company is under-capitalised, the rate of dividend is higher, so a bonus issue lowers the rate of dividend, which in turn goes to preserve cash.

Rifling through a rights issue

A rights issue is a way for a company to raise cash by selling additional shares to existing shareholders in proportion to their current shareholding. As an incentive for the shareholder to take up a rights issue, the shares are usually sold at a discount (in other words, at a price set lower than the current share price), but this isn't prescriptive and companies can offer a rights issue to existing shareholders at market value if they so choose.

If a shareholder does *not* take up an offer of a rights issue, her shareholding becomes diluted because the shares will go to other shareholders.

Seeing a Sample Equity Section of the Balance Sheet

Figure 9-3 shows you how to prepare the equity section of a balance sheet for a company. While assets and liabilities are merely a line item in Figure 9-3, you can go to Chapter 7 to see the asset section fully developed, and Chapter 8 shows the liability section in all its debt-filled glory!

First up is always the issuing of shares by a company. As you can see from the captions, the company has issued 250 ordinary shares and additional paid-up share capital of £5,000 means that investors paid £5,000 over par value (sometimes called *face value*) for shares purchased. The company also has a revaluation surplus from the revaluation of fixed assets of £1,500 (which means fixed assets have risen in value). Profit and loss account reserves tells us that the company has £47,500 of earned profit from the day it opened its doors to 31 December 2012. Plus, the company has lost a bit of money on Investment sales and foreign currency transactions. Finally, the balance in treasury shares tells you that the company purchased back some of its shares.

	£
Total assets	105,245.00
Total liabilities	58,966.12
Net assets	46,278.88
Capital and reserves	
Ordinary shares (250 shares at £75 per share)	18,750.00
Share premium	5,000.00
Revaluation reserve	1,500.00
Profit and loss account	47,500.00
Net unrealised loss on available for sale investments	(7,500.00)
Unrealised loss from foreighn currency translation	(3,971.12)
Treasury shares	(15,000.00)
Shareholders' funds	46,278.88

Figure 9-3: The equity section of a balance sheet.

Part IV
Investigating Income and Cash Flow

Bart Baling Equipment Limited
Profit and Loss Account
For the year ended 31 March 2013

		31.03.13		31.03.12
	£	£	£	£
Turnover		7,283,681		7,037,637
Cost of sales		5,968,041		5,586,593
Gross Profit		1,315,640		1,451,044
Distribution costs	68,937		61,373	
Administrative expenses	1,118,641		897,665	
		1,187,578		959,038
		128,062		492,006
Other operating income		21,289		17,196
Operating profit		149,351		509,202
Interest payable and similar charges		10,377		6,440
Profit on oridinary activities before taxation		138,974		502,762
Tax on profit on ordinary activities		25,779		119,283
Profit for the financial year		113,195		383,479

Go to www.dummies.com/extras/financialaccounting for online bonus content.

In this part . . .

✔ Learn how to prepare an income statement and a statement of cash flows.

✔ Understand profit and loss.

✔ Get a handle on revenue and expenses.

✔ Deal with and account for inventory.

✔ Appreciate depreciation.

✔ Go to www.dummies.com/extras/financial accounting for online bonus content, including an extra Part of Tens chapter: 'Ten Differences Between Some National Standards and IFRS'.

Chapter 10

Understanding Profit or Loss

*T*his chapter gives you a comprehensive overview of how to prepare an *income statement* (statement of profit or loss): the financial document that reflects a company's revenue and expenses (it's also known as a *profit and loss account*). The ultimate purpose of an income statement is to show how the company has performed during an accounting period.

In this chapter, you see the difference between a profit and loss account under the UK's format one (the most commonly used format) and format two methods. You also discover what an income statement prepared under IFRSs looks like.

I introduce each section commonly found in the income statement, and I discuss unusual items that sometimes show up. Finally, the income statement in all its glory is laid out on the table, from the start – revenue (or turnover) – to the end – net profit after taxes.

Presenting the Profit and Loss Account in One of Two Ways

Before I get into the details of what you find in a profit and loss account, I want you to understand that not every profit and loss account looks exactly the same. That's because in the UK you can prepare the basic profit and loss account in one of two ways: format one and format two (formats three and four also exist, but those are beyond the scope of this book as they're rarely used). The format one method is most commonly used. Format one reports the classification of expenses by *function* (cost of sales, distribution costs and administrative expenses). Format two reports the classification of expenses by *type* (raw materials and consumables, staff costs and depreciation).

In this section, I show you an example of each profit and loss format. Looking at them, you may think that even format one isn't all that informative – neither type of statement contains very many numbers. But as I show you later in the chapter in the section 'Examining Income Statement Sections', the income statement/profit and loss account is actually full to the brim with information.

Figuring out format one

In Figure 10-1, I offer an example of a profit and loss account prepared under format one. All the main players in the profit and loss account are present – notably turnover and net profit. I offer more details later in the chapter, but for now just keep in mind that *turnover* is gross sales less sales returns and discounts, and *net profit* is what the company has made at the end of the day after deducting all expenses.

Completing the statement is the calculation for *basic earnings per share*, which shows net profit allocated to investors based on the number of shares they own. This bottom line number is very important to the users of financial statements (see Chapter 1) because it tells them how well their investment in the shares of the company is performing.

For the Year Ended 31 December 2012

	£	£
Turnover		150,000
Cost of sales		45,000
Gross profit		105,000
Distribution costs	10,000	
Administrative expenses	12,000	
		22,000
		83,000
Other operating income		1,000
Operating profit		84,000
Interest receivable and similar income		500
		84,500
Interest payable and similar charges		250
Profit on ordinary activities before taxation		84,250
Tax on profit on ordinary activities		23,200
Profit for the financial year		61,050
Basic earnings per share		20.5p

Figure 10-1: A format one profit and loss account.

Working through format two

Using the same facts and circumstances as in Figure 10-1, Figure 10-2 shows the profit and loss account prepared under format two. The big differences between format one and format two are the following:

✔ Format one has a line item for gross profit. This information is very helpful when doing ratio analysis (see Chapter 14).

✔ Format two breaks down operating costs in greater depth, allowing the user to see a more detailed make up of costs.

✔ Format two profit and loss accounts also contain categories for 'Change in stocks of finished goods and in work in progress' (which is shown directly underneath turnover). This figure is shown within cost of sales in format one profit and loss accounts.

ABC Limited
Profit and Loss Account
For the Year Ended 31 December 2012

		£	£
Turnover			150,000
Operating costs	Note 1		(66,000)
Profit on ordinary activities before interest and taxation			84,000
Net interest receivable			250
Profit on ordinary activities before taxation			84,250
Tax on profit on oridinary activities			(23,200)
Profit on ordinary activities after taxation			**61,050**
Basic earnings per share			20.5p

Note 1
Operating costs

Other operating income		(1,000)
Raw materials and consumables		37,000
Other external charges		18,000
Staff costs:		
Wages and salaries	6,000	
Social security costs	900	
Other pension costs	100	
		7,000
Depreciation of tangible fixed assets		2,500
Operating lease rentals		2,500
		66,000

Figure 10-2: A profit and loss account prepared under format two.

Because the UK's Companies Act permits these formats, it must seem that these differences are therefore insignificant. But they're worth noting from the start of our discussion because in your career you'll probably come across both types of income statements.

Seeing an example IFRS income statement

The section above discusses the profit and loss accounts prepared under formats one and two. These two formats are very much UK-specific, but you also need to know how a profit and loss account prepared under IFRSs looks. A profit and loss account in international lingo is known as the *income statement* or *statement of comprehensive income* or (more recently) *statement of profit or loss*. For simplicity, I stick to using just *income statement*. Figure 10-3 provides an illustration of an income statement under IFRSs.

ABC Limited
Income Statement
For the year ended 31 December 2012

	£
Revenue	150,000
Cost of sales	(45,000)
	105,000
Other income	1,000
Distribution costs	(10,000)
Administrative expenses	(12,000)
Finance costs	250
Profit before tax	84,250
Income tax expense	(23,200)
Profit after tax	61,050
Basic earnings per share	20.5p

Figure 10-3: An illustrative income statement.

Defining Different Types of Businesses

Every business can be allotted to one of three types: service, manufacturing and retail. It's important to realise which type you're working with when reviewing or creating any financial statement – including the income statement. That's because not every type of account (which I introduce in Chapter 5) shows up on the financial statements for every company.

Peeking at service providers

When the true value of what a business provides derives from any type of personal service rather than a tangible product, that business is a *service* provider. Accountants, lawyers, doctors and hair stylists are examples of people who run service businesses.

Here's an example: as a chartered certified accountant working for an accountancy practice, I create reports that are on paper and bound in folders for my clients. Each folder is a tangible product, but the client isn't paying me for the relatively small cost of the paper and ink; he's paying me for the intellectual product I provide on the paper.

One major giveaway that a company is a service provider is if it doesn't have any inventory. Most service providers make purchases only for the job at hand so they won't carry any inventory; the purchases are simply expensed to each job. If the company does retain some purchases, the amount is inconsequential, especially when compared to a *retail* company (which sells products another company makes) or a *manufacturing* company (which makes the products it sells). I discuss these two types of companies next.

Selling goods to Joe Public

A *retailer* is a business like Marks and Spencer or your local supermarket. The business purchases goods from a manufacturer (see the next section) and in turn sells them to the end user – a customer like you or me.

Unlike a service business, the retailer has inventory. The inventory consists of goods available for sale, which are ready to be put on the shelves of the shop. So your local supermarket's inventory includes milk, fresh produce, tinned goods, baked produce, and so on. I show you how to account for retail type inventory in Chapter 13.

Manufacturing a product

The finished goods sold by retailers have to come from somewhere, and that somewhere is the manufacturer. Because the manufacturer makes products from scratch, accounting for this type of inventory is much more complicated than accounting for products held by a retailer.

Manufacturers have three types of inventory:

- **Raw materials:** This is the inventory the company purchases to make the products. For example, to make a dress, it purchases fabric, thread and buttons.

- **Work in progress:** This inventory category includes all materials that have been partially but not completely made into finished products. A work-in-progress item could be a dress whose sleeves have not yet been sewn to the body of the dress.

- **Finished goods:** Finished goods are all products that are completely assembled but not yet sold to a customer. So our dresses are ready to leave the manufacturing plant as soon as a buyer puts in an order.

You learn how to account for manufacturing inventory in Chapter 13.

Examining Income Statement Sections

As you see in Figures 10-1 and 10-2, income statements are broken down into different sections. The main reason that items of revenue and expense are separated and reported in distinct sections is so that the business owner can better use the income statement to make decisions and to isolate problems with the way the business is being run. (Fear not – this will make more sense after you review all the income statement parts in this section.)

Before you get into the nitty gritty – all the different types of revenues and expenses – you have to know how to prepare a heading for a particular financial statement. The first line of the heading is always the name of the company. The second line identifies the type of report – in this case, Income Statement. The third line in an income statement heading indicates the period covered by the statement; for example, 'For the year ending 31 December 2012'. (Note that the date on the report is *not* the date when the report itself was prepared.)

Revenue and other income

In this section, I explain two revenue accounts that appear on an income statement: revenue from sales and other income.

Revenue from sales

The first line item in the income statement is always *revenue*, which is the amount of income the company generates by doing whatever it's in the business of doing. Some accountants refer to revenue as *turnover*. Both names mean the same thing.

Revenue is derived from a sale (whether a good or service) and a sale will start with an implicit or written contract between a company and its customer (and end with reporting the sales after they're earned and realisable, which I discuss in a moment). The contract states that an agreed-upon good or service is to be provided for a set amount of money.

Here's an example of an implicit contract: I walk into a department store and buy a pair of trousers. It's implicitly understood that when I take the trousers to the checkout, I'll exchange cash or cash equivalent (a credit or debit card transaction) for the amount on the price tag.

An example of a written agreement is a contract for sale. Say that a department store signs a contract stating it wants to buy 500 pairs of trousers from the manufacturer. This contract states all the expenses and obligations on the side of both the seller and the purchaser.

A company's sales revenue includes only transactions that relate to the purpose of the business. In the department store example, revenue includes the amount of products sold to customers. If that same company sells one of its company cars, you record the gain or loss on that transaction in the line called 'profit or loss on disposal of non-current assets', not within sales. That's because the company isn't in the used car sales business. Profit or loss unrelated to the business purpose isn't part of sales. Find out more about this subject in the upcoming 'Other income' section.

Financial accounting uses the accruals method of accounting (see Chapter 6) so a company can't record sales unless that money is earned and realisable. Here's what these terms mean:

- ✔ For revenue to be *earned*, the job, whether it involves goods or services, has to be complete based upon the terms of the contract between the company and the customer.

- ✔ For revenue to be *realisable*, it means an expectation exists that the company performing the service or providing the goods will be paid. When might revenue *not* be realisable? If, after the job is complete (but before the company is paid), a customer closes its doors and disappears or becomes bankrupt, the revenue is no longer realisable.

Based on the above information, you can understand that cash doesn't have to change hands for sales to be earned and realisable. To address this fact, a company has a 'trade receivables' account holding the monetary amount of revenue that hasn't been paid. I discuss accounts receivable in Chapter 7.

Other income

You classify all other income the company brings in peripherally as *miscellaneous income*, *sundry income* or *other income*. (All of these names are fine.) During your accounting studies, or day-to-day working life in accountancy, you may come across three kinds of other income:

✔ **Interest:** Revenue a company earns from money in a bank deposit account

✔ **Dividends:** Revenue a company earns on investments it owns, such as shares in other businesses

✔ **Gain on disposal of an asset:** Revenue a company earns when it sells one of its assets, such as a car or machine, and makes money on the deal

Note that while the sales account is your first income statement account, other income doesn't appear until later in the statement. That's because, frankly, it's not quite as significant as some of the other financial facts about the business. But the main reason in financial accounting is because that's what generally accepted accounting practice (GAAP) dictates. (I explain why following GAAP is important in Chapter 4 but in a nutshell, everyone doing the same thing enables comparability between businesses.)

Contra revenue accounts

In Chapter 5, I give you the lowdown on the rules of debits and credits. One of the immutable rules of accountancy is that revenue accounts normally carry a credit balance. However, in the wonderful world of accountancy, you have what are called *contra accounts*, which means the account carries a balance contrary to the normal balance. So a contra revenue account carries a debit balance instead of a credit balance.

The two contra revenue accounts you're most likely to encounter are 'sales discounts' and 'sales returns and allowances', which I discuss here.

Sales discounts

Sales discounts reflect any discount a business gives to a good customer who pays early. For example, a customer's invoice is due within 30 days of receipt of the good or service. If the customer pays early (what's considered *early* is spelt out in the terms of the contract), it gets a 2 per cent discount. So if the invoice is for £100, the customer has to pay only £98. This doesn't seem like such a big deal, but consider the difference between the invoice amount and payment amount if the invoice is for £10,000 or £100,000.

Sales returns and allowances

Sales returns reflect all products that customers return to the company after the sale is complete. For example, after I buy a pair of trousers for my father, perhaps I decide purple trousers are a fashion faux pas and I no longer want them. Back to the department store I go to return the trousers and get a full refund for the purchase price.

Sales allowances reflect a discount in price given to a customer wanting to purchase damaged goods. A perfect example is that some shops sell slightly damaged appliances (sometimes referred to as *seconds goods*).

Gross sales less sales discounts and sales returns and allowances equals *net sales*. Figure 10-4 shows an example of how this calculation looks if a company has gross sales of £300,000, sales discounts of £25,500 and sales returns of £1,000.

Figure 10-4:
Net sales.

Sales			£300,000
Less:	Sales discounts	£25,500	
	Sales returns and allowances	£1,000	
			(26,500)
Net sales			£273,500

If you're a student accountant, the examples of income statements in your textbook may show all three accounts (gross sales, sales discounts and sales returns and allowances) with a net sales total like I show in Figure 10-4 and Figure 10-8 at the end of this chapter. Or your textbook may show just the consolidated line item 'net sales', which I show in Figures 10-1 and 10-2. Depending on what level of study you're up to, either method of presentation may be fine as long as you understand the accounting behind how gross sales turns into net sales. It's important to be aware that many professional level exams (such as chartered courses) tend to just show the total net revenue figure as it's assumed you already know the ins and outs of how revenue figures are reported.

If a business is registered for value added tax (VAT) with HM Revenue and Customs, the sales figure in the profit and loss account (income statement) is always shown net of VAT. When I say *net* of VAT I mean the amount of the sale *before* VAT is charged.

Cost of sales

The *cost of sales figure* in the income statement reflects all costs directly tied to any product a company sells, be it a retailer or a manufacturing company. A service company generally doesn't have a cost of sales line because it doesn't sell a tangible product.

Because retailers sell products they purchase from manufacturers, their cost of sales is fairly easy to calculate. That's because retailers have only one type of inventory to keep track of: goods they purchase for resale. As I note in the 'Manufacturing a product' section earlier in the chapter, a manufacturer has several different types of inventory, so calculating its cost of sales is a little trickier.

In this section, I talk about the easier cost of sales (for retailers) first and then tackle the more difficult cost of sales for the manufacturing company.

Retailing cost of sales

Calculating cost of sales for a retailer starts with *opening inventory*, which is the stock the company has available for sale at the beginning of the month (in other words, the leftover inventory from the prior month). I discuss inventory in depth in Chapter 13.

Next, you have to work out the cost of purchases. To do so, you add together two items:

- ✓ **Purchases:** Any new goods the company buys during the current month

- ✓ **Freight costs:** The shipping expense the business incurs in order to get the goods from the manufacturer to their location

For example, if purchases for the month of April are £125,000 and freight costs are £10,500, your cost of purchases is £135,500.

Your next step is to work out *net purchases*, which means cost of purchases less contra purchases. Once again, contra accounts raise their ugly heads! Two contra purchase accounts exist:

- ✓ **Purchase discounts:** This contra account reflects any discount a company receives because it pays a supplier's invoice early. It's the flip side of the contra revenue account 'sales discount' – looking at the same event from the eyes of the customer rather than the seller.

- ✓ **Purchase returns and allowances:** This contra account consists of items a retailer orders that it returns to the supplier. Items may be returned if an order arrives too late to use, arrives damaged or doesn't contain what the company actually ordered. This account is the flip side of 'sales returns and allowances' – looking at the same event from the side of the customer instead of the seller.

Because purchases are an expense and normally carry a debit balance, a contra purchase expense will carry a credit balance.

Cost of purchases less the two contra purchase accounts equals *net purchases*. For example, start with our cost of purchases of £135,500. Assume that purchase discounts are £5,000 and purchase returns and allowances come to £7,000. Your net purchases amount is £123,500.

Adding net purchases to opening inventory gives you *cost of goods available for sale*. So if opening inventory is £5,000, cost of goods available for sale is £128,500 (£123,500 + £5,000).

Okay, just one more calculation! Subtract *closing inventory*, which is the stock of goods the company still has available for sale on the last day of the accounting period, from cost of goods available for sale. (Because the closing inventory wasn't sold, we're subtracting its costs from the goods available for sale.) Then you have your cost of sales! Continuing our example, if closing inventory is £10,000, your cost of sales is £118,500 (£128,500 – £10,000).

Manufacturing cost of sales

Manufacturers have three types of inventory: raw materials, work in progress and finished goods. To work out a manufacturing company's cost of sales, you first have to calculate the cost of goods manufactured. What appears to be a simple single line item in the cost of sales for a manufacturing company is really a calculation in which many different variables are added and subtracted.

Check out Figure 10-5 to see how the manufacturing company's cost of sales shows up in the income statement. Looks pretty bare-boned, doesn't it?

Figure 10-5:
Computing cost of sales for a manufacturing company.

Opening finished goods in inventory		£X
Add:	Costs of goods manufactured during the period	£X
Equals:	Cost of goods available for sale	£X
Minus:	Closing finished goods in inventory	(£X)
Equals:	Cost of sales	£X

Here, I walk you through the preparation of the cost of sales line item 'cost of goods manufactured during the period'. Most of the terms I use in this calculation have already been explained in this chapter, but I throw in a couple of new ones too:

- ✔ **Direct labour:** This expense includes only what the company pays to workers who are directly involved in making the items the company manufactures. So if the company makes blouses, direct labour includes the payroll for the employees who make the blouse patterns, cut out the fabric pieces and assemble the fabric pieces into a wearable garment.

- ✔ **Factory overhead:** This expense includes all manufacturing costs except those you include in direct materials and direct labour. It also includes indirect materials and labour:

  - • *Indirect materials:* These are materials that a manufacturer would use for more than one product. For example, your blouse manufacturer has to use thread to sew the pieces of the blouse patterns together to make a complete, wearable garment. If the thread is a generic colour (such as black or white) that the company uses to make various other garments such as jackets, it would properly be classed as indirect materials. That's because the thread is not directly associated only with the blouses.

- *Indirect labour:* This item includes employee payroll that doesn't directly tie to a specific finished product. A good example of an indirect employee is a quality control inspector who makes sure the goods flowing down the assembly line are made properly.

Another example of factory overhead is *depreciation of factory equipment*, which is the process of spreading the cost of the factory equipment over its useful life. For example, you include the depreciation of the sewing machines the company uses to make the blouses in factory overhead. Depreciation of the computers that the number-crunchers use in the accounts department *isn't* included. I explain different methods of depreciation in Chapter 12.

Utilities you include in factory overhead are the heating and air conditioning, lights, power to run the factory machines and factory water. These expenses are classed as overhead because while the business incurs them when manufacturing products, it cannot tie these expenses to one particular product (unless the company makes only one product).

Other overhead items can include any other manufacturing costs that can't be attributed to a specific product. One example is repair and maintenance expense to keep the factory machines running smoothly. A good example is if the company buys the same brand of lubricant to oil all the machines.

Now that you know all the terms you see when preparing the 'cost of goods manufactured during the period', I walk you through the preparation itself in Figure 10-6.

Opening direct materials inventory			£X	
Plus:	net purchases		£X	
Equals:	total direct materials available		£X	
Less:	closing direct materials in inventory		(£X)	
Equals:	direct materials used			£X
Plus:	direct labour			£X
Plus:	items of factory overhead:			
		Depreciation of factory equipment	£X	
		Utilities	£X	
		Indirect factory labour	£X	
		Indirect materials	£X	
		Other overhead items	£X	
Equals:	manufacturing cost incurred during the period			£X
Plus:	opening work in progress			£X
Less:	closing work in progress			(£X)
Cost of goods manufactured during the period				£X

Figure 10-6: The step-by-step preparation of cost of goods manufactured during a period.

Gross profit

Well, this is an easy one! On the multiple-step income statement (refer back to Figure 10-2), *gross profit* is what's left over after you subtract the cost of sales from revenue. Basically, gross profit shows you how much money the company makes if it doesn't have any other expenses such as office rent, salaries and so on. (Note that this line doesn't appear on the format two profit and loss account format, such as the one shown in Figure 10-2.)

Gross profit is very important in financial accounting because it gives the users of the financial statements a measurement upon which to compare this company to others. (See Chapter 14 for information about ratio analysis.) A company showing a higher gross profit than others in its industry will be more likely to attract investors, as long as expenses other than cost of sales are kept in line.

Distribution and administrative expenses

First up, in order to set the context, think of this section as *selling* and *distribution* expenses. Two principal categories of operating expenses show up in the income statement and follow on from each other:

- ✔ **Distribution costs:** Any expenses a company incurs to sell its goods or services to customers. Some examples are salaries and commissions paid to sales staff, shipping costs to get the goods to the customer and storage costs.
- ✔ **Administrative expenses:** All expenses a company incurs to keep up the normal business operations. Some examples are office supplies, general administrative wages/salaries, non-factory rent and utilities, and accountancy and legal services.

Heading toward the bottom line

If you've gone through this chapter section by section, you've worked through a lot of different income statement accounts so far. Bet you never thought that making money could be so complicated! However, you're fast approaching the finish line where you find out if the company has made or lost money during the accounting period (and the point at which many directors' nerves start to kick in!).

Other income and expenses

In the earlier section 'Revenue and other income', I explain that *revenue* includes only the amount of money the company brings in doing whatever it's in the business of doing; it doesn't include any investment income. Well, here's the section of the income statement where you record all the other types of revenue.

This line of the income statement also includes expenses that the company incurs other than costs associated with normal operations. Here are two types of expenses you typically see reflected on this line:

- ✔ **Interest payable:** This includes the cost of using borrowed funds for business operations, expansion and cash flow. Why wouldn't interest expense be included as an operating expense? Well, operating expenses are for the day-to-day activities involved in running a business. Per generally accepted accounting practice (GAAP, which I explain in Chapter 4), interest expense is not considered to be a day-to-day activity unless the company is in the business of lending money.

- ✔ **Loss on disposal of a fixed asset (non-current asset):** I talk about 'gain on disposal of an asset' earlier in the chapter (see the 'Other income' section). Loss is the flip side of the coin. If a company sells an asset it no longer needs and loses money on the transaction, the loss reflects in the income statement as 'loss on disposal of fixed asset'.

Profit before tax

The sum total of all income less cost of sales less expenses gets you to the *profit before tax* figure. The profit before tax figure is an important number because it's generally what most investors are interested in seeing. HM Revenue and Customs (HMRC) is also very interested in this figure because this is the baseline that will be used in calculating the company's corporation tax (see Chapter 18 for more on a company's corporation tax provision).

Provision for income taxes

Before you can arrive at the final total for net profit or loss, you have to reduce profit before tax by subtracting a provision for the corporation tax the company will pay when it files its corporation tax return. I discuss accounting for income taxes in Chapter 18.

If you're a student accountant and are studying financial reporting, you probably won't be asked to calculate corporation tax as this exercise will be covered in your tax studies. You'll more than likely be given the corporation tax charge to include in the financial statements. For example, if profit from continuing operations before taxes is £10,000 and you have a corporation tax rate of 24 per cent, your provision for corporation tax is £2,400. That makes profit from continuing operations after taxes equal to £7,600 (£10,000 – £2,400). To get the £2,400 tax charge in the financial statements you debit income tax expense in the income statement of £2,400 and credit income tax payable as a current liability in the statement of financial position with £2,400.

Finally – net profit!

If no unusual items are listed in the income statement, such as *discontinued operations* (which are segments of a business that a company has disposed of), the income from continuing operations after taxes is called *net profit* (or *profit after tax*). That line in the income statement reflects all revenue less all expenses incurred in the production of that revenue.

If expenses are more than revenue, the company has a net loss rather than net profit.

Earnings per share

Earnings per share (EPS) shows the spread of net profit when you divvy it up among shareholders. Potential investors in a company like to see this type of information so they can make informed investment decisions. If your motivation for buying shares in a company is to bring in some dividend income, you want to be able to compare what level of dividends shareholders are currently getting.

Before I get into the discussion of earnings per share, it's important to understand the two types of shares an investor may own in a company:

- ✔ **Ordinary shares:** People who own ordinary shares are the ultimate owners of the company and have voting privileges. For example, ordinary shareholders can elect the company's board of directors.

- ✔ **Preference shares:** This type of share gives shareholders a claim to the company's assets. In case of *liquidation* (when the company shuts its doors and disposes of all its assets), the preference shareholders are paid back for their ownership in the company first, and any leftovers go to the ordinary shareholders. Be very careful with preference shares because if they entitle the preference shareholder to receive cash (such as dividends or by way of redemption at a later date) this means that they must be treated as a liability in the company's accounts and not shown within the equity section of the statement of financial position. This is the case for companies that report under UK GAAP and IFRSs.

    Preference shareholders have a much more favourable position when it's time for the company to pay dividends. If a company decides it's going to pay dividends, the preference shareholders normally get their share of the pie first, with any leftover cash then paid to the ordinary shareholders.

When you're doing the EPS calculation, you must only ever use the ordinary shares figure – you ignore preference shares for the purposes of calculating EPS.

Here's an example of how to calculate the EPS figure:

Heaton Enterprises Limited makes a profit for the year ended 31 December 2012 before tax of £11,100 and a profit after tax amounting to £10.6 million. It has 12 million ordinary £1 shares and 3 million £1 preference shares in issue. To work out the EPS figure, take the following steps:

1. **Find the profit (the *earnings*) to be used in the calculation.** This must always be the profit attributable to the shareholders, which is the profit *after tax* figure of £10,600.

2. **Find the amount of issued ordinary share capital.** You must take only the *ordinary* shares – you ignore the preference shares for the purposes of the basic EPS calculation. So Heaton Enterprises has 12 million ordinary shares.

3. **Divide the profit after tax (the *earnings*) into the ordinary shares figure.** The calculation is therefore earnings (£10,600,000) divided by shares (£12,000,000), which equals 88.3 pence per share.

Watching Out for Unusual Income Statement Items

You're almost done! Only a few more issues to get to grips with where unusual items are concerned. I discuss two in this chapter: Discontinued operations and exceptional items. These items are broken down into 'profit from continuing operations' to give users of the financial statements a better idea of the probable results of future operations. Separating out non-recurring events from regular recurring business results makes it easier for the users of the financial statements to form an accurate opinion about the company.

Discontinued operations

Discontinued operations take place when a segment of a business is regarded as *held-for-sale*. This term means that either the business has some sort of legal obligation to sell the segment (for example, the shareholders voted on the sale) or that the segment has been disposed of during the accounting period and the following criteria are met:

✔ The discontinued operation represents either a separate major line of business or a geographical area of operations.

✔ The discontinued operation is part of a single co-ordinated plan to dispose of a separate major line of business or geographical area of operations.

✔ The discontinued operation is a subsidiary acquired exclusively with a view to resale and the disposal involves loss of control.

Here's an example to breathe a little life into this concept for you. Say a company that manufactures shoes has four different segments: boots, tennis shoes, women's sandals and men's walking boots. The company decides to sell its tennis shoe segment to a well-known manufacturer of sports shoes.

Disclosure of revenue, expenses, pre-tax profit or loss and related income taxes is required on the face of the income statement (profit and loss account), or in the notes to the financial statements distinct from continuing operations and such disclosures must cover both the current and the prior periods presented in the financial statements.

Exceptional items

To meet the criteria laid out by GAAP for *exceptional item* treatment, the item in question must be something that occurs infrequently and is by its very nature unusual. To meet both criteria is very hard.

An example that could possibly meet these strict criteria is when a company makes a profit or loss on the sale of a business operation. A company selling off part of its operations is likely to be an infrequent transaction and GAAP requires such profits or losses from the sale or termination of an operation to be shown separately on the face of the income statement (profit and loss account).

The important thing to remember is the fact that you report exceptional items that are material separately on the face of the income statement (profit and loss account). Figure 10-7 shows how to represent an exceptional item relating to the sale of a business operation in the income statement under UK GAAP.

Turnover	£X
Cost of sales	£X
Gross profit	£X
Administrative expenses	£X
Operating profit	£X
Profit and loss on sale of operations	£X (this is an exceptional item)
Interest payable and similar charges	£X
Profit on ordinary activities before taxation	£X
Tax on profit on ordinary activities	£X
Profit for the financial year	£X

Figure 10-7: Reporting an exceptional item.

Arriving at the Final Product

Ta-da! Here you are, ready to take everything you know from this chapter and use it to produce your final product: an income statement or profit and loss account (depending on which title you prefer).

Every company may have a slightly different system to handle the financial accounting work that begins with sales and purchase invoices and ends with all transactions being recorded in the accounting records. In the past, I've worked for a very large company where my only job was to manage trade payables (trade creditors), and I've also worked for a business where I was the only finance department employee doing everything from opening the mail to producing the financial statements. How the finance function works varies from company to company.

Figure 10-8 provides an example income statement for a company with no exceptional items or discontinued operations prepared under UK GAAP. Figure 10-9 provides an example of an income statement for a company prepared under International Financial Reporting Standards (IFRSs).

Bart Baling Equipment Limited
Profit and Loss Account
For the year ended 31 March 2013

	£	31.03.13 £	£	31.03.12 £
Turnover		7,283,681		7,037,637
Cost of sales		5,968,041		5,586,593
Gross Profit		1,315,640		1,451,044
Distribution costs	68,937		61,373	
Administrative expenses	1,118,641		897,665	
		1,187,578		959,038
		128,062		492,006
Other operating income		21,289		17,196
Operating profit		149,351		509,202
Interest payable and similar charges		10,377		6,440
Profit on ordinary activities before taxation		138,974		502,762
Tax on profit on ordinary activities		25,779		119,283
Profit for the financial year		113,195		383,479

Figure 10-8:
A profit and loss account under UK GAAP.

Bart Baling Equipment Limited
Statement of Profit or Loss
For the year ended 31 March 2013

	31.03.13	31.03.12
	£	£
Revenue	7,283,681	7,037,637
Cost of sales	5,968,041	5,586,593
Gross profit	1,315,640	1,451,044
Distribution costs	68,937	61,373
Administrative expenses	1,118,641	897,665
Other operating income	21,289	17,196
Finance costs	10,377	6,440
Profit before tax	138,974	502,762
Tax on profit on ordinary activities	25,779	119,283
Profit after tax	113,195	383,479

Figure 10-9:
An income
statement
prepared
under IFRSs.

Chapter 11

Figuring Out the Statement of Cash Flows under UK GAAP and IFRS

In This Chapter

▶ Separating cash from profit and costs from expenses

▶ Joining the dots with the statement of cash flows

▶ Learning about the sections of the statement of cash flows

▶ Presenting cash flow using the direct or indirect method

*W*hile financial accounting is all about the *accruals* method, which means revenue is recorded when it is earned and realisable and expenses are recorded when they're incurred, the missing piece of the jigsaw is cash changing hands. For the financial statements used to get a complete picture of the health of the business, cash payments and receipts have to be reconciled with accruals-based transactions.

You accomplish this reconciliation by preparing a statement of cash flows. In this chapter, you find out about the three sections of the statement of cash flows – operating, investing and financing – and what types of accounting information are reported in each. I also show you how the statement of cash flows looks when prepared under UK accounting standard FRS 1 *Cash Flow Statement*.

To mix things up a little bit, two acceptable ways to prepare the statement of cash flows exist: using the direct method and using the indirect method. The International Accounting Standards Board (IASB) and the UK's Financial Reporting Council (FRC) prefer the direct method because they believe this method provides the user with more standardised information so companies can more accurately be compared. However, most companies use the indirect method because compiling the information is less expensive than using the direct method.

Fear not! Before you finish the chapter, you find out how the statement of cash flows is prepared using both methods. If you're a student accountant studying IFRS, you need a sound grasp of IAS 7 *Statement of Cash Flows* and this chapter fits nicely around that.

Understanding the Difference between Cash and Profit

Accountancy is all about the accruals method of accounting. As I explain in Chapter 6, with the accruals method, you record revenue when it's earned regardless of whether money changes hands. Plus, you record expenses when you incur them regardless of whether they're paid. (As I also note in Chapter 6, another accounting method exists – the cash method – which uses the criterion of cash changing hands to record revenue and expenses.)

Because recognising accounting transactions for financial accounting doesn't hinge on cash being exchanged, chances are that there will always be a difference between a company's cash balances and profit shown in the income statement (see Chapter 10). That's because all costs aren't expenses, and until a cost *is* an expense, it doesn't hit the income statement.

In this section, I start off by showing you how non-cash transactions influence a company's net profit. Then I illustrate the difference between costs and expenses.

Seeing how non-cash transactions affect profit

The statement of cash flows homes in on the difference between cash a company receives and profit it's earned. Profit shows the real net income for the accounting period – factoring in revenue earned but not yet collected from customers and expenses incurred but not yet paid – rather than reflecting only transactions involving cash.

For example, assume that in June a company pays £2,000 into its bank current account and writes cheques to pay bills for £1,800. If you only look at the cash flowing in and out of the business, the company spent £200 less than it made, so it shows a profit of £200. But what if, in June, the company also used a credit card it doesn't intend to pay for until August (or a loan it took out in May or any other non-cash resource) to pay monthly bills amounting to £1,000? Taking this transaction into account, the company actually spent more than it made, resulting in a loss of £800.

Distinguishing costs from expenses

Generally accepted accounting practice (GAAP; see Chapter 4) pretty much dictates the accruals method for financial accounting. Some variations on this theme do exist, however, which you can find out about in Chapter 22. However, your number-one focus when talking about costs and expenses is to remember that, in the world of business, costs are not the same as expenses.

Let's say a company buys a new car for £25,000 cash. A company car is an example of a fixed asset (sometimes called a non-current asset) (see Chapter 7), which goes on the balance sheet (or statement of financial position if you're talking in international lingo). When the company buys the car, the price it pays, or promises to pay, is a *cost*. Then, as company employees drive the car on company business, the company depreciates the car.

Depreciation (see Chapter 12) is the process of reclassifying the cost of buying the asset as an expense of doing business. So over time, the resources (in this case, £25,000 cash) that the company uses to purchase the car are reclassified from the balance sheet (where they're a cost) to the income statement (where they're an expense).

Assume that the amount the company depreciates the car in the year of purchase is £4,500. So in that first year, the company's *expense* is £4,500 and the *cost* is £25,000. Big difference, eh? That's why the statement of cash flows is so important; it ties together the costs shown on the balance sheet with the expenses shown in the income statement.

Make sure you don't get confused about the difference between costs and expenses! A *cost* is the value of money the company uses to produce or buy something – money that is not available to use anymore. Costs are the ways a company uses cash, be it to purchase inventory, make investments or pay back debt. *Expenses* are costs that directly tie back to revenue the company earns during an accounting period.

Getting to Grips with the Statement of Cash Flows

The primary purpose of the statement of cash flows is to show how a company has made cash and what it has spent that dosh on during the accounting period. While cash can come from many different origins, such as customer payments, loans and sales of assets and equity, uses of cash directly trace back to costs. This information is very interesting to the external users of the company's financial statements, who aren't privy to the day-to-day operations of the business, because it provides a basis for understanding how wisely a company manages its cash.

A company can be a real go-getter in the business world, but if cash is thrown around unwisely, the business may not be able to give the external users what they're looking for, which is basically a return on their investment. This holds true for both potential investors looking for dividend payments and potential lenders wanting to make sure the company can pay back the capital part of any loan plus any interest the lender charges.

A third category of external users of financial statements is HM Revenue and Customs (HMRC). Its main focus is whether the company is reporting taxable profit correctly, a topic I discuss in Chapter 18. In that respect a statement of cash flows has limited value.

The statement of cash flows provides guidance for the following questions:

✔ **Does the company have the ability to generate positive cash flow in the future?** You don't want to invest in a one-hit wonder. Viewing a current statement of cash flows does give a hint as to the company's future prospects.

✔ **Does the company have enough cash to make loan or dividend payments?** Obviously, if you're a potential investor or lender for a company, it's probably not your idea of a good time to let the business use your money for free. You want to check out the statement of cash flows to see how the business manages its money and gauge the probability of the company having enough cash to satisfy its obligations and pay dividends.

✔ **Is the reason for the difference between net profit and cash transactions indicative of a healthy business?** All cash is not created equal. Cash a company brings in from gross receipts is a lot more exciting to me as a potential investor than cash the company has left over because it sold some assets. After all, the business can own only a finite number of assets, while with a well-run business the sky's the limit for bringing in revenue from operations.

You dig out this information by reviewing the different sections of the statement of cash flows. Each section ties back to how accounting transactions affect the income statement and balance sheet. So you're not looking at new information; instead, you're looking at the same information shown in a different way.

Walking through the Cash Flow Sections

A statement of cash flows, prepared under IAS 7, has three sections: operating, investing and financing:

✔ The sources and uses of cash in the **operating** section come from revenue, expenses, cash received from gains and losses shown in the income statement and cash paid out for other costs.

✔ The **investing** section shows sources and uses of cash from debt and equity investment purchases and sales; purchases and sales of property, plant and equipment; and collection of the capital element on debt.

✔ The **financing** section shows long-term liability (paying or receiving loans beyond a period of 12 months from the balance sheet date) and equity items (the sale of company shares and payment of dividends).

Under UK accounting standard FRS 1, the cash flow statement is prepared differently and I look at this issue in the upcoming section 'Getting a heads up on the different headings in a UK GAAP cash flow statement'.

Some of these terms may be unfamiliar to you. Don't worry, by the time you finish reading the rest of this section, you'll be a whizz on cash flow. First, I satisfy your curiosity about the operating section.

Knowing about net cash from operating activities

GAAP's guide to what shows up in the operating section is simply this: the operating section contains transactions not listed as investing or financing transactions – in other words, income statement items. Here, I offer examples of operating sources and uses of cash.

Operating sources of cash

Here are examples of operating sources of cash:

✔ **Cash receipts from the sale of goods or services:** This source is the cash that customers pay the company at the point of contact or what the company collects at a later date from existing trade receivables. For example, I go into an electrical goods shop and buy a new DVD player. It costs £65. I hand over the cost of the purchase plus value added tax in cash. The shop then records this receipt as a source of cash.

On the flip side, assume that on 12 October I go into another electrical appliance shop to buy a new washer and dryer. The shop is holding a 'buy now pay later' interest-free promotion for 90 days, which means that as long as I cough up the cash for the washer and dryer within 90 days, I pay no interest. On 12 October, the electrical shop has no cash source from me, and it won't have that source until I pay for my purchase on or before 12 January.

✔ **Cash receipts from contracts held for dealing or trading purposes:** *Contracts held for dealing or trading purposes* are assets a business purchases to make a profit in the short term. What usually happens is that a business has some spare cash lying around that it doesn't need access to in the immediate future. Rather than leaving the cash in the bank earning little or no interest, the company buys *highly liquid* (easily convertible to cash) shares, bonds or loans.

The business tries to invest in something that won't go down in value during the holding period. Then, when the company sells the investment, the cash it receives goes on the statement of cash flows in the operating section rather than investing. The key here for operating section placement is that the investment is *short term*. See Chapter 7 for more information about short-term investments.

✔ **Interest and dividends:** If the company makes loans to other businesses or individuals, any interest income it receives on those loans goes in the operating section. An example is a loan to a shareholder who is also an employee and needs cash beyond what she's receiving in her salary. This situation happens often in a smaller, owner-managed company.

Also, some companies make loans to key suppliers needing a short-term influx of cash to keep their doors open. A company will take this step if it's in the company's best interest to keep an essential supplier in business. After all, if you like to buy your widgets from Joe's Widget Shop and Joe goes out of business, you'll have to find another widget supplier, and you might not like working with that supplier (or paying its prices) as much as you liked working with Joe.

As reported in the income statement, *dividends* are income paid to shareholders based on their proportional ownership of the company. For example, ABC Limited owns 2,000 shares of XYZ Limited. ABC receives dividends from XYZ at £2 per share totalling £4,000 (£2 × 2,000 shares); this amount shows in the operating section as a source of cash. You can find out more about the process behind declaring and paying dividends in Chapter 9.

Trading at a personal level

Even though you're not a business, you may have put the principles of contracts held for dealing/trading to work for you. For example, let's say your great auntie Dot was feeling flush while visiting your parents for Christmas and gave you £5,000 to put towards your university tuition. Your tuition is already paid for the next 12 months. So, since you know you won't need this money until then, you put the money into a high-interest savings account that matures just in time to make your next tuition payment. That way, you have both the £5,000 gift from Dot and the interest you earn on the high-interest savings account at your disposal instead of just hiding the cash under your bed or allowing it to languish in a non-interest-bearing bank account.

Operating uses of cash

Next, I look at uses of cash showing up in the operating section of a statement of cash flows. The cash outflows are the flip side of the cash inflows. For example, trade receivables from customers is an inflow, and trade payables paid to suppliers is an outflow.

Here are the operating cash outflows you'll come across in your dealings with the statement of cash flows:

- **Satisfying trade payables:** *Trade payables* (or *trade creditors*) is the amount a company owes suppliers for services and products the suppliers render to the company. When the original purchase takes place, no money changes hands between the customer and the supplier. Rather, a promise to pay within a certain amount of time exists.

  For example, I buy £500 of office supplies from a stationery shop to replenish the stationery supply at the office. When I come back to the office with that £500 receipt in my hand, my firm doesn't record this amount as a cash outlay. That's because the stationer hasn't been paid yet; it merely has my promise to pay within 10 days (or 30 days, or whatever). This £500 will be a cash outlay only after I sign and post the cheque to the stationer.

- **Purchases of contracts held for dealing or trading:** Just as sales of contracts held for dealing/trading are a cash source, the amount of money the company pays to buy any contract is a use of cash. No securities other than contracts held for dealing/trading go in the operating section of the statement of cash flows. Again, the key here for operating section placement is that the investment is *short term*. See Chapter 7 for more information about short-term investments.

- **Payments for other business expenses:** This category includes any cash outlays to buy inventory, pay employees, pay taxes or pay any other suppliers (such as utility providers or the telephone company). You can find out more information about inventory purchases in Chapter 13. Chapter 18 shows how to account for income taxes.

- **Interest payments:** Any cash paid to lenders in the form of interest also goes in the operating section. It doesn't make any difference what the purpose of the loan or source of the loan is. So interest paid to a related party, such as a shareholder, for an *operating capital* loan (cash made available for day-to-day business functions) is treated in the same way as interest paid to a vehicle financing company for the lease of the company car.

- **Corporation tax:** Payments made to HM Revenue and Customs for corporation taxes should be separately disclosed within operating cash flows.

What about dividends, which I list as a source of cash? Did I forget to add them here as a use of cash? Nope! Remember, the main thrust of the operating section of the statement of cash flows is to reconcile the cash versus accruals treatment of income statement items. Because paying dividends to shareholders is not a business expense, it doesn't show up in the income statement, so it's not an operating use of cash.

Gaining an understanding of investing activities

Investing transactions are those involving the purchase and sale of non-current assets (see Chapter 7). *Non-current assets* (sometimes called *fixed assets*) are assets the company anticipates owning for more than one year past the date of the balance sheet. Examples of non-current assets are long-term debt and equity investments; property, plant and equipment; and intangible assets such as patents and copyrights.

What exactly are 'debt and equity investments'?

- ✔ Ordinary shares are an example of an *equity* investment. Let's say you buy some ordinary shares in a company. As a shareholder, you don't have a payable/creditor and receivable/debtor relationship with the company. Instead, you are an investor who'll be paid back for the purchase of the shares only if you sell them to someone else.

- ✔ Bonds are *debt* investments. For example, say a public authority sells bonds to the public for the purpose of financing a new hospital. The public authority eventually has to pay the bonds back plus interest. Companies generally issue bonds to raise money for capital expenditures, operating expenses and acquisitions. Bondholders receive interest payments at the bond's stated interest rate. When the bond matures, the company pays the bondholder back the face value of the bond.

Investing sources of cash

Here, I show you specifically how investing transactions show up as sources of cash:

- ✔ **Long-term debt sales and collection:** A company's investments in debt may fall into three categories: outright loans, held-to-maturity debt investments and available-for-sale debt portfolios. Here's how they differ:

  - *Loans* are easy to understand; they're merely money the company loans to others that will not be paid off within 12 months of the balance sheet date. You know from your own personal debts (such as car loans) that, when you owe money, you periodically have to make payments on the capital element of the loan. The same holds true with businesses. So any collection of capital on loans is a cash source for the company lending the money.

- *Held-to-maturity debt investments* are those the company anticipates holding onto until the debt matures. For example, ABC Limited buys five-year bonds to build a new sports arena. When the bonds mature, the cash proceeds go in the investing section. See Chapter 8 for the whole story on bonds.

  Sometimes a company receives cash on held-to-maturity investments because of a prepayment of the capital or scheduled payments of capital and interest. Additionally, sometimes bonds are *called*, which essentially means that the issuer pays them off early.

- *Available-for-sale debt portfolios* are one of those accounting topics defined by what they aren't rather than what they are. They don't fall into the held-to-maturity or trading category. However, as with the held-to-maturity investments, any cash the company receives from their sale or collection of capital prior to or at maturity reflects as a cash source in the investing section of the statement of cash flows.

✔ **Sales of equity investments:** If the company sells shares it owns in other companies, the cash it receives is an investment source. So suppose your company owns 500 shares of ABC Limited, and you decide to sell all 500 shares to finance another purchase. Any money you receive for the sale of your shares goes in the investing section.

✔ **Sales of property, plant and equipment (PP&E) and intangibles:** The cash proceeds from any PP&E the company owns and sells (such as cars, buildings or equipment) is an investment source of cash. Ditto if the company sells an intangible such as a patent. (A *patent* provides licensing for inventions or other unique processes and designs, thus limiting who can profit from them.)

Investing uses of cash

Here are the potential uses of cash that would appear in the investing section of the statement of cash flows:

✔ **Loans and debt purchases:** Any cash the company loans to another company is a cash outlay. So is any cash the company uses to buy bonds.

✔ **Purchase of equity investments:** This category includes any cash the company uses to buy shares in another company.

✔ **Purchase of PP&E:** If the business pays cash for any non-current asset acquisition or an intangible asset, this outlay of cash must appear in the investing section.

Finding out about financing activities

If your head is spinning at this point, I have some good news for you! You're on the last section of the statement of cash flows. In addition to that uplifting piece of information, financing activities are the flip side of investing, so if you've managed to get a grip on investing you'll be able to whizz through financing activities.

Okay, so in a nutshell, what are these financing activities? Financing activities show transactions with lenders such as long-term liabilities (paying or receiving loans beyond a period of 12 months from the balance sheet date) and equity items (the sale of company shares and payment of dividends). Sound familiar from the investing section?

Just one main financing cash source exists: *cash proceeds if a business issues its own shares or debt.* For example, ABC Limited sells £3,000 of shares to XYZ Limited. The cash ABC receives from XYZ for this transaction is a financing source of cash on ABC's statement of cash flows.

Both short-term and long-term debt the company becomes liable for goes in the financing section. How long the creditor plans to hold the debt determines whether it goes on the creditor's books as short- or long-term debt.

Now, here are the uses of cash that would appear in the financing section of the statement of cash flows:

- ✔ **Treasury share transactions:** *Treasury shares* are shares that were previously sold and have since been bought back by the issuing company. The use of the cash is to buy back shares from shareholders. See Chapter 9 for more information about treasury shares.

- ✔ **Cash dividend payments:** *Cash dividends* are earnings paid to shareholders based on the number of shares they own. Remember, only cash dividends go in the financing section. You find more information about cash dividends, plus some info on stock splits (also a non-cash transaction), in Chapter 9.

- ✔ **Paying back debt:** Any capital payments a company makes on bonds or loans constitute a financing activity. Capital payments on finance lease obligations are financing activities as well. *Finance leases* take place when the renter (lessee) assumes the risks and rewards of ownership of the leased asset; see Chapter 19.

Getting a heads up on the different headings in a UK GAAP cash flow statement

The earlier sections in this chapter cover a statement of cash flows prepared under IAS 7. However, currently in the UK, companies that don't follow IFRS need to follow UK GAAP. FRS 1 outlines the method for preparing the *cash flow statement* (as it's referred to in UK speak) for UK GAAP.

More headings are needed under FRS 1 than under IAS 7. The format for preparing the cash flow statement under FRS 1 is shown in Figure 11-1.

	£
Operating activities	X
Returns on investments and servicing of finance	
Interest received	X
Interest paid	(X)
Taxation	(X)
Capital expenditure and financial investments	
Purchase of tangible fixed assets	(X)
Sale of tangible fixed assets	X
Purchase of fixed asset investment	(X)
Acquisitions and disposals	
Acquisition of subsidiary	(X)
Disposal of subsidiary	X
Equity dividends paid	(X)
Management of liquid resources	
Withdrawals from short-term deposits not qualifying as cash	X
Payments into short-term deposits not qualifying as cash	(X)
Movement in cash and overdrafts	X/(X)
Cash and cash equivalents at beginning of year	X/(X)
Cash and cash equivalents at end of year	X/(X)

Figure 11-1: An FRS 1 cash flow statement

Recognising Methods for Preparing the Statement of Cash Flows

A statement of cash flows can be prepared in two ways: the indirect and direct methods. The International Accounting Standards Board (IASB) and the UK's Financial Reporting Council (FRC) (see Chapter 4) prefer the direct method, while the business community prefers the indirect method. Regardless of which method you use, the bottom-line cash balance is the same, and it has to equal how much cash you show on the balance sheet.

At the end of this chapter, I show you how to prepare a statement of cash flows using both the direct and indirect methods. Whichever method you use in your day-to-day work, or in your accountancy studies, you must have a grip on how both methods work. In your accountancy studies, chances are both methods will be examinable.

Using the direct method

The direct method of preparing the statement of cash flows shows the net cash from operating activities, so it shows all operating cash receipts and payments. Some examples of cash receipts you use for the direct method are cash collected from customers, interest and dividends the company receives, and other operating cash receipts such as cash received if the company sells an asset. Examples of cash payments are cash paid to employees and other suppliers and interest paid on bank loans, finance leases (see Chapter 19) or other loans.

Here are three key facts to remember about the direct method:

- ✔ You present cash received and paid – not net profit or loss as shown in the income statement (see Chapter 10).

- ✔ Any differences reflecting when using the direct versus the indirect method take place only in the operating section of the statement of cash flows. The financing and investing sections are the same regardless of which method you use.

- ✔ The IASB and FRC prefer the direct method because they believe the direct method gives the users of the financial statements a more complete picture of the health of the business.

Using the indirect method

When you use the indirect method to prepare the statement of cash flows, the operating section starts with net profit from the income statement. You then adjust net profit for any non-cash items hitting the income statement. Your two biggies are depreciation (see Chapter 12) and amortisation (see Chapter 7) expense, both of which are non-cash transactions.

Other common items requiring adjustment are gains and losses from the sale of assets (see Chapter 10). This is because the gain or losses shown in the income statement for the sale will rarely, if ever, equal the cash a company receives. In other words, gain or loss is based on the difference between the asset's *net book value*, which is cost less accumulated depreciation and (where relevant) impairment, and the amount the item was sold for – not how much cash the buyer hands over to the seller.

For example, say that a business has a machine it previously used for a product it no longer makes. Because it no longer needs the machine, the business sells it to another company for £1,500. The cash received is £1,500, but what about gain or loss on disposal? To work out that amount, suppose the company originally paid £3,000 to purchase and install the machine. During the time it owned the machine, it *depreciated* the machine (spread the cost of ownership over the machine's useful life) to the tune of £2,000, making its book value £1,000 (£3,000 – £2,000). Gain on disposal is £500, which is the difference between book value and the purchase price (£1,500 – £1,000). So a £500 difference exists between the gain in the income statement (£1,000) and the cash inflow of £1,500.

Interpreting the Statement of Cash Flows

Users of the statement of cash flows are primarily interested in whether the company has positive cash flows from operations. As a general rule, a company should be covering its costs by cash it brings in from the day-to-day running of the business rather than from borrowed funds. As a potential investor or creditor, I want to see that cash the company brings in through operations exceeds any cash brought in by selling assets or borrowing money. This is because selling assets or borrowing money can never be construed as a continuing event like bringing in cash from selling goods or services.

A company may issue shares or bonds in order to expand. The amount it generates may well exceed the net cash from operations. On a non-recurring basis, that situation can be okay because successful expansion is a good thing for investors and creditors. However, unless cash from operations regularly exceeds cash from other sources, a company will be paying back debt with debt, which is decidedly not a good thing.

Here's how an investor and a creditor use the statement of cash flows:

- ✔ **Investor:** An investor wants to make sure the company has enough cash flow to pay an adequate return on investment. In other words, can the investor anticipate getting a cash dividend each year? Also important is using the statement of cash flows to evaluate how well the company is managing its cash because investors will eventually sell their shares, something that won't be possible if the company mismanages its cash to such a point that it goes out of business.

- ✔ **Creditor:** The creditor also has a vested interest in making sure the company has sound cash management. After all, in addition to the interest income the debtor pays for the use of the loan, the creditor wants to make sure it also gets paid back the capital portion of the loan. It's never a good sign if a business is paying back debt by taking on more debt.

Looking at Two Sample Statements of Cash Flows

Here, I show you what the statement of cash flows looks like when you use both the direct and indirect methods of preparation. Figure 11-2 is the statement of cash flows using the direct method, and Figure 11-3 is the statement of cash flows using the indirect method. As you look at both, note that the cash balance at 31 December 2012 is the same for both methods.

Cash Flows from Investing Activities:	
Proceeds from sale of property, plant and equipment	25,000
Purchase of property, plant and equipment	(60,000)
Net cash used in investing activities	35,000
Cash Flows from Financing Activities:	
New long-term borrowing	350
Payment of long-term borrowing	(200)
Purchase of treasury shares	(175)
Equity dividends paid	(50)
Net cash used in financing activities	(75)
Increase (decrease) in cash	10,212
Opening cash balance at start of year	35,620
Closing cash balance at end of year	45,832
Note 1	
Net profit	43,987
Adjustments for:	
Depreciation	2,150
Gain on sale of property, plant and equipment	(150)
Increase in trade receivables	(3,500)
Increase in trade payables	2,800
Net cash from operating activities	45,287

Figure 11-2: A direct method statement of cash flows.

Purchase of property, plant and equipment	(60,000)	
Net cash used in investing activities		(35,000)
		10,287
Financing Activities:		
New long-term borrowing	350	
Payment of long-term borrowing	(200)	
Purchase of treasury shares	(175)	
Equity dividends paid	(50)	
		(75)
Increase (decrease) in cash		10,212
Opening cash balance at start of year		35,620
Closing cash balance at end of year		45,832

Figure 11-3: An indirect method statement of cash flows.

The increase in cash of £10,212 is the sum of the net cash provided by operating activities, net cash used for investing activities and net cash used for financing activities (£45,287 − £35,000 − £75).

When you prepare a statement of cash flows using the direct method, you also have to include a section reconciling accruals-based net profit to cash provided by operating activities.

As you can see, the indirect method operating section is the same as the statement you prepare reconciling cash to accruals for the direct method. Cash flows from investing and financing remain the same regardless of which method you use.

Chapter 12

Discovering and Understanding Depreciation

....

In This Chapter

▶ Seeing how depreciation affects the financial statements

▶ Knowing the ins and outs of costs

▶ Calculating depreciation

▶ Looking at a schedule of depreciation

....

This chapter is your introduction to a company's *tangible* assets, which you can touch and feel – they have a physical presence. Tangible assets, also called *fixed* assets (or in international lingo, *non-current assets*), include property, plant and equipment (PP&E). Many fixed assets are used for years, and a company relies on a mysterious accounting concept called *depreciation* to keep its financial statements in line with the reality of how long those assets may be used for in a business.

If you read this entire chapter, depreciation won't seem so mysterious anymore. I help you understand what depreciation is, how it affects all three financial statements, and how it connects a business's costs to its expenses. (Yes, costs and expenses are two different things in the business world – but hey, surely you didn't expect it to be anything else than less than straightforward!) I also show you the various depreciation methods financial accountants use: the straight-line method and the reducing balance method (sometimes called the *diminishing balance method*), and show you how the methods compare. And I walk you through what information you find in a schedule of depreciation.

The presentation in this chapter follows the setup of most financial accounting textbooks, so you can relate the information you find here back to your accountancy studies. With this chapter's help, you should be able to discuss depreciation with confidence in any exam (or work) situation.

Intangible assets, which are assets that you can't see or touch, receive an accounting treatment similar to depreciation that's called *amortisation*. See Chapter 7 for the lowdown on intangibles.

Discovering How Depreciation Affects All Financial Statements

Let me start with a simple definition of depreciation: it is a method of allocating a company's costs to the relevant accounting period. Later in the chapter, I define the word *costs* and help you understand what the *appropriate accounting period* may be for a given item. For now, sit tight with this definition, and keep in mind that depreciation is *not* used to find out an asset's *fair* (sometimes called *market*) *value* (the amount of money the company could receive upon the sale of that asset to an unconnected, willing third party in an arm's length transaction). Companies depreciate the fixed assets which they own. (Only under certain circumstances, which I explain in Chapter 19, do they depreciate fixed assets they lease.)

Many financial accounting transactions affect more than one financial statement. Depreciation is a *non-cash transaction* (no money changes hands when you account for depreciation), and it affects all three financial statements: the balance sheet (see Part III), the income statement (see Chapter 10) and the statement of cash flows (see Chapter 11). So getting your depreciation calculations right is quite a big issue in the world of financial accounting.

If you're a student accountant and have perhaps taken some tax exams, or if you work in practice doing accounts and tax returns for clients, you're probably familiar with the term 'capital allowances', which are basically HM Revenue and Custom's version of depreciation but are instead used for tax purposes. An important point to keep in mind is that a tax authority's depreciation methods (sometimes called *tax allowable depreciation*) are quite different to the financial accounting depreciation methods you get to grips with in this chapter.

How does depreciation take place and affect all three financial statements? When a company buys something that it anticipates being able to use for more than one year, generally accepted accounting practice (GAAP; see Chapter 4) spells out that this purchase must not be taken as a reduction to income all at once (in other words, posted to the income statement in one go). (Keep in mind that *income* is the operating and non-operating revenue the company brings in.) Accountants refer to the process of recording the cost of an asset on the balance sheet as *capitalisation*.

When an asset is *capitalised*, here's how the purchase affects each financial statement:

- ✔ **Balance sheet:** The purchase goes on the balance sheet as a fixed (non-current) asset.

- ✔ **Income statement:** Through the process of depreciation, the purchase eventually moves from the balance sheet into the income statement. (The 'Distinguishing among Depreciation Methods' section, later in this chapter, shows you exactly how this process happens.)

- ✔ **Statement of cash flows:** At the time of purchase, the asset's cost goes on the statement of cash flows as a reduction in cash for the entire purchase price. (If cash doesn't change hands at the time of purchase, the transaction still shows up on the statement of cash flows – just in a slightly different manner.) As the asset is depreciated, the depreciation amount has to be added back onto the statement of cash flows if you use the indirect rather than direct method to prepare the statement of cash flows. (That's because it's a non-cash transaction that has been included as an expense that makes up the final profit (or loss) figure.) See Chapter 11 for a run through on the indirect versus direct method of presenting the statement of cash flows.

When determining what items should be capitalised, common sense has to come into the equation. For example, I have a litter bin in my office that I've used for over three years. Does that mean that the bin should have been capitalised at the time of purchase? Well, unless this was some sort of expensive designer bin costing a lot of money, the answer is no. Most companies have a capitalisation policy setting a monetary benchmark for items to be capitalised rather than expensed – for example, items that cost under £100 are automatically expensed no matter how long a company will use them for. Larger companies may have a higher monetary benchmark capitalisation policy than smaller companies, but so long as the capitalisation policy is reasonable and appropriate to the size and complexity of the company, there shouldn't be a problem. Companies take into consideration the *materiality* of such transactions when they are devising their capitalisation policy. Something is *material* when it can influence the decisions third parties make about the financial state of a company. For example consider a company that doesn't capitalise anything below £300. If it bought 20 laptops for £250 and wrote the entire cost of these off to the income statement, this treatment wouldn't be appropriate; it should capitalise the entire £5,000 and write this off over the useful economic life of the laptops.

Mastering Costs

You probably use the terms *cost* and *expense* interchangeably to describe a situation where you're paying cash, or a promise of cash, in order to purchase a good or service. For example, you buy a pint of milk at the supermarket and pay cash, or you fill up your car at the petrol station after swiping your credit card. In either situation, you may have a moan about the *cost* of the item you're buying or how that *expense* seems too high. In the business world, costs and expenses are two separate things. I explain why in Chapter 11, and I start this section with a refresher about the difference.

Defining costs and expenses in the world of business

In the world of business, day-to-day costs are not the same as expenses. When a business incurs a *cost*, it exchanges a resource (usually cash or a promise to pay cash in the future) to purchase a good or service that will allow the company to generate revenue. But in the future the cost will probably turn into an expense. That's because all expenses have to be matched with revenue for the financial period. You may have heard the phrase the *matching concept*. Well, this is a particularly important concept where the depreciation of fixed (non-current) assets is concerned, and I discuss this principle further in the next section 'Making sense of the matching principle'.

Confused? Well, keep reading, and hopefully all will become clear.

Here's an example of how a common business transaction can initially record as a cost and eventually migrate into an expense.

Amanda is the owner of Female Funky Fashions, a manufacturer of women's designer clothing. Demand for her products has been very high and she has decided to add a new line of women's formal clothing. She needs to purchase five new sewing machines, which for this type of business are fixed assets as they will be used to make the clothes to sell to retailers to generate money for Amanda's business.

When Amanda buys the sewing machines, the price she'll pay (or promise to pay) is a cost. Then, as the company uses the sewing machines in the normal activity of her business, she'll *depreciate* them: in other words, she'll reclassify the cost of buying the assets as an expense of doing business. So the resources Amanda uses to purchase the sewing machines move from the balance sheet (cost) to the income statement (expense).

The income statement shows revenue and expenses. The difference between those two numbers is the company's *net profit* (when revenue is more than expense) or *net loss* (when expenses are higher than revenue).

Still wondering what the big deal is with financial accountants having to depreciate fixed assets? Well, the process ties back to the matching principle, which I discuss in the next section.

Making sense of the matching principle

In financial accounting, every transaction you work with has to satisfy the matching principle (see Chapter 5). You have to associate all recognised revenue (both earned and realisable) during the accounting period to all expenses you incur to produce that revenue.

Continuing with the sewing machine example in the last section, assume that the life of the sewing machine – the expected amount of time the company will be able to use the sewing machine before having to replace it – is five years. The average cost of a commercial sewing machine is £1,500. If the company expenses the entire purchase price (cost) of £1,500 in the year of purchase, the net profit for this particular year is understated and the net profit for the next four years is overstated.

Why? Because while the company forked out £1,500 in year one for a machine, the company anticipates using the machine for another four years. So to truly match the sales the company generates from garments made using the sewing machine, the cost of the machine has to be allocated over each of the years it will be used to churn out those garments for sale.

Identifying the different types of costs

How a company classifies a cost depends on the category it falls into. Using generally accepted accounting practice (GAAP; see Chapter 4), business costs fall into three general categories: product, period and systematic. The subject of this chapter, depreciation, is a *systematic cost*, which means it's a cost expensed over time. I discuss depreciation in more detail in the next section.

Here, let me briefly define product and period costs so you can see how they differ from a systematic cost such as depreciation:

- ✔ **Product costs:** Any costs that relate to manufacturing or buying an item for resale to customers. A common example is inventory (sometimes called *stock*) (see Chapter 13), which reflects costs a manufacturing company incurs when buying all the different items or raw materials it needs to make the items it sells to its customers. For a retailer, the cost of inventory is what it pays to buy the finished goods from the manufacturer.

- ✔ **Period costs:** Costs that, while necessary to keep the business going, don't relate to any specific item the company sells. Examples of period costs are rent, telephone expenses and office salaries.

Learning which items are depreciated

When a company purchases a fixed asset (internationally known as a *non-current asset*; see Chapter 7) like a computer or a machine, the cost of the asset is spread over its useful life, which may be years after the purchase. Therefore, depreciation is a *systematic cost*: it's is allocated to different accounting periods based on when the company receives the benefit of the cost.

Your next question may be this: 'Which costs associated with purchasing a fixed asset do you bring in to work out the total cost of the fixed asset? Just the purchase price? Purchase price plus VAT and shipping? Other costs?'

Except for the allocation of cost between land and buildings, which I discuss in the next section, working out a total cost price which will be depreciated over an asset's useful life is straightforward. Following GAAP, the business has to record all fixed asset purchases on its balance sheet at their original cost plus all the ordinary and necessary costs to get the fixed asset ready to use (these additional costs are sometimes known as *incidental* or *incremental* costs). The total cost of the fixed asset is referred to as its *depreciable amount* (also known as its *base cost*).

Pat's Pencil Company Ltd makes pencils and buys a new machine to automatically separate and shrink-wrap ten pencils into saleable units. Here are examples of various costs of the machine: the purchase price, VAT, shipping costs, and assembly of the shrink-wrapping machine on the factory floor. (*Shipping costs* are Pat's Pencil Company's cost to get the machine from the seller to the pencil company.)

Allocating costs between land and building

A question that's commonly asked by both student accountants and professional accountants is how to work out the allocation between land and building. After all, you work in the world of accounting; you're not a building surveyor! How do you manage to get your head around whether the company appropriately allocates costs between the land and the building? The best way to do this is for the business to have a valuation done during the purchasing process.

A *valuation* occurs when a professional building surveyor/valuer determines the value of the property. If you've ever purchased a house and applied for a mortgage, you're probably familiar with surveys. Basically, the survey provides assurance to the mortgage company that you're not borrowing more than the property is worth.

Even if a business doesn't have to secure a mortgage to purchase a property, it still gets a valuation to make sure it's not overpaying for the property. Alternatively, the Land Registry may show an allocation of building to land. However, that allocation (where it exists) may not be materially correct for depreciation purposes.

If you're a student accountant, the allocation information will be given. Just remember to subtract land cost from the total if working out a property depreciation question.

Handling property depreciation

Now, what about *property* – land and buildings? Both are clearly fixed (non-current) assets, but the cost of the land a building sits on is not depreciated because land doesn't have a finite useful life and therefore has to be separated from the cost of the building for the purposes of depreciation. Why? The answer is that GAAP mandates that separation – no *if*s or *but*s about it.

The cost of land is never depreciated under GAAP. That's because the land a building stands on is assumed to retain its value. In other words, it won't be used up or run down through use over time – it has an indefinite lifespan whereas buildings don't.

So, in the example above, if Pat's Pencil Company Limited pays £250,000 to purchase a building to manufacture its pencils and the purchase price is allocated 90 per cent to building and 10 per cent to land, how much of the purchase price is spread out over the useful life of the building? Your answer is £250,000 multiplied by 90 per cent: £225,000.

However, just to keep you on your toes, land *improvements* are depreciable. Examples of land improvements are fences, roads and gates. If a business purchases a piece of raw land and constructs its own building, the accounting for this is dead easy because you have a sales price for the land and construction costs for the building – bonus!

Expensing repairs and maintenance

Repair and maintenance costs are expenses of the period in which they are incurred and not systematic depreciation costs. For example, on 14 June 2013, a floristry business has the oil changed and purchases a new set of tyres for the delivery van. The cost of the oil change and tyres goes in the income statement as an operating expense for the month of June.

The next month, the delivery van's engine blows up, leaving the driver and flowers on the hard shoulder of the motorway. Replacing the engine significantly increases the useful life of the delivery van, so you have to add the cost of the new engine to the net book value of the van on the balance sheet. *Net book value* (also shortened to just *book value*) is the difference between the cost of the fixed asset and its accumulated depreciation at any given time.

I discuss accumulated depreciation in the 'Preparing a Depreciation Schedule' section later in this chapter. For now, just remember that *accumulated depreciation* refers to how much depreciation has been charged to a particular asset so far since the asset's purchase.

Distinguishing between Depreciation Methods

Financial accounting generally uses two methods of depreciation, which are based on time: the straight-line method and the reducing balance method (sometimes called the *diminishing balance* method).

Depreciation is the systematic allocation of the depreciable amount of an asset over its expected useful life. The *depreciable amount* of an asset is the cost of the asset (including incremental costs such as non-refundable taxes and shipping costs) less the amount of money at the end of the asset's useful life that can be expected to be received when the asset is sold (this amount is often referred to as the *residual* amount). The total cost less residual value is then subjected to systematic depreciation (see later in this section for an illustration of how depreciable amount is calculated).

Here's a brief explanation of each method of depreciation:

- ✔ **Straight-line method:** This method spreads out the cost of the fixed asset evenly over its useful life.

- ✔ **Reducing balance method:** This is an *accelerated* method of depreciation, meaning the depreciation expense is higher in the earlier years of ownership but lower in the later years.

Depletion, which is the annual expense for the use of natural resources, is based on actual physical usage. Examples of natural resources subject to depletion are oil, timber and minerals.

Don't worry, I walk you through an example of each of the above methods of depreciation in detail later in this section. And to show how the choice of a depreciation method can greatly affect the amount of depreciation expense taken in each year, I use the same asset facts and circumstances for each depreciation example to show you a comparison of the two methods.

First, however, you need to understand what information you need to know about each fixed asset before you calculate depreciation. For the purposes of calculating depreciation for this chapter, here are the facts and circumstances for your sample fixed asset – a delivery van that the company buys on 1 January 2013:

- ✔ **The cost of the asset:** In the earlier section 'Learning which items are depreciated', I explain what costs have to be included in the *depreciable amount* – the total cost of the fixed asset. The cost of the delivery van is £30,000.

- ✔ **How long the company anticipates being able to use the fixed asset:** The company may measure the length in years, in production hours or in miles driven. For this example, the business anticipates using the delivery van for five years.

- ✔ **The value of the asset after the company has finished using it (known as its residual value):** The *residual value* is an estimate that management makes for how much the fixed asset will be worth when it has served its purpose. When the delivery van is replaced, the company anticipates receiving £3,000 in trade-in value.

- ✔ **The depreciation method the company uses:** I introduce the two GAAP methods earlier in this section. The method the business uses is a matter of choice as long as the method is appropriate for the asset. For financial accounting purposes, the standard of appropriateness is met if the company uses the method that most closely matches expenses to revenue.

  A business could switch methods after it's started using one depreciation method for an asset. However, to do so would be a change in estimation technique (see Chapter 15).

- ✔ **Date of purchase and whether the company is on a calendar or other year-end:** The date is when the fixed asset is ready for use. Calendar year-end is on 31 December. These annual accounting periods are known as *financial year-ends*. For example, many companies have a 31 March financial year-end; others have a 30 September financial year-end. This business has a calendar year-end of 31 December. The delivery van is purchased on 1 January.

Ready? Well, start your engines and let's depreciate this delivery van!

Walking through the straight-line method

When using the straight-line method, the residual value reduces the depreciable amount. So the cost of the delivery van (£30,000) less its salvage value (£3,000) gives you a depreciable amount of £27,000.

The expected useful life is five years. So depreciation expense for the van would be £27,000/5 or £5,400 depreciation expense per year for each of the five years. The van's book value at the end of year five is £3,000.

Running through the reducing balance method

Unlike the straight-line method, you don't deduct residual value when calculating the depreciable amount with the reducing balance method. However, you do have to limit depreciation so that, at the end of the day, net book value is the same as the residual value. Clear as mud? Stick with me.

For your depreciation rate, you take a multiple of the straight-line method (for student accountants, this will more than likely be given to you in any practice questions you're set or in an exam situation). In this example, I'm going to use the *double reducing balance method*, which is twice the straight-line rate. All will become clear very soon – trust me!

Because the delivery van has a useful life of five years, shown as a percentage, the straight-line rate is 1/5 or 20 per cent per year. Double that to get your double declining balance rate of 40 per cent. That's not so bad to work out!

Figure 12-1 shows how to calculate double reducing balance depreciation. Note that in year five, the rate doesn't matter because you have to limit the depreciation to residual value. Because the closing net book value is £3,888 in year four, depreciation is limited to £888 in year five.

		Opening Net Book Value	Rate	Depreciation Expense	Accumulated Depreciation	Closing Net Book Value
		£		£	£	£
	2012	30,000	40%	12,000	12,000	18,000
Figure 12-1: A double reducing balance depreciation calculation.	2013	18,000	40%	7,200	19,200	10,800
	2014	10,800	40%	4,320	23,520	6,480
	2015	6,480	40%	2,592	26,112	3,888
	2016	3,888	*	888	27,000	3,000

Seeing how the methods compare

Just for fun, Figure 12-2 shows how the different depreciation methods result in a different amount of depreciation expense per year. You'll see that over the entire five-year useful life of the van, the total depreciation is £27,000 regardless of the method used. Thus, the different methods result in different depreciation expense amounts in each of the years, but not in a difference in total depreciation over the life of the asset.

Pretty cool, eh! Depending on the depreciation method the company uses for the fixed asset, depreciation expense can be all over the place. A business can use a different depreciation method for different types of assets as long as the depreciation method fairly shows the use of the asset over time. You'll see the same method and expense variations in Chapter 13 when you learn about stock/inventory cost flow assumptions.

		Straight-line	Reducing Balance
		£	£
	2012	5,400	12,000
Figure 12-2: Comparison of depreciation expense between methods.	2013	5,400	7,200
	2014	5,400	4,320
	2015	5,400	2,592
	2016	5,400	888
	Total	27,000	27,000

You can also see from Figure 12-2 that the reducing balance method charges more depreciation in the earlier years and less depreciation in the later years. 'Why?' I hear you ask! Well, the reason is that (particularly for motor vehicles which are often subjected to the reducing balance method of depreciation) in the early years, when the asset is new, it will require less maintenance and servicing. However, in the later years as the asset becomes worn out through use, it will require more maintenance and servicing so what you'll see in a company income statement is repairs and maintenance costs increasing (because of additional maintenance and servicing costs of the asset), but less depreciation being charged. The reducing balance method recognises that, in the later years, more costs will be incurred for repairs, so this method reduces depreciation as a direct result.

More depreciation expense in an accounting period means less net profit, and vice versa.

Pro-rating the depreciation charge

The delivery van example above was neat and tidy because the company purchased the van on 1 January (the first day of its financial accounting year). What happens, then, if the company buys a fixed asset mid-year?

Well, all that would actually depend on the company's accounting policy for depreciation. Some companies have a policy of charging a full year's depreciation in the year of purchase, even if the asset has been purchased mid-way through the financial year. The flip side to this approach is that many companies don't charge any depreciation in the year they dispose of the asset (either by sale or as scrap), which then levels out the depreciation charge. However, some companies are known to charge depreciation on a *pro-rata* basis, which means the cost of a particular item is divided in proportion, according to a factor that can be calculated exactly. If you come across a situation where depreciation is charged on a pro-rata basis in the year of acquisition, then you pro-rate the depreciation expense among the accounting periods involved. For example, if a company with a 31 December year-end buys a new machine on 1 June, the first year of depreciation is pro-rated using the fraction 7/12 (because seven months remain in the financial year). Any surplus depreciation is charged in year 6.

Consider the delivery van example above while using the straight-line method. Depreciation expense in year 1 is now £3,150 (£5,400 × 7/12). For years 2 to 5, the depreciation expense remains £5,400. In year 6, you finish up by charging the remaining £2,250 (£5,400 × 5/12).

The journal entry (see Chapter 5) to get the depreciation charge into the accounts is to debit depreciation expense and credit accumulated depreciation.

Preparing a Depreciation Schedule

All businesses keep a depreciation schedule for their assets showing all relevant details about each asset. The depreciation schedule is also known as the *fixed assets register* or *non-current asset register*. Here are some of the more common examples of items that show up on a basic depreciation schedule:

- **Description:** The type of asset and any other identifying information about the fixed asset (such as an asset number).

- **Cost:** The purchase price of the asset plus any other costs requiring capitalisation. While most additions to purchase price take place when the company acquires the asset, the fixed asset cost can be added to after the event if material renovations are performed. (Think about the new engine in the van example from the earlier section 'Expensing repairs and maintenance'.)

- **Life:** How long the company estimates it will use the fixed asset.

- **Method:** The method of depreciation the company uses for this fixed asset.

- **Residual value:** The estimated value of the fixed asset when the company gets rid of or replaces it.

- **Date purchased:** The day the asset was purchased.

- **Current depreciation:** The depreciation expense charged in the current period.

- **Accumulated depreciation:** The total amount of depreciation expensed from the day the company started to use the fixed asset to the date of the financial report.

- **Net book value:** The difference between the fixed asset cost and its accumulated depreciation.

Depending on the size of the company, the depreciation schedule may also have the fixed asset's identification number, the location where the fixed asset is kept and other relevant facts about the asset.

Having a nicely organised depreciation schedule allows the company to keep an accurate record of activity for each fixed asset. Why is this information important? As you find out in Chapter 7 (when learning how companies account for fixed assets), this info cannot be obtained by looking at the balance sheet.

Check out Figure 12-3 to see the basic organisation for a depreciation schedule.

Figure 12-3:
Example
of a depre-
ciation
schedule.

Date of Purchase	Description	Cost	Residual Value	Depreciation Method *	Useful Life (years)	Opening Depreciation	Current year Depreciation Expense	Accumulated Depreciation	Net Book Value
01.05.12	Delivery van	30,000	2,000	25% RB	5	7,500	5,625	13,125	16,875
20.05.12	Computer	1,500	0	3 yr SL	3	500	500	1,000	500
15.09.12	Furniture	2,500	300	3 yr SL	3	733	733	1,466	1,034
03.10.12	Fixtures	700	100	10 yr SL	10	60	60	120	580

*

RB = reducing balance
SL = straight line

See Chapter 18 if you're wondering how to account for the difference between GAAP and tax allowable depreciation (sometimes called *capital allowances*).

Chapter 13

Dealing with and Accounting for Inventory

In This Chapter

▶ Seeing how inventory calculations impact the financial statements

▶ Focusing on service companies

▶ Recognising a variety of inventory types

▶ Getting to grips with the inventory valuation methods

▶ Looking at an inventory worksheet

Some people think that inventory is only the products available for sale in a retail shop or supermarket. I discuss that kind of inventory (called *retail inventory*) in this chapter, but I also introduce you to other kinds of *product inventory* used by manufacturers, which includes raw materials, work in progress and finished goods.

You also find out in this chapter about two methods a company may use to keep track of retail inventory, as well as the three methods businesses may use to value their closing inventory: first-in, first-out; last-in, first-out; and weighted average. Some businesses actually won't have *any* inventory, and I explain when you can expect this situation to occur and how to handle any minimal amounts of inventory this type of business may keep on hand.

Discovering How the Valuation of Inventory Affects the Accounts

In financial accounting, you're preparing financial statements for external users, such as investors and lenders (see Chapter 1). They need accurate financial statements to make informed decisions as to whether they want to invest in the company or lend it money.

For *manufacturing* companies (which make products) and *retail* companies (which sell the products made by the manufacturers), inventory can be a large number on the balance sheet. Actually, it may be their largest current asset account. So proper accounting for inventory is very important – including determining what costs go on the balance sheet rather than in the income statement to making sure the client values its closing inventory properly because inventory affects both the profit and loss account (income statement) and the balance sheet (statement of financial position). A company can inadvertently prepare a set of highly inaccurate financial statements by writing off purchases to the income statement rather than keeping them on the balance sheet as inventory.

So what costs are okay to write off directly to the income statement, and which costs should stay on the balance sheet? Here's a full and frank answer: any items a company buys to sell that it will put to use in periods beyond the current accounting period are taken to inventory.

Inventory ties into the revenue process and to cost of sales (see Chapter 10). Putting inventory hand in hand with cost of sales makes common sense – you have to buy something before you can sell it. But you may be wondering how revenue and inventory relate to each other. Well, remember that you need to use generally accepted accounting practice (GAAP), which I introduce in Chapter 4. GAAP dictates that expenses are matched with revenue earned for the period.

How does inventory come into the revenue equation? In Chapter 10 I show you how to prepare a cost of goods sold for a retailing and manufacturing company. Product costs are part of the cost of goods sold. Product costs that relate to inventory are any costs that a company incurs when purchasing or manufacturing an item for sale to customers. The cost of sales in the income statement is what the company pays to buy or manufacture the goods that it sells to its customers *in that specific accounting period only*. The rest of the cost of the product purchases stays on the balance sheet as a current asset.

Seeing How Service Organisations Deal with Inventory

While discussions of inventory focus on manufacturing and retail companies, you also need to consider *service organisations*: those that don't provide a tangible good and normally won't have any type of appreciable inventory. Service companies provide more of a knowledge-based work product. (Think about what you get from your dentist or doctor.) However, if a service company keeps a large amount of office or other supplies on hand, it may account for them as inventory at the end of the accounting period instead of just taking the cost of supplies purchased to the relevant expense account each month.

If you're a student accountant, you'll probably be asked to demonstrate your knowledge on accounting for inventory. A typical scenario you may come across in your accountancy studies or bookkeeping studies is as follows.

The facts will generally be that the company purchases a certain amount of supplies in a month. The question will ask you to set up the journal entry to record both the purchase and expense of the supplies in that month. In this example, let's say the company purchases supplies *on account*, which means the company promises to pay for them at a later date. The supplies cost £700 at the beginning of September. On the last day of September, an inventory count is done and supplies amounting to £230 remain in stock.

Your journal entry to record the purchase is to debit 'inventory' (an asset account) and credit 'trade payables' for £700. So far you have not affected the income statement.

Now at the end of the month, you have to adjust closing inventory to the actual value you've got left over, which involves expensing the portion of supplies used to the income statement. The company purchased £700 of supplies and only £230 remains, so you know that £470 (£700 – £230) of supplies were used and should be expensed for the month of September. So your journal entry is to debit 'purchases' (an income statement account) and credit 'inventory' (the asset account).

Technically, anything the company purchases that will not be used up in the current period should go to some sort of inventory account. However, retail shops sometimes take shop supplies (such as carrier bags, price tags and cash register receipts) to the income statement expense when they're purchased instead of to a balance sheet account such as shop supplies inventory. Doing so is not normally a big deal provided that the expense is not a material amount (*material* means the significance of the item on the accounts). For a larger retailer like Tesco, the amount would be material because it purchases everything in huge volumes.

Classifying Inventory

Depending on the type of business, you'll encounter different sorts of inventory. To make life easier, in this section I break the subject down into inventory for retail companies and inventory for manufacturing companies.

Accounting for the purchase of goods

Accounting for goods in a retail company, while it has its moments, is easier than accounting for manufacturing inventory. That's because a retail company, such as a home improvements store, has only one class of inventory to keep track of: goods the business purchases from various manufacturers for resale.

Here's an example of the basic flow of inventory for a retailer. A sales assistant in the pet outlet within a major department store notices and informs her manager that they're running low on a certain brand of dog food. The manager follows the department store's purchasing process, and the end result is that the department receives a shipment of dog food from its supplier.

This transaction is a purchase (cost), but it's not an expense until the department store sells the dog food. So the business records the entire shipment of dog food on the balance sheet as an addition to both inventory and trade payables (see Chapter 8). I use *trade payables* instead of *cash* because the department store has payment terms with this supplier and money has yet to change hands during the transaction.

Say that, in August, the store sells dog food to customers for £150 that cost the company £75 to purchase from the supplier. Sales revenue increases by £150, cost of sales increases by £75 and inventory decreases by £75. Matching the expense to revenue, the effect to gross profit is £75 (£150 – £75).

Pretty basic stuff, eh? The company buys inventory and sells it. Next, I talk about how retail shops normally keep track of their inventory. Two major types of inventory monitoring system exist: perpetual and periodic.

Perpetual system

Most larger retailers have electronic cash registers (ECRs). If you've used a self-checkout at a supermarket, you're familiar with them. The checkout features a glass window with a red beam of light. You run the bar code of a product over the red beam, and the selling price of the item automatically records as a sale for which you are charged and the business receives revenue.

If the business also uses a *point-of-sale system*, which means transactions at the register automatically update all accounting records, the inventory count is updated constantly, *perpetually*, as the ECR records the item sold. This means that the cost of the item sold is taken out of the asset inventory account and moved to cost of sales.

With point-of-sale systems, transactions taking place at the cash register update all inventory, cost of sales and sales information throughout the system in real time as the transactions occur.

Let's say you go into John Lewis and buy a birthday card for a friend. As you check out, the point-of-sale software is updating the greeting card department records showing that one less birthday card is available for sale. The software is also updating cost of goods sold showing the cost for the card, and it's updating revenue to reflect the retail price (what you just paid) for the birthday card.

Even if a company uses a point-of-sale system, undertaking a physical inventory count at year-end (or periodically) is still very important to verify that the perpetual system is working correctly. Doing a physical inventory count is also the best way to identify breakage and employee or customer theft issues, and certainly your external auditors will need one doing at the year-end to corroborate the year-end inventory valuation (they'll more than likely attend the count as well!).

Periodic system

With a periodic system of inventory counting, the physical inventory count is carried out periodically, and the resulting figure is used to adjust the balance sheet 'inventory asset' account. Retail shops using periodic inventory usually count their inventory at their particular year-end. However, inventory could be taken more often, such as quarterly or at the end of every heavy sales season (such as Valentine's Day, Mother's Day and the Christmas holidays).

Here's how the periodic system works. The business counts *closing inventory*, arriving at a final monetary amount for all unsold inventory as at the last day of the accounting period. Next, the company's accounts department deducts closing inventory totals from the opening inventory after adding in all inventory purchases made during the period. The resulting number is the cost of sales. The balance sheet inventory account is reduced by the cost of sales figure and the income statement expense account 'cost of sales' is increased by that number to match expenses with revenue.

Using the periodic system, cost of sales can be determined with a fairly high degree of accuracy, but only after the physical inventory is counted and valued. When companies prepare financial statements and a physical inventory is not carried out, they use an estimate, which is basically a 'best guess' for inventory and cost of sales (see Chapter 15). For example, they may use past history or experience to estimate cost of sales. If in prior years cost of sales for the month of May was 75 per cent of gross sales, the company uses the same percentage for current cost of sales, adjusting that figure to actual at year-end using the physical inventory figures.

Consignment goods, those a retailing business offers for sale but does not officially own (often seen in car dealerships), aren't included in inventory. With a consignment arrangement, the retailer (consignee) is acting as a middleman between the owner of the goods (consignor) and the customer.

Accounting for the manufacturing of goods

To account for all expenses it incurs while making products for resale, a manufacturing company has a 'cost of goods manufactured' account. (See Chapter 10 to see how to go about preparing the cost of goods manufactured section of the income statement.) The cost of goods manufactured contains three types of inventory: raw materials, work in progress and finished goods.

Raw materials

The *raw materials* inventory reflects all the materials the company uses to make a product. For example, for a car manufacturer this includes the steel to form the body, leather or fabric for the seats, and all the bits and bobs that go under the bonnet. (Hey, I'm an accountant – not a mechanic!) In essence, any materials that you can directly trace back to making the car are raw materials inventory.

Keep in mind that manufacturing companies can use the perpetual inventory method of keeping track of their inventory, which I describe in the previous section. For example, components that a computer manufacturer needs to assemble laptops for sale to retail stores will have serial numbers that are scanned in when purchased from the component manufacturer and scanned back out when put into the computer made by the computer manufacturer. Thus, the manufacturer keeps a running total of components in inventory.

Work in progress

At any point in time during the manufacturing process, the company probably has items that are in the process of being made but are not yet complete, which is *work in progress*. With a car manufacturer, imagine the car going down the production line. At the stroke of midnight on the last day of the accounting period, there will be cars up and down the production line at various stages of completion. The company values its work in progress based on how far each product has been completed.

If you're a student starting out in the world of financial accounting, chances are you'll be given the value of work in progress. The calculation of this figure is usually dealt with in management accounting subjects.

Finished goods

Finally, the costs you associate with goods that are completely ready for sale to customers, but haven't yet been sold, are classified as *finished goods* inventory. For the car manufacturer, this category consists of cars not yet sold to individual dealerships.

Working out who owns the finished goods

Obviously, any finished goods that haven't been matched with a customer are part of the manufacturer's inventory. But suppose the finished goods have a buyer and are in transit to that customer. Who owns the finished goods then?

To make this determination, you need to find out whether the terms of the sale are ownership *at the shipping point* or when the goods reach their *destination.* If the terms state that it is at the shipping point this means the customer owns the item as soon as it leaves the manufacturer's loading bay; ownership transfers to the buyer at the shipping point to the freight company. Ownership which passes when the product reaches its destination is the opposite: the customer owns the inventory only after it has hit its own loading bay; any goods in transit to the customer will still be counted as part of the supplier's/manufacturer's inventory.

Getting to Know Inventory Valuation Methods

In the world of financial accounting you'll come across three methods to value closing inventory: first-in, first-out (FIFO); last-in, first-out (LIFO); and weighted average. Like depreciation (see Chapter 12), depending on the method the company uses, the amount transferring from the balance sheet inventory account to the income statement cost of sales can vary wildly.

Because of this fact, the user of the financial statements must know which inventory valuation method a company uses. The method is always spelt out in the accounting policies note which is found in the notes to the financial statements (see Chapter 15). If the method used is unclear, any comparison between one company's financial statements and another's will be inaccurate because the user may be comparing financial results from dissimilar valuation methods.

In this section, I walk you through each method, show you how to calculate it for your accountancy studies or day-to-day working life, and show you the monetary amount differences when the same number of items in closing inventory is treated using the three methods.

First-in, first-out (FIFO)

Using the FIFO method, the company assumes that the oldest items in its inventory are the ones first sold. Consider buying a bottle of milk in a supermarket. The cartons or bottles with the most current sell-by date are pushed ahead of the cartons that have more time before they go sour. The oldest cartons of milk may not always actually be the first ones sold (because some people dig around looking for later sell-by dates), but the business is basing its numbers on the oldest bottles of milk being sold first.

The *inventory assumption* here states that, under FIFO, the oldest units are presumed to be sold first, regardless of whether they actually were.

Last-in, first-out (LIFO)

With this method, the company assumes that its newest items (the ones most recently purchased) are the first ones sold. Imagine a large stack of timber in a hardware store. If a customer wants to buy a plank of wood, for convenience sake, he takes one from the top. As customers purchase the planks, more planks are added on top of the old ones instead of redistributing the old planks so they move to the top of the pile. Therefore, the newest planks of wood are consistently sold to customers rather than the oldest.

Quite a few companies use LIFO because it more closely matches expenses to revenue than does FIFO. Why? The cost of the item being sold has been incurred more closely time-wise to the sale, so a better matching of pound to pound value exists. Be careful with this method, though – if your company reports under IFRS, you'll have to do a bit more pondering. See the 'Doing It Right Under IFRS: Knowing the Restrictions' section later in this chapter.

Weighted average

When a company uses the weighted average method, inventory and the cost of sales are based on the average cost of all units purchased during the period as well as those held in opening stock/inventory. This method is generally used when inventory is substantially the same.

If the company sells running shoes, the total cost of all running shoes available for sale is divided by the total pairs of running shoes available for sale. Multiply that figure by the number of running shoes remaining in inventory at the end of the period to get your closing inventory figure.

In the section below, you can find an example of this method in action.

Comparing inventory assumptions

It's easier to understand how to value closing inventory using FIFO, LIFO and weighted average if you have an example of each method. (The specific identification method is pretty straightforward, so I don't include it here.) In this section, I offer some practical calculations that should help you along the way.

For the closing inventory calculation examples, I use a retail sports shop called Fast Feet Sports Goods, which sells a variety of items – specifically running shoes. Ready to start? Let's figure out this shop's closing running shoe inventory!

Figure 13-1 shows opening inventory and purchases from 1 July 2013 to the end of the calendar year (no purchases took place in December). Your job is to calculate closing inventory and cost of goods sold as at 31 December 2013.

Date of purchase	Number	Cost per unit £	Total cost £
1st July (opening inventory)	200	10	2,000
15th July	250	12	3,000
5th August	100	15	1,500
6th September	450	9	4,050
3rd October	325	13	4,225
21st November	50	11	550
Total available for sale	1,375		15,325
Pairs sold	600		
Pairs remaining in inventory at 31 Dec 2012	775		

Figure 13-1: Fast Feet inventory analysis.

Calculating closing inventory and cost of goods sold using FIFO

Using FIFO, you start at the top of the running shoes list because the shoes in opening inventory are first in, followed by the shoes purchased on 15 July, those purchased on 5 August, and 50 of the 450 purchased on 6 September. As you can see from Figure 13-2, cost of goods sold is £6,950. That means closing inventory is £8,375 (£15,325 – £6,950).

FIFO

Date of purchase	Number	Cost per unit £	Total cost £
1st July (opening inventory)	200	10	2,000
15th July	250	12	3,000
5th August	100	15	1,500
6th September	50	9	450
Total	600		6,950

Figure 13-2: FIFO cost assumption.

Calculating closing inventory and cost of goods sold using LIFO

Using LIFO, you start at the bottom of the running shoes list because the company assumes that the last shoes purchased are the first ones sold. That gives you the running shoes purchased on 21 November, 3 October, and 225 of the shoes purchased on 6 September. As you can see from Figure 13-3, cost of goods sold is £6,800. That means closing inventory is £8,525 (£15,325 – £6,800).

LIFO

Date of purchase		Number	Cost per unit £	Total cost £
21st November		50	11	550
3rd October		325	13	4,225
6th September		225	9	2,025
	Total	600		6,800

Figure 13-3: LIFO cost assumption.

Calculating closing inventory and cost of goods sold using weighted average

Last but not least, here's the calculation for the weighted average method: the total cost of £15,325 divided by the total number of running shoes available for sale (1,375) equals £11.15 per unit. The shop sells 600 pairs of shoes in the second half of the year. Multiply 600 pairs sold times an average cost of £11.15 to get a cost of goods sold of £6,690. Closing inventory is £8,635 (£15,325 – £6,690).

Depending on which method a business uses, closing inventory for the same facts and circumstances ranges from £8,375 to £8,635. While this isn't a dramatic difference, consider what a difference the accounting method makes when a company has sales in the thousands or millions of units!

The accounting inventory methods shown in this example assume the inventory is valued at cost rather than *net realisable value*, which is the price the company can charge when it sells its goods (the official definition of net realisable value is *the estimated selling price in the ordinary course of business, less the estimated costs necessary to make the sale*). If your client sells items whose net realisable value is less than what the company paid for the inventory, your client may have to value its inventory using the lower of cost or net realisable value, which is stipulated in IAS 2 *Inventories* and in UK GAAP SSAP 9 *Stocks and Long-Term Contracts* (in the new UK GAAP, inventories are dealt with in Section 13). You can check out IAS 2 at www.iasb.org.uk and SSAP 9 at www.frc.org.uk.

Preparing an Inventory Worksheet

I want to show you what a simple inventory worksheet looks like. Using Fast Feet from the previous section as an example, Figure 13-4 shows all running shoes theoretically in stock as at 31 December 2013. The last column, 'Actual Count', is filled in by Fast Feet employees while counting the physical inventory.

Even if a retail shop uses the perpetual method, it's important to take a physical inventory at year end to identify thefts and breakages. If, after totalling up the 'Actual Count' column, the company has a figure less than 775, it'll know that running shoes have left the shop in other ways than by being bought by paying customers. Under GAAP, the company has to prepare a journal entry (see Chapter 5) to record the cost of the missing footwear – in other words, it adjusts the inventory balance to the actual count.

Fast Feet Sports Goods Ltd
Inventory Worksheet

Item Name	Item Description	Qty on Hand	Actual Count
Running Shoes:			
Ladies	Ladies XYZ brand running shoes	210	_____
Ladies	Ladies ABC brand running shoes	125	_____
Mens	Mens XYZ brand running shoes	250	_____
Mens	Mens ABC brand running shoes	115	_____
Childrens	Childrens Lil' Mite running shoes	75	_____
		775	

Figure 13-4: Partial inventory worksheet.

Doing It Right Under IFRS: Knowing the Restrictions

This chapter covers the three cost methods that a company can choose from to value its closing inventory: FIFO, LIFO and weighted average. I wrap up this chapter by explaining some important restrictions that you'll come across when you deal with inventory using IFRS. The main restriction will also kick in when the UK moves over to its new UK GAAP in 2015.

Under IAS 2 *Inventories*, the use of the LIFO method is strictly prohibited. Companies reporting under IFRS can only use FIFO or the weighted average method. The same applies in the new UK GAAP – LIFO is a no, no! Currently in the UK, SSAP 9 permits the use of LIFO, but it doesn't like it and the directors of a company that uses LIFO as a cost method must be able to justify its use. The reason SSAP 9 doesn't like LIFO is because it believes this method doesn't reflect actual cost, which means that inventory can often be stated in a company's balance sheet at amounts that bear little relation to recent cost levels.

Part V

Analysing the Financial Statements

Alicia Antiques Limited
Income Statement Horizontal
Analysis for the years ending
31 December 2011 and
31 December 2012

	2011	2012	% change
Sales	500,000	475,000	-5.00%
Cost of sales	269,000	265,000	-1.49%
Gross profit	231,000	210,000	-9.09%
Wages	163,000	154,000	-5.52%
Repairs	4,150	5,800	39.76%
Rent	12,000	13,000	8.33%
Taxes	17,930	16,940	-5.52%
Office expenses	587	1,023	14.14%
Total expenses	197,667	190,763	-3.49%
Net profit	33,333	19,237	-42.29%

Go to www.dummies.com/extras/financialaccounting for online bonus content.

In this part . . .

- ✔ Use your accounting skills to judge the merit of companies.

- ✔ Pick your way through the annual report.

- ✔ Understand how to file documents with Companies House.

- ✔ Grasp the importance of liquidity, profitability and gearing.

- ✔ Find your way through disclosures and explanatory notes.

- ✔ Go to `www.dummies.com/extras/financial accounting` for online bonus content, including an extra Part of Tens chapter: 'Ten Differences Between Some National Standards and IFRS'.

Chapter 14

Using Ratios and Other Tools

In This Chapter

▶ Measuring liquidity

▶ Putting profitability measures to the test

▶ Focusing on the flow of cash

▶ Preparing vertical and horizontal analyses

The information in this chapter helps you understand why financial accounting rules are so nit-picky. Properly classifying accounting transactions is key for user analysis, which is the subject of this chapter. Here, you learn about key measurements that financial statement users perform to gauge management's effectiveness and efficiency in running the company.

Three major measurement categories are a company's liquidity, profitability and cash flow. You may assume that all investors care about is how profitable a company is, but that's not necessarily true. *Liquidity*, which indicates how well a company can cover its short-term debt, and *cash flow*, which shows how well a company is collecting its cash and paying its suppliers, have to be considered along with profitability to form a complete picture of how well the business is performing.

Wrapping up this chapter, you find out about horizontal and vertical analyses of the income statement, which is an excellent way to zoom in on profitability issues.

Ready to get started? The next stop on your exciting financial accounting journey is . . . liquidity measurements!

Learning about Liquidity

Liquidity is a company's ability to free up cash to meet its business obligations. Liquidity measurements reflect a company's ability to meet its short-term obligations. These measurements are important because a company that can't pay its bills in the short term more than likely has going concern problems. The phrase *going concern* means the company is likely to continue in business for at least 12 months beyond the date of the balance sheet. If a company has going concern problems, you can't be certain it's going to stay in business for very long and the more worrying the going concern problems might be, the higher the exposure to risk is.

The account balances you use to measure liquidity are taken from the balance sheet. Because liquidity is concerned with the short term, the accounts you use for these measurements are all current rather than long term.

A quick heads up: later in this chapter (in the 'Measuring Profitability' section), I talk about *trend analysis*, which is looking at ratios over a period of years. Trend analysis isn't normally applicable to liquidity measurements because, when it comes to liquidity, financial statement users are looking at what's going on in the short term – not over a long period of time.

Accounting reference material may discuss three principal evaluations to measure liquidity: current ratio, acid-test ratio and working capital. The first two show up in the form of (you guessed it!) ratios. You express working capital as a monetary amount. These measurements are all easier to understand if you use account balances to work through them, so let's get to work calculating some figures!

Conquering the current ratio

You find a company's current ratio by dividing its current assets by its current liabilities. I discuss current assets in Chapter 7 and current liabilities in Chapter 8, but here are some quick examples of each:

- **Current assets:** Accounts such as cash, trade receivables, inventory and short-term investments.

- **Current liabilities:** Trade payables and all other debt that's due within 12 months of the balance sheet date, such as *accrued payroll*, which is wages employees have earned but not yet been paid.

So, you're looking at a balance sheet. A company's current assets are £120,000, and its current liabilities are £57,000. The current ratio is 2:1 (£120,000 divided by £57,000).

The current ratio tells you a lot about how liquid a company is because current assets are either cash or are easily converted to cash in the short term; in theory, they can be used to pay short-term obligations. Being able to meet short-term obligations is crucial to a company remaining a going concern.

The theory behind the current ratio is pretty simple. If you're a student accountant and financial reporting is on your syllabus, the chances are you're definitely going to have to calculate some ratios – one of which will undoubtedly be the current ratio. Getting to grips with ratio analysis (sometimes called *financial statement interpretation*) is very important. Below is an example similar to what you may be asked during your studies, or in accountancy practice if a client is potentially thinking about investing in a business.

Weavers Wedding Dresses has current liabilities on 31 December of £140,000, and its current ratio at that time is 2:2. What are the company's current assets?

Okay, you know that current assets divided by current liabilities equals the current ratio. You are trying to find out the value for current assets (the unknown variable x), so your equation is x divided by £140,000 equals 2:2.

$$x/140,000 = 2:2$$

Isolating x on one side of the equation gives you £140,000 times 2:2.

$$x = 140,000 \times 2:2$$

So your current assets are £308,000 (£140,000 × 2:2).

You can prove this by plugging that figure into the first equation: £308,000 divided by £140,000 does equal 2:2. Hooray!

Don't forget that the method a company uses to value its closing inventory affects the carrying amount of inventory on the balance sheet. (I discuss inventory valuation methods in Chapter 13.) That is one of the reasons why spelling out inventory valuation methods is a required disclosure in the notes to the financial statements, as I explain in Chapter 15.

Putting the acid test to work

As I explain in the previous section, a company whose current assets are £120,000 and whose current liabilities are £57,000 has a current ratio of 2:1. This business appears to have more than adequate resources available to pay any short-term debt. However, one current asset account, *inventory* (goods that a company holds for resale to customers), isn't always all that easy to convert to cash quickly because the company would first need to sell it, which then turns it into a receivable, and then collect any accounts receivable resulting from the sale. So the acid-test ratio is used in conjunction with the current ratio to evaluate the worst-case scenario: that the company can't sell any of its existing inventory. If it can't sell any of its existing inventory, can it still pay its bills?

To work out the acid-test ratio, you first add together cash, all short-term investments, and trade receivables. *Short-term investments* are those that the company is willing and able to sell within one year of the balance sheet date. Next, you divide that figure by the company's current liabilities.

So assume a company has current assets worth £120,000 and inventory is valued at £40,000. That means its other current assets (cash, short-term investments and trade receivables) are £80,000 (£120,000 – £40,000). Dividing £80,000 by the company's current liabilities of £57,000 gives you an acid-test ratio of 1:4.

As a general rule, if a company has both a current ratio of at least 2:0 and an acid-test ratio of at least 1:0, that shows it has adequate liquidity to pay current obligations as they fall due. You may be asking, 'What if ratios are less than these targets – should the investor or lender walk away or pull the plug?' This question is difficult to answer; it depends on the investor and that person's goals. Certainly an interested party should consider doing trend analysis before making a firm decision (see the upcoming 'Measuring Profitability' section).

Working with working capital

The working capital measurement is simply current assets less current liabilities. If a company has current assets of £120,000 and current liabilities of £57,000, working capital is £63,000 (£120,000 – £57,000).

It's not rocket science to realise that most healthy companies have positive working capital. In your personal life, you work to maintain positive working capital so you can pay your bills. Likewise, a business very much wants, and needs, to have enough cash rattling around in the bank accounts to pay its bills. When the coffers get too low, some businesses take out *working capital loans*, which are short-term loans that carry companies through a rough patch.

Many businesses won't have enough cash on hand to cover all their short-term debts. The assumption is usually that its trade receivables will be collected and its inventory sold, thus converting those current assets to cash.

Always keep in mind that you express the working capital measurement as a monetary amount, not a ratio. In the real world, a client (or one of your non-financial colleagues) could ask you to explain how working capital is affected by the payment of short-term debt. Always remember this immutable fact of accounting: working capital is never affected by the payment of short-term debt because both current assets and current liabilities decrease by the same amount.

Below is an example.

On 1 December 2012, Byrne Breeze Blocks Limited has current assets of £50,000 and current liabilities of £10,000. Working capital is £40,000 (£50,000 – £10,000). Now assume that Byrne Breeze Blocks pays £5,000 of the current liability balance on 15 December 2012. Does this payment affect its working capital? No, it does not, because now current assets are £45,000 (£50,000 – £5,000) and current liabilities are £5,000 (£10,000 – £5,000). Working capital remains at £40,000 (£45,000 – £5,000).

While the payment of short-term debt doesn't affect working capital, it does affect the current ratio. Using the same example, on 1 December 2012 Byrne Breeze Blocks' current ratio is 5 (£50,000 divided by £10,000). On 15 December 2012, Byrne Breeze Blocks' current ratio is 9 (£45,000 divided by £5,000). Quite a difference!

Grasping the gearing ratio

Gearing refers to the proportion of finance provided to a company by debt relative to the amount of finance provided to it by equity (by the company's shareholders). While the gearing ratio is concerned with how liquid a business is, it also focuses on the long-term financial stability of a company, so is a ratio that's crucial to investors such as a bank who may be considering offering the company a long-term loan. They'll be very much interested in the gearing ratio to make sure that the company can afford the loan it may be offered.

In a nutshell, the higher the level of borrowing (gearing), the riskier is the business because the payment of the capital amount of a loan and the interest portion are not optional (as dividends are). Gearing is calculated by taking a company's long-term liabilities (non-current liabilities) and dividing this number into a company's *capital employed* (share capital plus retained earnings plus long-term liabilities) and multiplying the result by 100 to turn it into a percentage. Here's an example.

You have obtained the following information for James Joinery Company Limited for the two years ending 31 December:

	2013	*2012*
	£,000	*£,000*
Long-term liabilities	1,300	1,500
Capital employed	5,765	4,895

To calculate the gearing ratio for both years, you divide long-term liabilities into capital employed and multiply by 100 to arrive at a gearing percentage. Here's how it is done:

31 December 2013:

£1,300/£5,765 × 100 = 22.5%

31 December 2012:

£1,500/£4,895 × 100 = 30.6%

You can see from the above information that James Joinery Co's gearing ratio has dropped from 30.6 per cent in 2012 to 22.5 per cent in 2013, which is a good sign! (Remember, the higher the gearing figure, the more risky the company.) The reason the gearing ratio has dropped is because long-term borrowings reduced in 2013 by £200,000 and the company added £870,000 to retained earnings.

The gearing ratio is one of the *position ratios* because it is the company's statement of financial position (balance sheet) that is being analysed.

Measuring Profitability

In addition to getting a grip on how well a company covers its current debt with current assets, most financial statement users want to be able to evaluate the relative robustness of a company's income over a series of years or financial periods. Looking at a company's performance over a long period of time is called *trend analysis*.

In this section, I explain how trend analysis works and why it's so important when evaluating profitability. Then, I move on to explain two profitability measures: return on investment and return on equity.

Explaining trend analysis

A single profitability measure standing alone doesn't really tell you much about a company or how it's performing compared to its competition. This is true for two reasons:

- ✔ **The company may have had an exceptionally good or bad year.** Unless a company's performance is static from year to year, looking at only one set of figures gives the financial statement user an inaccurate picture of the company as a whole.

  Consider a personal example. Assume you have a windfall in 2013: you win £50,000 on the lottery, making your total income (after adding in your earnings from your part-time job) £62,000. The next year and the year after that, you don't have any winning lottery tickets and your average income is £13,000 per year. Clearly, looking only at your income for 2013 doesn't give anything near an accurate picture of your income because that year's income includes an unusual, one-off event.

- ✔ **Under generally accepted accounting practice (GAAP), companies are allowed to use various methods to estimate some expenses.** If a financial statement user is trying to compare Company A to Company B by using a single set of profitability ratios, he's not going to see the whole picture.

  For example, Chapter 13 talks about inventory valuation methods. A company's decision to use one method against another can cause a wild variation in net profit. The same holds true for depreciation of non-current assets, which I discuss in Chapter 12. Different options are also available for recording an estimate for the *allowance for receivables* (or *bad debt expense*), which is the money the company reckons it won't be able to collect from credit customers (see Chapters 7 and 10). Many more differences may exist using allowable GAAP methods, but you can see where I'm coming from.

  Trend analysis gives much more meaningful information to the financial statement user because differences in accounting methods tend to smooth out over time. For example, while whichever method a company uses for depreciation affects the amount of depreciation expense by year, it never affects the original historic cost. In other words, an asset costing £1,000 can never be depreciated for more than £1,000. So, factoring in any alternative financial accounting methods in use, ratios over a period of several years should be somewhat consistent, which permits the financial statement user to do some useful trend comparisons.

 Using trend analysis means looking at profitability ratios over a number of years. Doing so is usually more helpful to the financial statement user than is any single ratio because everything is relative. Seeing how profitability ratios go up and down (when comparing current performance to past performance and when comparing the company with other companies in the same industry) is more meaningful than just looking at one stand-alone ratio. Most investors consider at least five years – sometimes up to ten or maybe more.

Going through the gross profit ratio

The gross profit ratio helps to assess how much gross profit (pence in the pound) a company is making on its sales. A key point to remember is that a company needs to make sufficient gross profit to enable it to make enough net profit to pay its expenses. It works a bit like your monthly salary: the higher your gross pay, the higher your net pay will be and the more surplus dosh you'll have available to fritter away (assuming your expenses don't also increase).

The gross profit ratio expressed as a percentage is calculated by taking gross profit (sales/revenue less cost of sales), dividing it into sales/revenue and multiplying it by 100 to arrive at a percentage. Let me show you a quick example.

Extracts from the financial statements of Daniel's Days Out are as follows:

	2013 *£,000*	*2013* *£,000*
Revenue	100,000	80,000
Cost of sales	75,000	70,000
Gross profit	25,000	10,000

From this information you can work out the gross profit, as follows:

31 December 2013:

£25,000/£100,000 × 100 = 25 per cent (or 25 pence made for every £1 sold)

31 December 2012:

£10,000/£80,000 × 100 = 12.5 per cent (or 12.5 pence for every £1 sold)

You can see that Daniel's Days Out's gross margins have increased considerably in 2013 as compared to those in 2012, which is encouraging. Companies want to make as much gross profit as possible and it could be that, in 2013, Daniel's Days Out increased its prices to increase its gross margins, or changed suppliers to reduce its cost of sales. Other issues could also have arisen in 2012 that dragged down margins, such as an incomplete sales figure or too much going into cost of sales (usually referred to as *cut-off errors*), which means invoices (sales and cost of sales) go into the wrong accounting period. Flick over to Chapter 10 for an insight as to what types of costs go into cost of sales and other types of expense.

Focusing on return on investment

Return on investment (ROI) is a tool investors use to see how well their investment in a particular company is doing – and to help them make that important decision of whether to sell an investment and move on or to stick with it. Potential investors also use ROI when trying to choose from among different companies in which to pump their spare cash.

Basically, investors want to see how well company management is using the company assets to make money. This information gives the investor some idea of the competency of management and the relative profitability of a business when compared to others the investor is considering.

Investors can calculate ROI, which is expressed as a percentage, in a few different ways. All the methods involve using some form of comparing profit to assets. Here are two methods that are fairly common:

- **Net profit divided by average total assets:** *Net profit* (see Chapter 10) is the bottom-line total of what's left over after you deduct all business expenses and losses from all revenue and gains for the same financial period. I discuss *assets* in Chapter 7; in a nutshell, they're all the resources a company owns. So if a company has net profit of £100,000 and average total assets of £27,000, its ROI is 3.7 per cent (£100,000 divided by £27,000).

  To work out the *average* figure, you do it by adding the account balance at the beginning of the financial period to the closing balance and dividing that figure by two. So, if total liabilities are £50,000 at 1 January 2012 and £75,000 at 31 December 2012, average total liabilities are £62,500 (£125,000 divided by 2).

- **Operating profit divided by average operating assets:** This form of ROI calculation starts with profit before tax and interest (see Chapter 10 for more info) and divides it by average *operating assets*, which are non-current assets such as property, plant and equipment (see Chapter 7). So if a company's operating income is £82,000 and its average operating assets are £12,000, ROI using this method is 6.9 per cent.

In real life, each method has its own characteristics and uses. However, if you want a fairly general perspective, as long as the chosen method is used consistently, trend analysis using any ROI method will give the investor a significant resource for making a decision as to which company to invest in.

Homing in on return on equity

Return on equity (ROE) measures the profit earned for each pound invested in a company's shares. You work out ROE by dividing net profit by *owners' equity* (see Chapter 9), which is what's left over in the business after all liabilities are subtracted from all assets.

The higher the ROE ratio, the more efficient management of the company is at utilising its equity base. This measurement is important to shareholders and potential investors because it compares earnings to owners' investments. Particularly because it takes into account *retained earnings* – the company's cumulative net profit less dividends – it gives the investors much-needed information on how effectively their capital is being used. Having net profit grow in relation to increases in equity presents a picture of a well-run business.

Let's walk through a quick calculation. If a company's net profit is £35,000 and the owners' equity is £250,000, ROE is 14 per cent (£35,000 divided by £250,000). Once again, to make wise investment decisions, users of this information will look at ROE as it trends over a series of years and will compare it to the ROE of other companies.

Exploring the Cash Position

In this section, I discuss *cash flow measures* that quantify the relationship between how well a company collects money in and how quickly it's able to meet its short-term obligations with suppliers. Here, I discuss the ones most commonly used: those measuring trade receivables, trade payables and inventory activity.

Ratio analysis that studies activity, as well as cash flow, shows you how well a company is using its assets to make money. This calculation is an expansion of the return on investment (ROI) measurement (see the above section 'Focusing on return on investment'). Basically, the premise is that how well a company uses its assets to generate revenue goes a long way towards telling the tale of its overall profitability. That's because a business that's effectively and efficiently operated, which activity measures show, will generally be more successful than its less effective and efficient competition.

Turnover analysis shows how quickly an asset comes in and goes out again. The quicker the better! By this, I mean that in normal circumstances, efficiently moving assets indicates a well-run business. The basic formula to calculate turnover is this: turnover equals sales divided by average assets.

Calculating debtor/receivables days

This calculation looks at how efficient the company is at collecting its debts from customers (receivables). You've more than likely heard the old phrase 'cash is king' – well, this is as appropriate today as it was 400 years ago and the trade receivables days calculation is a valuable tool in helping companies set credit and collection policies. If a company runs out of cash it's going to be in dire straits, and even the most profitable of companies have been known to go bust in that circumstance. Trade receivables days is worked out by dividing trade receivables as at the last day of the financial period by revenue/sales (all sales in the financial period) and then dividing this by 365 to represent the number of days in the year. The number calculated is expressed in *days*.

Let me walk you through an example.

The financial statements for Westhead Group Limited show that in 2013 revenue is £1.2 million (in 2012 it was £975,000) and trade receivables were £175,000 (in 2012 they were £125,000). You can calculate the receivables days as follows:

2013:

(£175,000/£1,200,000) × 365 = 53 days

2012:

(£125,000/£975,000) × 365 = 47 days

You can see that in 2013 it takes an average of 53 days to collect debts in from trade receivables, but in 2012 it only took 47, so it may be that the credit control system at the company needs to be improved, or customers are suffering from cash flow difficulties which result in them paying much more slowly.

Working out creditor/payables days

In the section above, I talk you through how to work out calculating receivables days – that is, how many days, on average, it takes the company to collect money from its customers. On the flip side of that process, interested parties also want to see how efficient the company is at sorting out its trade payables (sometimes known as *trade creditors*). Like trade receivables days, this number is expressed in *days* and is calculated by taking the trade payables figure in the financial statements and dividing it into trade purchases (or cost of sales) and multiplying it by 365.

Here's an example.

The Westhead Group had trade payables of £15,000 in 2013 and £128,000 in 2012. Cost of sales in 2013 were £170,000 and £530,000 in 2012. The trade payables days is calculated as follows:

2013:

(£15,000/£170,000) × 365 = 32 days

2012:

(£128,000/£530,000) × 365 = 88 days

You can see from the above that a drastic reduction in trade payables days has occurred, which means that either the company is paying its suppliers too quickly in 2013, or they've had credit terms seriously squeezed. Either way, such a reduction isn't good news. But on the flip side, you don't want to increase your payables days to such an extent that supplier goodwill suffers because, if you do, the supplier won't supply goods, or will reduce your credit terms, which is never a good thing.

These sorts of calculations are all about the *working capital cycle*. The working capital cycle measures the amount of time that elapses between the business buying a product or providing a service to payment being received from its customer. A short working capital cycle means the business has good cash flow, whereas a long working capital cycle can result in the business suffering from cash flow problems. The working capital cycle is calculated as inventory turnover days *plus* receivable days *less* payable days. Inventory turnover days is calculated as cost of sales divided by average inventory multiplied by 365.

Inventory turnover

This activity measure shows how efficiently the company is handling inventory management and replenishment. The less inventory a company keeps on hand, the lower are the costs to store and hold it, thus lowering the cost of inventory having to be financed with debt or *owners' equity* (the ownership rights left over after deducting liabilities).

However, keep in mind that running out of inventory is not a good place to be either. Depleting inventory could cause a company to deliver an order late to a customer, resulting in the loss of customer goodwill. Also, running low on inventory may cause the company to panic and buy the same inventory for a higher price to get it *right now*. Too much of that sort of thing can play havoc with the bottom line.

To work out inventory turnover, you divide sales by inventory value and the number is expressed in *times*. So if a company's sales are £35,000 and inventory is £8,500, inventory turnover is 4.12 times (£35,000 divided by £8,500).

Some financial analysts use cost of sales instead of sales when calculating inventory turnover. That's because inventory is reported at cost, not at its selling price.

Analysing Financial Statements

A good way to do some ratio and trend analysis work is to prepare both horizontal and vertical analyses of the income statement. Both analyses involve comparing income statement accounts to each other in monetary amounts and in percentages.

If this type of analysis reveals any unexpected differences in income statement accounts, management and accounting staff at the company should isolate the reasons and take action to fix the problem.

Using horizontal analysis

Horizontal analysis compares accounts over different periods. For example, you compare a company's sales in 2011 to its sales in 2012.

Figure 14-1 is an example of how to prepare a horizontal analysis for two years. For useful trend analysis, you need to use more years (most investors use five), but this example gives you all the info you need to prepare one for an unlimited number of years. In this figure, all expenses are expressed as a percentage of sales. Net profit is 6.67 per cent of sales in 2011 and 4.05 per cent of sales in 2012 – not a stunning difference on the face of it, but whether any of these percentages is significant depends upon the company and management expectations.

Comparing with vertical analysis

Vertical analysis goes up and down the income statement for one year comparing all other accounts to sales. This analysis gives the company a heads up if cost of sales or any other expense appears to be too high when compared to sales. Reviewing these comparisons allows management and accounting staff at the company to isolate the reasons and take action to fix the problem.

Alicia Antiques Limited
Income Statement Horizontal
Analysis for the years ending
31 December 2011 and
31 December 2012

	2011	2012	% change
Sales	500,000	475,000	-5.00%
Cost of sales	269,000	265,000	-1.49%
Gross profit	231,000	210,000	-9.09%
Wages	163,000	154,000	-5.52%
Repairs	4,150	5,800	39.76%
Rent	12,000	13,000	8.33%
Taxes	17,930	16,940	-5.52%
Office expenses	587	1,023	14.14%
Total expenses	197,667	190,763	-3.49%
Net profit	33,333	19,237	-42.29%

Figure 14-1:
Income statement horizontal analysis for 2011 and 2012.

Figure 14-2 is an example of how to prepare a vertical analysis for two years. As with the horizontal analysis, you'll need to use more years for any meaningful trend analysis. This figure compares the difference in accounts from 2011 to 2012, showing the percentage change from one year to the next. Of concern should be that, while gross profit decreased by only 9 per cent, net income decreased by 42 per cent. Whether any of these percentages is significant depends upon the company and management expectations.

Alicia Antiques Limited
Income Statement Vertical Analysis
For the years ending 31 December 2011
and 31 December 2012

	2011		2012	
Sales	500,000	100.00%	475,000	100.00%
Cost of sales	269,000	53.80%	265,000	55.79%
Gross profit	231,000	46.20%	210,000	44.21%
Wages	163,000	32.60%	154,000	32.42%
Repairs	4,150	0.83%	5,800	1.22%
Rent	12,000	2.40%	13,000	2.74%
Taxes	17,930	3.59%	16,940	3.57%
Office expenses	587	0.12%	1,023	0.22%
Total expenses	197,667	39.53%	190,763	40.16%
Net profit	33,333	6.67%	19,237	4.05%

Figure 14-2:
Income statement vertical analysis for 2011 and 2012.

You can do the same types of analyses for balance sheet accounts. For a horizontal analysis, you compare like for like accounts to each other over periods of time – for example, trade receivables in 2011 to trade receivables in 2012. To prepare a vertical analysis, you select an account of interest (comparable to total revenue) and express other balance sheet accounts as a percentage. For example, you may show inventory or trade receivables as a percentage of total assets.

Chapter 15

Delving into the Disclosures

This chapter begins with a quick overview of corporate governance and ends by shedding light on the explanatory notes and other information found in most companies' annual reports. I provide the complete picture on companies' annual reports in Chapter 16. Basically, they give shareholders an insight into the company's operations for the past financial year.

Also in this chapter, you learn how a business becomes a company, and you review four characteristics of a company: continuity, easy transferability of shares, separation of ownership and control and (the biggie) limited liability.

The complete list of notes and disclosures that may appear in a company's annual report is quite long, so I can't cover every one here. Instead, I focus on the most common explanatory notes and disclosures popping up in various companies' annual reports.

Touching on How Corporate Governance Works

Put simply, *corporate governance* is the framework under which a company operates. At its core, this framework involves establishing financial *controls* (policies and procedures that govern how the company's finances are handled), showing accountability to the shareholders, and making sure the management acts in the best interest of the shareholders and the community in which it operates. I talk about financial controls and accountability in the upcoming sections 'Reviewing the Notes to the Financial Statements' and 'Looking for information about important events'.

Enron: A cautionary tale of corporate governance at its worst

The fact that Enron represented such a massive failure to safeguard investors' interests still continues to fascinate. Here's just a glance at how financial reporting played a part.

A primary contributor to the problem was the use of *mark-to-market accounting*, which essentially means accounting for expected profits before they're earned. It's actually a fairly easy concept to understand if you break it down to its lowest common denominator. Here's an example of how it works.

Let's say I invent a machine that will rearrange the molecules in the fabric of a pair of jeans so that the jeans fit your body perfectly every time you wear them. I have a five-year contract with a retailer for the sale of this machine. My best guess is that sales over five years will be £50 million. Instead of waiting and recording the profits as the machine is sold, under mark-to-market accounting I can record the entire £50 million at the time the contract is signed with the retailer.

You may be wondering, why would I want to do this? What would be the purpose? After all, the £50 million was just my best guess – a figure I wrote down on a scrap piece of paper at the local coffee shop while drinking a cup of coffee. Why not wait and see what sales are really going to be?

Here's the deal: high-ranking employees at most listed companies (by *listed* I mean the company's shares are publicly traded on a stock market) are rewarded by methods other than their agreed-upon salaries. This reward system allows for millions of pounds of incentive payments and share options to be given to those employees as they deliver faster and faster revenues and earnings growth. Meeting and exceeding revenue projections has only one effect on the price of shares as traded on the open market: the price goes up. The increase in share price will have a direct effect on the amount of money I make when I exercise and sell any share options tied to an incentive plan.

At Enron, mark-to-market accounting treatment was a condition of the (then) CEO Jeffrey Skilling accepting employment at Enron. Enron's accountants, Arthur Andersen, signed off the treatment, and the US Securities and Exchange Commission (SEC) approved it. Unfortunately for the lower-ranking employees at Enron, Enron's top management lacked corporate governance awareness. Large bonuses were paid to top management based on excessively optimistic revenue stream projections that never came to fruition.

In the end, all employees at Arthur Andersen and Enron lost their jobs and health insurance benefits. Many Enron employees and retirees lost their entire pensions, these having been invested in Enron shares whose value bottomed out at 40 cents per share.

Part of a company's self-regulation includes fully disclosing information in its financial statements. Hence the focus on corporate governance in a chapter about financial statement notes and disclosures.

I cannot cover the subject of corporate governance in depth here; I'd need another book to do so. But here are just a couple of examples of ways that companies need to self-regulate:

✔ **Acting in the best interests of the shareholders:** The company should operate so that the shareholders can expect a reasonable rate of return. For example, the company doesn't pay excessive bonuses to directors that reduce cash flow to such an extent that the business can't effectively operate.

✔ **Being sensitive to environmental concerns:** The company shouldn't pollute or cause health issues through its business waste or other by-products for those living in the communities in which the business operates.

Recognising How Companies Work in the UK

Many trainee accountants only have a basic understanding of how a business becomes a company and what it means to be a company. I quickly walk you through the process in this section and explain the characteristics of a company to provide a broader context for understanding corporate governance and financial statement disclosures.

Incorporation – the process of turning a regular old business into a company – is governed by companies' legislation. If a business wants to set up shop as a company, it must play by the rules of the Companies Act 2006 (or whatever company legislation is in force in its country if not UK-based).

In the UK, the whole process kicks off when the company files information with Companies House notifying them of:

✔ Company name and address
✔ Details of the director(s) and company secretary (where appropriate)
✔ Company share capital and shareholders' details

Companies House will then send a certificate of incorporation and the company's memorandum and articles of association The memorandum and articles of association contain all pertinent facts about the new company, including its objectives, its name, address and information about the type and number of shares it's issued. The person who initiates the process and files the required information is called the *formation agent*. This might be an outside body, but there is no reason why any member of the public with a great idea can't go about this themselves (but they should be sure to check up on the finer details). The company must also have a *registered office*: the address which the Registrar of Companies contacts with questions about the company or where the Registrar will send documentation. After the company is formed, the new shareholders then elect a board of directors, and the company is up and running!

This is a very simplified version of the whole process, which can also vary by country. An initial public offering (IPO) – when a company offers shares to the public for the first time – is much more complicated than the previous paragraph may lead you to believe. However, these basic facts are what you need to know in your day-to-day dealings with companies.

Four characteristics of a company are:

- **Limited liability:** This term means that the shareholders in a company normally can't be pursued for corporate debt. If the company is sued by a supplier, a financier or some other entity to which it owes money, the individual shareholders are generally off the hook.

    However, exceptions to this general rule can exist, which hinge on the company managing itself according to company law. In certain situations, usually when some dodgy goings on have occurred at the company, the government and HM Revenue and Customs (HMRC) can go after the directors, or possibly the shareholders for certain types of unpaid taxes, such as unpaid corporation tax or pay as you earn (PAYE).

- **Easy transferability of shares:** This characteristic means that, if a person has the money, he can purchase shares in any company – with the expectation of selling the shares in the future if he needs the money. However, for *close companies* (those with few shareholders), this characteristic doesn't quite ring true. If you're the majority shareholder in a private company, you don't have to sell shares to just anyone.

    Easy transferability of shares applies more to the purchase and sale of shares in listed companies. For example, if you want to buy shares in Sainsbury's, you don't have to get permission from the CEO at Sainsbury's. You just call your stock broker – or go online – and cough up the cash for the shares.

- **Separation of ownership and control:** The management of a company shouldn't be divided among many different groups. Therefore, for the company to function at full efficiency, shareholders give up the right to be involved in every decision it makes. The shareholders elect the board of directors, who oversee the company's operations and choose the management to handle the day-to-day business operations.

✔ **Continuity:** Until the company is formally dissolved, it's assumed to have unlimited life, continuing out into perpetuity. The members of the board of directors can change, management can change, or a different mix of shareholders may exist, but the company just keeps going on and on.

Reviewing the Notes to the Financial Statements

As I note earlier in the chapter, one aspect of corporate self-governance is giving financial statement users the complete information they need in order to accurately gauge the company's performance and financial health. Some of that information comes in the form of explanatory notes contained within the annual financial statements.

Knowing how the notes interact with the accounts

Explanatory notes are discussions of items accompanying the financial statements; they contain important disclosures that aren't presented in the financial statements themselves. The financial statements are the income statement (or *statement of profit or loss* or *profit and loss account*; see Chapter 10), balance sheet (or *statement of financial position*; see Part III) and statement of cash flows (or the *cash flow statement*; see Chapter 11).

The notes to the financial statements are essential to fulfil the needs of the external users of the financial statements: people like you and me who may be interested in investing in the business, banks thinking about lending the company money or governmental agencies making sure the company has complied with reporting or taxation issues. External users don't work for the company, so they aren't privy to the day-to-day accounting transactions taking place within the business.

Information that can't easily be gleaned from reviewing the financial statements has to be spelt out in notes and disclosures, which explain how or why a company handles a transaction. Full disclosure allows external users to understand what's going on at the company and creates a level playing field so an external user can compare the financial statements of one company with those of another company.

Such notes are part of the company's annual report, which provides share-holders with both financial and non-financial information about the company's operations in the past year. I discuss this report in Chapter 16.

The notes come after the financial statements in the company's annual report and are ordered to mirror the presentation of the financial statements. In other words, notes for income statement accounts come first, followed by balance sheet notes and then items reflecting on the statement of cash flows.

In the next section, I explain the six explanatory notes that are commonly seen in the world of accountancy. Most of these subjects are presented else-where in this book in more detail, so I offer just a brief overview here and let you know where you can find more info.

Keep in mind that I merely gloss over each of these explanatory notes. Depending on the company and the complexity of the underlying accounting transaction, explanatory notes can be long and boring to wade through for all but the most diligent and experienced investor. For each type of note, I give you a simple version of what you see in real life, which is more than sufficient for your initial dealings with financial statements.

Some explanatory notes are required only for listed companies by the London Stock Exchange, which I introduce in Chapter 4.

Explaining significant accounting policies

The first thing a business has to do when it prepares its explanatory notes is to explain in general the business and its significant accounting poli-cies. These are split into two different notes. The first is called the 'Basis of Preparation' or 'Accounting Convention' and the second 'Accounting Policies'.

Taking this first step creates a more fair presentation of the financial state-ments. Information about accounting policies helps financial readers to better interpret the statements. A note is needed for each significant account-ing policy adopted by the company.

At the very least, the explanatory notes should include the basis of consolida-tion, the company's revenue recognition policies, the depreciation methods in use, the way the company accounts for intangible assets, how it recognises lease transactions and how the company values its closing inventory. I touch on each of these subjects in turn.

Consolidating financial statements

Consolidation is what happens when companies acquire one or more smaller ones. In the context of GAAP and financial accounting, *consolidation* refers to the aggregation of financial statements of two or more companies so those financial statements can be presented as if a group were one, single reporting entity. In this section of the notes, the company confirms the fact that the consolidated financial statements do indeed contain the financial information for all its subsidiaries. Any deviations from including all subsidiaries would have to be explained. See Chapter 17 for more information about consolidation.

Here's a basic example of how a note addressing consolidation appears:

NOTE 1: BASIS OF CONSOLIDATION

All companies over which the group is able to exercise a dominant influence are consolidated as subsidiary undertakings. Dominant influence is defined as the right to give directions with respect to operating and financial policies.

Reporting revenue recognition policies

Revenue (or turnover) is often a company's largest number in its financial statements; therefore adequate disclosure of a company's revenue recognition policy is essential. This will enable the user to understand at what point the company recognises revenue and how the revenue is calculated.

Here's a basic example of how a typical accounting policy note may appear (please note that I use the term *turnover* as opposed to revenue as the Companies Act 2006 in the UK refers to turnover):

NOTE 2: TURNOVER

Turnover is stated net of value added tax and trade discounts. The company recognises turnover when its contractual obligations are fulfilled, which is usually at the point the goods are shipped to the customer. Turnover in respect of service contracts is recognised when the company receives a right to consideration. Deferred income is recognised in the period to which the income relates.

Reviewing depreciation methods

In Chapter 12, I discuss *depreciation*: spreading the cost of a non-current (fixed) asset over its useful life, which may be years after the purchase.

The methods a company chooses to use for depreciation expense can cause significant fluctuations for the amount of assets shown on the balance sheet and the amount of net profit (or loss) shown in the income statement. Because of this fluctuation, the financial statement user needs to know which methods the company uses in order to more fairly compare one company's financial statement figures to another's. Differences in net profit could merely be a function of depreciation methodology – a fact the user would be unaware of without the explanatory note.

Here's an example of what you might see:

NOTE 3: TANGIBLE FIXED ASSETS

Depreciation is provided at the following annual rates in order to write off the cost less estimated residual value of each asset over its estimated useful life:

Plant and machinery: 5 years straight line

Computer equipment: 3 years straight line

Motor vehicles: 25 per cent reducing balance

Tangible fixed assets are initially recognised at cost and subsequently measured in the financial statements at depreciated historic cost.

Walking through intangibles

Intangible assets aren't physical in nature like a desk or computer. Two common examples of intangibles are *patents*, which license inventions or other unique processes and designs, and *trademarks*, which are unique signs, symbols or names that the company uses. (See Chapter 7 for more information about intangibles.) Besides explaining the different intangible assets the company owns via an explanatory note, the business also needs to explain how it's determined the intangible asset's value showing on the balance sheet.

Here's a truncated example of how such a note looks:

NOTE 4: INTANGIBLE ASSETS

The company values its intangible fixed assets based on the intangible asset's cost. The company's policy of writing off the costs incurred in respect of the development costs is to write this off over ten years. The directors consider this amortisation policy to be adequate based on the useful economic life of the development costs.

Looking at leasing transactions

Lease transactions are very topical at the minute because such transactions can be deliberately engineered to achieve what's known in the profession as *off balance sheet finance*. This is when a company will deliberately keep a lease off the balance sheet so it doesn't report additional liabilities. The fact of the matter is that, if a lease is a finance lease (where such a lease transfers the risks and rewards of ownership of the leased asset to the lessee), the lease should appear as an asset on the balance sheet, with a corresponding creditor. If the risks and rewards of ownership have not passed to the lessee, then it's recorded as an operating lease (where the payments simply get expensed to the profit and loss account).

Here's an example of a typical disclosure:

> NOTE 5: HIRE PURCHASE AND LEASING
>
> Assets obtained under hire purchase contracts and finance leases are capitalised as tangible fixed assets. Assets acquired under finance leases are depreciated over the shorter of the lease term and their useful lives. Assets acquired under hire purchase contracts are depreciated over their useful lives.
>
> Finance leases are those where substantially all of the benefits and risks of ownership are assumed by the company. Obligations under such agreements are included in creditors, net of the finance charge, allocated to future periods. The finance element of the rental payment is charged to the profit and loss account so as to produce a constant periodic rate of charge on the net obligation outstanding in each period.
>
> Rentals applicable to operating leases where substantially all of the risks of ownership remain with the lessor are charged to the profit and loss account as incurred.

Investigating inventory policies

Inventory (or *stock*) is another thorny issue because of the ease in which this figure can be manipulated. Again, companies have been known to inflate, or reduce, profit disproportionately by manipulating the closing inventory figure in the balance sheet and the income statement (though not all companies are guilty of this dodgy practice). Financial statements need to adequately disclose the policy of inventory valuation by a company so users can see exactly how the closing inventory figure is made up.

Here's a basic disclosure of inventory valuation (please note, again I used UK terminology due to the Companies Act wording):

NOTE 6: STOCK

Stock is valued at the lower of cost and net realisable value and is valued using the first-in first-out method of valuation. Cost comprises the cost of products plus other direct costs involved in getting stock to its saleable condition and shipping the goods to the company. Net realisable value is based on an estimated selling price, less further costs to be incurred to completion and disposal. Provision is made for obsolete, slow-moving or defective items where appropriate.

Looking for information about important events

A company must also provide information in its annual report explaining the following issues: accounting changes, business combinations, contingencies, events after the balance sheet date and segment reporting.

Various accounting reference/textbooks usually cover events after the balance sheet date separately from the discussion of explanatory notes that accompany financial statements. But keep in mind that events after the balance sheet date disclosure information goes in the notes to the financial statements.

Accounting changes

A company may have up to three types of accounting changes to report: a change in accounting policy, a change in an accounting estimate or a change in a reporting entity. Narrative descriptions about accounting changes go in the explanatory notes to the financial statements very early in the game – usually in the first or second note.

Below is an explanation of each type of accounting change:

- ✔ **Accounting policies** guide the way the company records its accounting transactions. Under generally accepted accounting practice (GAAP), a company is usually allowed different ways to account for transactions. For example, in Chapter 12, I discuss depreciation, which is the way a company expenses the cost of non-current (or *fixed*) assets. That chapter lays out the various depreciation methods allowable under GAAP.

  For the financial statements, changes in accounting policies have to be shown by retrospective application to all affected prior periods (unless doing so is not practical). This process involves three steps:

- Adjust the carrying amounts of affected assets and liability accounts for the cumulative effect of the change.

- Take any offset to opening retained earnings.

- Disclose why each new accounting policy is thought more appropriate, together with the effect of the change on the financial statements in the prior period, and (where practical) an indication of the effect of a change in accounting policy on the results for the current period.

I discuss each of these steps in more detail in Chapter 20.

✔ **Accounting estimates** are numbers a company enters into the financial records to reflect its best estimates as to how certain transactions will eventually pan out. For example, going back to the depreciation example, consider the estimate for *residual value*, which is how much a company assumes it will be able to get for a non-current asset when it comes to dispose of it. If something happens to make you believe your original estimate of residual value was wrong and you change it, that's a change in accounting estimate.

A change in accounting estimate has to be recognised currently and prospectively. For example, if residual value is recalculated, the current and future financial statements show the residual value as corrected. No change is made to prior period financial statements. You can find more on this topic in Chapter 20.

✔ **Reporting entities** reflect what combinations of businesses are shown combined in the financial statements, also known as *consolidated* financial statements. When a business owns more than 50 per cent of another business, the investor business is called a *parent* and the investee is the *subsidiary*. If something changes in the way the subsidiaries show up in the financial statements, that's a change in reporting entity.

Business combinations

In your early days as a trainee accountant, you'll come across some basic *business combinations*, which include these three:

✔ **Mergers:** Two or more companies combine into a single entity. Mergers are usually regarded as friendly combinations – not hostile takeovers.

✔ **Acquisitions:** One company acquires another business. The business doing the acquiring takes over, and in essence the *target* (acquired) company ceases to exist. Acquisitions are usually not quite as friendly as mergers.

✔ **Disposals:** A company transfers, sells or otherwise gets rid of a portion of its business. For example, a shoe manufacturer makes dress shoes, slippers and tennis shoes and decides to sell its slipper division to another company.

If a company involves itself in any of these three activities during the financial reporting period, it has to explain the transaction and spell out the effect of the business combination in the financial statements. Business combination information goes in the explanatory notes to the financial statements and could well involve more than one disclosure depending on the information required to be disclosed.

If you're a trainee accountant studying for more advanced financial reporting examinations, be sure to check out Chapter 17, where I go over this topic in quite a bit more detail.

If a company is involved in a disposal, GAAP dictates that it discloses not only the facts and circumstances surrounding the disposal but also any anticipated operational losses from getting rid of a portion of its business. Such losses should only be provided for if a decision has been made, by the year-end, to close the relevant part of the business, but the closure is not made until the following period. Take care here! A *demonstrable commitment* must exist, which means that the company must be committed to completing the termination. UK GAAP provides two specific examples of what might be regarded as sufficient evidence of a demonstrable commitment:

- A public announcement of specific plans.
- Commencement of implementation.

The company must also show any loss or gain on the sale of that portion of the business in the income statement. These results are pulled out and reported separately because they won't continue into the future. See Chapter 10 for more information on how this type of event shows up on the income statement.

Contingencies

A *contingent liability* exists when an existing circumstance may cause a loss in the future depending on other events that have yet to happen (and, indeed, may never happen). For example, the company is involved in a corporation tax dispute. Disclosing this contingent liability is a requirement if the company will owe a substantial amount (often referred to as a *material* amount) of additional tax penalties and interest should the unsolved tax inspection end up in HMRC's favour. See Chapter 8 for more information about reporting contingencies.

Here's a basic example of how a contingency note looks:

NOTE 10: CONTINGENT LIABILITIES

As at 31 December 2012, the company was contingently liable for guarantees of indebtedness owed by third parties in the amount of £3 million. These guarantees relate to third-party suppliers and customers and have arisen through the normal course of business. The amount represents the maximum future payments that the company could be responsible for making under the guarantees; however, the directors do not consider it probable that the company will be required to satisfy these guarantees.

A contingent liability is only reported as a disclosure note in the financial statements (amounts aren't recognised as a liability in relation to the contingent liability). It becomes a liability, and hence a monetary amount recognised in the financial statements, if the company has an obligation to the third party, it's probable that the company will need to cough up some dosh (or another asset) to settle the liability and the amount of loss that may be sustained is reasonably estimated (see Chapter 8). This 'liability' is known as a *provision*.

Events happening after the balance sheet date

The company also has to address any subsequent events happening after the close of the accounting period but before the financial statements are approved. Such events are also known in the UK as *post balance sheet events* or *subsequent events*. Like contingent liabilities, depending on their nature, post balance sheet events may just need a disclosure in the notes to the financial statements, or they may require both a disclosure and an adjustment to the figures in the financial statements to reflect the monetary amount effect of the subsequent event.

How the company handles the event happening after the balance sheet date depends on whether the event is classified as an *adjusting* event or a *non-adjusting* event:

✔ **Adjusting events:** These are events after the reporting period that provide further evidence of conditions that existed at the end of the reporting period. A good example is the estimate for uncollectible receivables. This estimate exists in the books at the balance sheet date, but the company can't be sure of the outcome of the estimate until a subsequent event occurs, such as a customer filing for bankruptcy. At that point, the company confirms that the amount is actually uncollectible.

If the adjusting event (such as the bankruptcy) occurs after the balance sheet date but before the financial statements are finalised, the company has to adjust its financial statements. Disclosure notes can be used to explain the event as well.

✔ **Non-adjusting events:** These events aren't in the books at all before the balance sheet date and have no direct effect on the financial statements under audit. The purchase or sale of a division of the company is a classic example of a non-adjusting event.

Material, non-adjusting events must be disclosed as a note to the financial statements even though the financial statements themselves are not adjusted.

Here's a basic example of how a note on an event taking place after the balance sheet date looks:

NOTE 21: POST BALANCE SHEET EVENT

On 1 February 2013, we entered into an agreement to sell our ownership interests in our ABC division to XYZ Manufacturing for approximately £5 million in cash. The transaction is subject to certain regulatory approvals. We expect the transaction to complete in the 4th quarter of 2013.

Segment reports

Business segments are components operating within a company. For example, a women's clothing manufacturer makes dresses, blouses, trousers and jumpers; these are all business segments. If a business has various segments, it must disclose information about each segment such as its type, geographic location and major customer base so that the users of the financial statements have sufficient information. Here's a basic example of how such a note looks:

NOTE 25: SEGMENT REPORTING

As at 31 December 2012, our organisational structure consisted of the following operating segments: North America and Europe. Our North American segment derives the majority of its revenue from the sale of finished women's clothing. Our European segment derives the majority of its revenue from the sale of fabric and ancillary items to other European companies.

Putting the Onus on the Preparer

Here's the million-dollar question: who's responsible for preparing the notes and disclosures to the financial statements? If you decide to pursue accountancy as your career, are you going to be stuck writing disclosure notes for the rest of your life?

Well, it depends. The answers to these questions take us back to the very purpose of financial accounting, which is the preparation of financial statements for a business. The explanatory notes and disclosures, like the financial statements themselves, are the responsibility of the company's management and its accounting staff. Management and the internal accounting staff prepare the explanatory notes and disclosures using a disclosure checklist. Sometimes, however, if you work in general accountancy practice, you yourself may prepare the financial statements and associated disclosures for a company.

After management prepares the financial statements and explanatory notes and disclosure information, the company often hires an independent auditor to evaluate management's work. The auditor is *independent*, which means she has no special relationship to, or financial interest in, the company (see Chapter 1).

An auditor must be appropriately qualified, for example a member of the Association of Chartered Certified Accountants (ACCA) with statutory auditor status, or a member of the Institute of Chartered Accountants in England and Wales (ICAEW), again holding statutory auditor status. However, chartered certified or chartered accountants can perform three major types of financial statement work:

✔ **Audits:** *Auditing* is the process of investigating information that's prepared by someone else, usually the company's management and the financial accountants the company employs, in order to determine if the information is fairly stated. Auditors performing audits must investigate the assertions that a company makes in its financial statements, including any notes and disclosures.

An audit provides a reasonable level of *positive assurance*, which means the financial statements are free from material errors and fraud and are stated in accordance with GAAP. An audit does not, however, provide an absolute guarantee that the financial statements contain no mistakes.

Financial statement assertions often relate to how the company conducts business, such as how it makes and spends money and how it records financial information about its property, plant and equipment; its long-term liabilities and equity; and its cash and investments.

While financial accountants employed by the business prepare the financial statements (including the notes and disclosures), only an independent qualified accountant who's a member of one of the Consultative Committee of Accountancy Bodies (CCAB) can audit them. Check out www.ccab.org.uk for a list of accountancy bodies that are members of the CCAB.

✔ **Reviews:** When an accountant conducts a *review*, he looks at the company's documents and provides *negative assurance*, which means the accountant finds no reason to believe that the information prepared by company management isn't correct. For example, the accountant looks over the company's financial statements, noting whether they appear to have been properly prepared. For example, do the financial statements contain appropriate explanatory notes and disclosures as required under the Companies Act 2006? Do they conform to UK or international GAAP? Reviews are usually performed for privately-owned companies when the users of the financial statements require some sort of assurance about the financial statements' assertions but don't require a full-blown audit.

✔ **Compilations:** Accountants can be engaged to prepare financial statements for a company and/or prepare the company's corporation tax return. Here, the accountant is not providing any form of assurance that the financial statements are completely correct – the accountant is merely compiling the financial statements based on information and explanations given to him by the client. This sort of work is usually done for smaller companies, such as those that are exempt from the statutory audit requirement, and the accountant's report that's attached to the accounts will confirm that no audit has been carried out and the financial statements have been prepared based on information and explanations provided by the client.

Chapter 16

Reporting to Shareholders

· ·

In This Chapter

▶ Staying private or going public: why annual reports differ among companies

▶ Identifying the three purposes of a company's annual report

▶ Looking at some common sections in an annual report

▶ Going through the auditor's report

· ·

Much of this book is devoted to explaining how financial statements (the income statement (profit and loss account or statement of profit or loss), balance sheet (statement of financial position) and statement of cash flows (or cash flow statement)) are prepared. But what happens to them after they're done? Do they just get filed away in case anyone asks to see them?

Absolutely not! The financial statements become the heart of a company's annual report to its shareholders. An annual report is a document that the company can share with its current owners, potential investors, creditors, the media . . . it can be an important public relations tool that shows the outside world how the company is doing. For many companies, the report is also a regulatory requirement.

In this chapter, I explain the ins and outs of an annual report, including the three key purposes it serves. As many big companies in the UK are listed on the US stock market (usually because their head office is based in the US), I also take a very brief look at Form 10-K, an annual filing that the US Securities and Exchange Commission (SEC) requires from most publicly traded companies.

Seeing Why Private and Public Companies Treat Annual Reports Differently

A company's annual report (which may also be called the *annual report*, the *annual report to shareholders* or the *annual review*) may look very different depending on whether the company in question is private or public.

The annual report for a *private* company – one whose shares aren't traded on the open market – is usually a bare-bones document that may just give users the mandatory information about how the company performed in the past year. You don't find many bells and whistles in a private company's report. That's because most private companies are *close companies* (they have a small number of owners), so they aren't too concerned about how a larger audience will react to the report. On the other hand, a public company's report is often loaded with extra flourishes, such as marketing material designed to tout the company to potential investors and creditors.

Another key difference between the annual reports of private and public companies is that a lot of private companies don't always have their financial statements audited, while public companies do. A private company usually has its financial statements audited only if doing so is legally required; for example, having turnover of more than £6.5 million and gross (fixed plus current) assets of more than £3.26 million means the company cannot claim audit exemption in the UK. As I explain later in this chapter, public companies' financial statements must always be audited in order to fulfil regulatory requirements. What does it mean for the statements to be audited? After the company creates the financial statements, it hires an independent professionally-qualified accountancy firm that's eligible to conduct audits to gather sufficient and appropriate information to express an opinion on whether the statements are materially correct. (In other words, they don't contain any misstatements that could significantly impact the decisions made by the financial statement users.)

Only after a public company's financial statements are audited can they be included in the company's annual report to the shareholders.

In this chapter, I focus on the annual reports that large public companies prepare. That way, you get a picture of what the most elaborate reports look like.

Finding annual reports online

If you want to see real-life examples of what an annual report looks like, you can easily access the annual report for just about any publicly traded company online.

Go to the home page of any company in which you have an interest. Look for an 'Investor' link on the home page, and click it. Voila! Chances are you're looking at the annual report. If you can't locate the 'Investor' link, just enter the key phrase '(Company name) company annual report' into a search engine and you'll probably then find it quite easily.

Fulfilling Three Purposes

In this section, I set out the three distinct goals of the annual report for a public company: to promote the company, to display its financial performance and goals, and to meet regulatory requirements.

Something to keep in mind: going forward, large public companies will undoubtedly turn increasingly to electronic media to distribute their annual reports. Doing so is a cost-saver and demonstrates a company's commitment to using resources wisely as environmental issues become more important for companies, particularly in the UK.

Serving a marketing and PR function

Who doesn't like to blow their own trumpet? A substantial portion of an annual report is devoted to the company's bragging about what it's accomplished during the preceding year and where it expects to go in the forthcoming year. The language can be quite full of hype and excitement. The purpose of this marketing and public relations material is to keep existing shareholders happy about the wisdom of their investment and to attract new shareholders to the fold.

Stating financial performance and goals

Less flashy but of decidedly more interest to serious investors are the sections addressing the company's financial performance in the past year and its financial goals. The information in these sections indicates how closely the company came to hitting projected revenue figures, where the company wants to be in the next 12 months and how it plans to get there. Additionally, the company addresses how it intends to measure its success in achieving these goals.

Here are some examples of financial goals:

- ✔ Increasing revenue by expanding into global markets.
- ✔ Becoming regarded as a premier employer.
- ✔ Managing operations for the greatest effectiveness.
- ✔ Increasing brand awareness. This phrase is a fancy way of saying the company wants to make sure consumers know about its products. The purpose of brand awareness is also tied to making the company's products preferred over similar ones marketed by the competition.

Meeting regulatory requirements

Most large companies would produce an annual report even if they weren't required to by the UK government. That's because an annual report is such a crucial marketing and PR tool. However, because stringent regulatory requirements for publicly traded companies exist, not issuing an annual report isn't an option.

Companies that issue securities that are traded publicly on the various stock markets have to meet certain deadlines when releasing information about their annual reports. Table 16-1 shows the deadines for PLUS quoted companies, AIM-listed companies and fully listed companies.

Table 16-1	Financial Statement Deadlines		
	Release of Interim Announcement	*Release of Preliminary Announcement*	*Release of Annual Accounts*
PLUS quoted companies	3 months	5 months	9 months
AIM-listed companies	3 months	Optional – no deadline	6 months
Fully listed	2 months	Optional – but as soon as possible	4 months

Accounts for all of the companies listed in Table 16-1 must be sent to the Registrar of Companies (Companies House) within six months of the accounting period/year-end and shareholders must receive the accounts at least 21 days before the annual general meeting (AGM). This requirement for shareholders to receive the accounts at least 21 days before the AGM under Section 424 of the Companies Act 2006 reduces the available time to finalise the company's financial statements by around three weeks.

Substantial penalties exist for both public and private companies that file their accounts late with Companies House! For delays of up to one month the fine is £750; between one and three months it's £1,500; between three and six months it's £3,000; and for more than six months it's £7,500 (yikes!). It doesn't stop there, either. Where accounts were also late in the previous year, the penalty doubles!

Reading the Annual Report to Shareholders

In this section, I take you through the sections that you most often find in a company's annual report. With the exception of the audited financial statements, the sections are put together in an effort to draw the external reader into the inner workings of the business in an attempt to raise the users' comfort with – and confidence level in – the company.

Keep in mind that this section contains just a brief overview of what you may expect to see in an annual report. Especially if a company is very large, it may include a plethora of additional information.

If you have the time, I recommend picking up *Reading Financial Reports For Dummies* by Lita Epstein (Wiley). While I touch on the fundamentals here, this book walks you through reviewing financial reports from A to Z.

Meeting the chair of the board of directors

Most casual investors in a company have absolutely no idea who or what the chairperson of the board of directors is. While the duties of the chairperson are quite similar from company to company, the individual holding the position is unique to the particular company.

The chairperson of the board of directors is the head honcho who oversees that board (and is usually elected by the other members of it). The board of directors consists of individuals elected by the shareholders to guide the overall philosophy of the business. The guidance as to how all this operates is the UK Corporate Governance Code a copy of which can be found at www.frc.org.uk.

The day-to-day activities of any business aren't handled by the board of directors; they're handled by company management. *Executive directors* handle the activities of the business whereas *non-executive directors* don't get involved in the day-to-day running of the company but instead monitor the work of the executive directors and contribute to the company's strategy. However, approving the hiring of upper management personnel, such as the chief financial officer (CFO) and chief executive officer (CEO), is a function of the board of directors.

In the annual report, you meet the chairperson via a letter whose salutation is something like 'Dear Fellow Shareholder'. The letter gives the company's top management team a chance to review for the users all the great accomplishments the company achieved during the last financial year. The letter also outlines the company's goals for the future. It ends by thanking the shareholders for their support and offering a firm promise to work tirelessly to continue earning the trust of the shareholders and growing their investment in the company's shares.

Highlighting key financial information

In the beginning of the annual review, the company gives the shareholders a very condensed version of how well the company performed during the last financial year. This condensed information provides the lazier readers with what the company perceives as the main points of interest. At the very least, this section contains a summary of operations, details of earnings per share and balance sheet information:

- **Summary of operations:** This summary shows the company's bottom line net profit for at least three years. *Net profit* is the excess of revenue and gains over expenses and losses during a financial period.

- **Earnings per share (EPS):** This calculation shows the distribution of net profit over all company shares that are in issue. Many investors home in on this figure, comparing it to their other investments and to other companies' EPS in the same industry. For example, an investor may compare the EPS of Manchester United Football Club to Chelsea Football Club to gauge the value of one company's shares over the other.

Three calculations you may see in an annual review are basic EPS, diluted EPS and dividends per share. Here's an example of each:

- *Basic EPS:* To work out basic EPS, take net profit for the financial period and divide it by the weighted average number of ordinary shares issued. The weighted average factors in the fluctuations of shares issued during the entire year instead of just taking shares issued as at 1 January and shares issued as at 31 December and dividing it by two.

  The 'Calculating weighted average' sidebar guides you through a simple example.

  If Lucas Lighting PLC has net profit of £10,000, and the weighted average number of ordinary shares is 21,833, basic EPS is 0.46p (£10,000/21,833).

- *Diluted EPS:* If the company has issued share options or long-term debt that the investor has the option to convert into shares, the company also has to show diluted EPS, which is a complicated calculation. (*Share options* are benefits allowing employees to purchase a certain number of shares in the company at a determined date.)

  Diluted EPS calculates earnings per share by estimating how many shares could theoretically exist after all share options and convertible debt have been exercised. So if Lucas Lighting PLC's weighted average shares after adding in these extras is 24,989, its diluted EPS is 0.40p (£10,000 divided by 24,989).

- *Dividends per share:* This calculation is the amount per share paid to investors in dividends. It usually isn't the same amount as EPS, although EPS is one tool the board of directors can use when deciding the dividend to pay to the shareholders. See Chapter 9 for more information about dividends.

✔ **Balance sheet information:** This section shows selected figures from the balance sheet in which the company believes the shareholders have an interest. For example, the company may show *total assets*, which are all assets (current and long term) that the company owns as at the balance sheet date. The company may also show *long-term debt*, which is any debt the company won't have paid off within 12 months of the balance sheet date.

Figure 16-1 shows an example of this condensed financial data.

Even though these figures are very compressed (check out Chapter 10 to see a full-blown income statement and Part III to see a fully-developed balance sheet), the figures are based upon – and must reconcile with – the audited financial statements.

Calculating weighted average

Say that on 1 January 2012, Breary Bricks PLC has 10,000 shares in issue. On 1 July 2012, it issues another 7,000 shares. You need to calculate the weighted average number of shares in issue during the year to 31 December 2012.

Date	No. of months	No. of shares in issue	Time fraction	No. of shares in issue × the time fraction
1.1.12 to 30.6.12	6	10,000	6/12	5,000
1.7.12 to 31.12.12	6	17,000	6/12	8,500
				13,500

So Breary Bricks PLC had a weighted average number of 13,500 shares in issue from 1 January 2012 to 31 December 2012.

Summary of operations	£	£	£
Net operating revenues	100,000	98,000	105,000
Earnings per Share:			
Basic	4.58	4.75	3.89
Diluted	4.00	4.25	3.97
Dividends per Share	1.75	1.62	1.24
Balance Sheet Information:			
Total assets	35,271	33,620	39,587
Long-term liabilities	5,060	3,782	1,318

Figure 16-1: Selected financial information.

Promoting company achievements

In this section, which has a distinct public relations purpose, the company expands upon any facts the chairperson of the board discusses in his letter to the shareholders. For example, this section may break down how the company has increased growth *per capita*, which is the average per person living in an area the company serves. Per capita growth could mean that the company sold more products to existing consumers or expanded its sales base into new markets or countries. Companies want to emphasise that they're attracting new customers while still maintaining a bond with existing customers.

Looking into the future

In its annual report, a company also addresses where it sees itself in the short- and long-term future. Doing so addresses any concerns that an investor may have that the business is a *going concern*: that it will be able to stay in business for at least 12 months beyond the date the financial statements are approved, generating or raising enough cash to pay its operating expenses and make appropriate payments on debt.

If the company's management decide that the company will *not* be able to stay in business for at least 12 months beyond the date the financial statements are approved, they cannot prepare the financial statements on a going concern basis. Instead, they'll prepare them on what's known as the *break-up* basis. This means that assets and liabilities are all reclassified as current (in other words *short-term*) and are stated at their recoverable amounts (the amount that will realistically be paid and received). Obviously, investors aren't going to get all fired up about their ownership in the company's shares if they believe the company will be around for only a few more years. Therefore, annual reviews normally give at least a ten-year plan on growth. Often, companies associate their growth predictions with social and economic transitions – for example, changes in population demographics such as aging and income.

Getting to know key management and board members

This section of the annual report introduces other members of the board of directors, the management team for each division of the company and committee members (such as members of the audit committee). It's not uncommon for the company to include pictures of all of them posed at the company headquarters.

Making Sense of Other Sections in the Annual Report

When you look at a company's directors' report, you see all sorts of bits and bobs from commentary about the company's financial performance, to details about where management want the company to be in the future. Some of these details are required to be included in the directors' report by company law; other details are included because the company's management team want them in for public relations purposes. Here are some of the more common types of disclosures you see in a directors' report:

✔ **Statement of directors' responsibilities:** This statement outlines the company directors' obligations in the preparation of the company's financial statements. These responsibilities include, among other things, preparing the financial statements in accordance with UK GAAP; selecting suitable accounting policies and applying them consistently; making judgements and accounting estimates that are reasonable and prudent; stating whether UK accounting standards have been followed, subject to any material departures disclosed and explained in the financial statements; and preparing the financial statements on the going concern basis unless it's inappropriate to presume the company will continue in business.

✔ **Statement of disclosure to auditors:** This statement confirms that the directors are not aware of any relevant audit information needed by the auditors of which the auditors are not aware. It also confirms that the directors have taken all necessary steps to make themselves aware of any relevant audit information and to establish that the company's auditors are aware of that information.

✔ **Principal activities and review of the business:** This disclosure outlines the day-to-day activities of the business (that is, what it does) and gives an overview of the financial results for the accounting period.

✔ **Principal risks and uncertainties:** In the annual report, the company must outline principal risks and uncertainties and explain to the user how the company manages them. For example, it may be that it conducts a lot of business overseas and acknowledges that foreign currency fluctuations pose a key risk to the company. The directors must outline these risks and what the company does to mitigate them. This information reassures the shareholders that the company has processes in place to manage those external risks that it can't control.

✔ **Future development:** The company should disclose where the company's directors wish the company to be in the future, details of planned expansions, and information about any projects that the company is currently undertaking that are expected to be finished or projects that the company is planning on undertaking.

✔ **Events that have happened after the year-end:** The company should disclose any material *events after the balance sheet date* (sometimes called *post-balance sheet events* or *subsequent events*). These are events that have occurred in the succeeding financial year that are considered to be significant (such as the acquisition or disposal of a subsidiary).

✔ **Creditor payment policies:** These are required to be disclosed by the Companies Act 2006 if the company is a public company or a large private company in a group that contains a public company.

Glancing at Form 10-K

The head offices of some companies in the UK are actually based in the United States. When a public company that trades its shares on the stock market is based in the US, it needs to file a Form 10-K with the US Securities and Exchange Commission (SEC).

Form 10-K consists of four parts:

- ✔ **Part I – the registrant:** This part contains information about the company, including an overview of what the company does and any risk factors surrounding it. An example of a *risk factor* may be heightened competition affecting the core business or a significant depletion of the raw materials needed to make its products.

- ✔ **Part II – the company's financial performance:** This part is really the meat of Form 10-K because it reveals a company's financial performance in the last financial year. It features information about where the company's shares are traded, analysis and discussion from company management, and the audited financial statements.

- ✔ **Part III – identifying management and corporate governance:** This part discusses management and governance. In this very short section, the company lists its directors and executive officers and will probably cross-refer to Part I, if that section has already provided sufficient information.

- ✔ **Part IV – exhibits, financial statement schedules and signature:** This part merely lists the documents that are part of Form 10-K and gives the exhibit number where each document can be found. The last page contains the signature of the chairperson of the board of directors, the chief executive officer, the chief financial officer, the principal accounting officer, all directors and the individual holding power of attorney attesting to the fact that the report does not contain any statements that are not factual or omit any necessary material facts.

Looking at the report of the auditors

Auditing is the process of systemically gathering enough evidence to support the facts a company is showing in any company-generated report, including the financial statements. The results of an audit are communicated to the company's shareholders.

The objective of a financial statement audit is for the auditor to form an opinion as to whether the financial statements are or are not free from error. Auditors aren't responsible for preparing the financial statements they're auditing. In fact, they *can't* prepare them for listed companies; to do so would violate the concept of independence (see Chapter 1).

Therefore, the items under audit are company management's responsibility. In other words, the financial statements contain *management assertions* – management's assurance that the information provided is materially correct. A financial accountant uses these assertions to produce the financial statements.

While the company's management assertions must be presented on the financial statements using generally accepted accounting practice (GAAP), auditors conduct their audits using international standards on auditing (ISAs) which are not to be confused with international accounting standards (IASs). In the UK and Ireland, these have been tailored to be UK and Ireland specific and are therefore known as ISAs (UK and Ireland). After conducting the audit of the financial statements, the auditor can express one of four basic options:

✔ **Unqualified:** An *unqualified* opinion is the best the client can get! It means the audit has been conducted in accordance with ISAs (UK and Ireland) *and* that the financial statements conform with GAAP in all material aspects.

✔ **Qualified:** An auditor may have to issue a qualified opinion when the company doesn't use GAAP consistently, or circumstances may have prevented the auditor from getting enough evidence to be able to issue an unqualified opinion. When the end user (a potential investor, for example) sees this opinion, she knows she can't rely on the information in the financial report as much as she could if the auditor offered an unqualified opinion.

✔ **Adverse:** As you can probably guess, an adverse opinion isn't good! The auditor issues an *adverse* opinion if the financial statements don't present the client's financial position, results of operations and cash flows in conformity with GAAP. This type of opinion is issued only when the financial statements contain material departures from GAAP. (In Chapter 4, I explain what constitutes an accounting fact being material. For now, just keep in mind that what's material for one business may not be material for another.)

✔ **Disclaimer of opinion:** This happens when the auditor can't form an opinion on a client's financial statements. For example, a disclaimer may be issued where the accounting records have been destroyed and the auditor can't gather sufficient and appropriate audit evidence.

I provide examples of properly prepared financial statements in Part III (balance sheet), Chapter 10 (income statement) and Chapter 11 (statement of cash flows). And if you're wondering what this opinion the auditor expresses looks like, wonder no more! Figure 16-2 shows an example of an unqualified opinion. The right-hand side shows the opinion letter; the left-hand side is merely a guide for you to see what auditors call each section. The left-hand side is *not* included in the actual audit report.

Title:	Independent Auditor's Report
Addressee:	To the shareholders of Breary Bricks PLC.
Introductory paragraph:	We have audited the financial statements of Breary Bricks PLC for the year ended 31 May 2012 set out on pages 12 to 13. The financial reporting framework that has been applied in their preparation is applicable law and International Financial Reporting Standards (IFRSs) as adopted by the EU.\n\nThis report is made solely to the company's members, as a body, in accordance with Chapter 3 of Part 16 of the Companies Act 2006. Our audit work has been undertaken so that we might state to the company's members those matters which we are required to state to them in an auditor's report and for no other purpose. To the fullest extent permitted by law, we do not accept or assume responsibility to anyone other than the company and the company's members, as a body, for our audit work, for this report, or for the opinions we have formed.
Responsibilities:	As explained more fully in the Director's Responsibilities Statement set out on page 10, the directors are responsible for the preparation of the financial statements and for being satisfied that they give a true and fair view. Our responsibility is to audit, and express an opinion on, the financial statements in accordance with applicable law and International Standards on Auditing (UK and Ireland). Those standards require us to comply with Auditing Practices Board's (APB's) Ethical Standards for Auditors.
Scope paragraph:	An audit involves obtaining evidence about the amounts and disclosures in the financial statements sufficient to give reasonable assurance that the financial statements are free from material misstatement, whether caused by fraud or error. This includes an assessment of: whether the accounting policies are appropriate to the company's circumstances and have been consistently applied and adequately disclosed; the reasonableness of significant accounting estimates made by the directors; and the overall presentation of the financial statements. In addition, we read all the financial and non-financial information in the Report of the Directors to identify material inconsistencies with the audited financial statements. If we become aware of any apparent material misstatements or inconsistencies, we consider the implications for our report.
Opinion paragraph:	In our opinion the financial statements: \n* give a true and fair view of the state of the company's affairs as at 31 May 2012 and of its profit for the year then ended; \n* have been properly prepared in accordance with IFRSs as adopted by the EU; and \n* have been prepared in accordance with the requirements of the Companies Act 2006.
Opinion on other matters:	In our opinion the information given in the Directors' Report for the financial year for which the financial statements are prepared is consistent with the financial statements.
Matters on which reports by exception are needed:	We have nothing to report in respect of the following matters where the Companies Act 2006 requires us to report to you if, in our opinion: \n* adequate accounting records have not been kept, or returns adequate for our audit have not been received from branches not visited by us; or \n* the financial statements are not in agreement with the accounting records and returns; or \n* certain disclosures of Directors' remuneration specified by law are not made; or \n* we have not received all the information and explanations we require for our audit.
Name of auditor:	John Smith (Senior Statutory Auditor) for and on behalf of An Audit Firm LLP
Date of report:	17th August 2012

Figure 16-2: An unqualified independent auditor's report for Breary Bricks PLC.

Part VI
Tackling More Advanced Financial Accounting Topics

Comparison of Income Statement to Corporation Tax Return
For the Year-Ended 31 December 2012

	Income Statement	Tax Return
Revenue	250,000	200,000 (a)
Cost of sales	75,000	82,000 (b)
Gross profit	175,000	118,000
Distribution costs	43,000	30,000 (c)
Fine	25,000	0 (d)
Profit before tax	107,000	88,000
Income tax expense	24,610	20,240
Profit after tax	82,390	67,760

Go to www.dummies.com/extras/financialaccounting for online bonus content.

In this part . . .

- ✔ Understand and learn to account for business mergers and acquisitions.

- ✔ Become a whizz on accounting for taxes.

- ✔ Grasp the differences between financial and operating leases.

- ✔ Put right errors and deal with changes in financial statements.

- ✔ Go to `www.dummies.com/extras/financial accounting` for online bonus content, including an extra Part of Tens chapter: 'Ten Differences Between Some National Standards and IFRS'.

Chapter 17

Accounting for Business Combinations

*T*his chapter discusses an advanced financial accounting topic: business combinations. Although some basic introductory accountancy lectures may not touch on this subject, outside of the classroom, most financial accountants specialise in this area because the rules are quite detailed. So if you're debating whether a career in financial accounting is for you, you may want to find out a bit about this topic now. (You'll more than likely encounter it if you work in an accountancy practice or study to become an accountant with one of the chartered accountancy bodies.)

Financial accountants must get information related to business combinations right because people using the information (such as potential investors) depend on it to understand the effect a business combination has on financial reports and operations.

In this chapter, you find out about some major revisions that took place in 2008 on how to report a business combination under International Financial Reporting Standards (IFRSs). In a nutshell, only one way to account for a business combination exists in IFRS 3 *Business Combinations*: the acquisition method. The changes didn't affect UK GAAP because FRS 6 *Acquisitions and Mergers* uses this method as a means of accounting for an acquisition. I also explain how to account for investments in equities and briefly touch on the two ways to set up a tax-free business combination – something investors in a business find extremely interesting. After all, who wants to pay taxes if they don't have to?

Explaining What Constitutes a Merger or Acquisition

Before I tackle accounting for business combinations, I want you to have a basic understanding of the lingo surrounding them. Here, I run through a list of key terms you need to know. (Mind you, these are just *key* terms. The list of all terms associated with business combinations is quite long. If you're really interested, you can augment this list with terms related to generally accepted accounting practice (GAAP; see Chapter 4).)

✔ **Acquisition:** This occurs when one company acquires another business. The business doing the acquiring (the *acquirer*) takes control. Obviously, if the target company doesn't want to be acquired, this can be a hostile situation.

✔ **Acquisition date:** The date control of a business passes from the acquiree (seller) to the acquirer.

✔ **Business:** Obviously the parties in a business combination actually have to be businesses. To qualify as a business, an entity must have assets and perform activities capable of providing a return to its investors. (The investors are either shareholders for a company, partners for a partnership or limited liability partnership, or the owner for a sole trader company.) Determining that all entities involved in a combination are actual businesses is really important because if the acquirer is not actually taking control of a business, this transaction must be handled as an asset acquisition rather than a share acquisition. (I explain these two types of acquisitions later in this section.)

✔ **Completion date:** The date the acquirer legally takes possession of the assets and assumes the liabilities of the acquiree.

✔ **Consolidation:** What occurs when many smaller companies are acquired by or merged into a larger one. The companies' financial statements must be aggregated so they appear as a consolidated whole. I cover this subject in the 'Consolidating financial statements' section later in this chapter.

✔ **Goodwill:** An intangible asset (see Chapter 7) that exists when the amount paid by the acquiring company during the business combination transaction exceeds the fair value of the net assets of the business being acquired. *Fair value* is what an unpressured person would pay in an open market to purchase an asset or transfer a liability.

✔ **Identifiable asset:** This is an asset in the control of the acquiree to which a fair value can be assigned or an asset that can legally be separated from the acquiree. For example, no weird legal circumstances prevent the acquiree from disposing of this asset.

✔ **Merger:** This business combination takes place when two or more companies combine into a single entity. Mergers are usually regarded as friendly – not hostile or unwanted takeovers. IFRS 3 *Business Combinations* does not recognise mergers, but UK GAAP at FRS 6 *Acquisitions and Mergers* does, and so does the new UK GAAP.

✔ **Parties to the business combination:** The two sides of a business combination are the acquirer and the acquiree. The *acquirer* is the business taking control and is also the party transferring the cash and/or assets – or assuming the debt – to obtain control in the combination. The *acquiree* is the business the acquirer is taking control of. Usually the larger business in the deal is the acquirer, and it's also the company initiating the deal.

Just to confuse things, here's a language note to keep in mind: even though each of these words means something specific, financial accountants often use the words *mergers*, *consolidations* and *acquisitions* interchangeably. In this chapter, I use the phrase *mergers and acquisitions* (or *M&A*) to refer to the process of combining two or more businesses.

As I touched on earlier in this section, M&As come in two different forms:

✔ **Asset acquisition:** One company acquires the net assets of another company, and at the end of the day only the acquiring company survives. For example, if X acquires Y's net assets, Y's books are closed and X is the surviving company.

✔ **Share acquisition:** The acquiring company purchases an investment in another company, which is now a subsidiary. The net assets of the subsidiary do not transfer to the purchaser. So if X purchases the investment in Y, Y is now a subsidiary of X. The value of Y reflects in X's financial statements in an account called 'investment in subsidiary Y'. In this case, you also have to prepare a set of *consolidated financial statements*, which shows the financial statements of the various businesses brought together by the M&A.

Now that you have the basic terminology in mind, I discuss some of the many issues facing a financial accountant while guiding a business through the combining process. These issues are the significant ones so having a sound understanding of them is important.

Dealing with a Business Combination

Companies that report under IFRSs saw a change in the way business combinations are accounted for. In 2008, the rules regarding how to account for business combinations changed and these changes were effective for annual periods beginning on or after 1 July 2009. The accounting method used when dealing with any new business combination is called the *acquisition method*.

UK GAAP at FRS 6 also uses the concept of *merger accounting* and *acquisition accounting*. Merger accounting is used for genuine business mergers (two businesses coming together to form one new business), and acquisition accounting is used when one company acquires a subsidiary. I go through the steps involved in applying the acquisition method in the next section.

Post 2008: The acquisition method

To better serve the external users of the financial statements, such as potential investors, the US Financial Accounting Standards Board (FASB) and the International Accounting Standards Board (IASB) worked together back in 2008 to form a new standard. This didn't really affect those companies that apply UK GAAP (FRS 6) because FRS 6 also uses the acquisition method, but it certainly did affect companies in the UK that report under IFRSs (and student accountants studying financial reporting papers under IFRSs).

The end result of the collaboration between FASB and IASB, for those companies reporting under IFRSs, was IFRS 3 (revised) *Business Combinations*.

The overriding objective of the new standard is to improve the relevance, representational faithfulness (that's a mouthful!), transparency and comparability of information provided in a company's financial statements about business combinations and their effects on the reporting entity.

IFRS 3 (revised) accomplishes this goal in these ways:

- ✔ It recognises and measures identifiable assets acquired, liabilities assumed, and the non-controlling interests in the acquiree (if any).
- ✔ It recognises and measures acquired goodwill or a gain from a bargain purchase.
- ✔ It determines the nature and extent of disclosures that are needed to enable the user to evaluate the nature of the business combination and its financial effect on the consolidated reporting entity.
- ✔ It accounts for and reports non-controlling interests in subsidiaries.
- ✔ It requires a subsidiary to be deconsolidated when the acquirer ceases to hold a controlling interest in it.

Following are the steps to account for business combinations using the acquisition method. As you walk through them, remember that while each step may seem straightforward, a multitude of factors make a business combination a very complicated accounting conundrum. A speciality within most accountancy firms, properly accounting for business combinations takes in-depth training and on-the-job experience.

Taking you through all the nooks and crannies of combinations is way beyond the scope of this book. But the information I present here will guide you through any basic consolidation exercise and serve as a jump-start for the more advanced consolidation issues you're likely to encounter as a financial accountant.

Without further ado, here they are! The steps to use the acquisition method to recognise a business combination are as follows:

1. **Identify the acquirer.** After you determine the transaction is a business combination, you have to identify the *acquirer*, which is the company taking over the *acquiree* (the target business). I explain these terms in the first section of this chapter.

2. **Decide on the acquisition date.** This is the date when control of the business passes from the acquiree to the acquirer. You may assume the acquisition date is also the *completion* date (the date the acquirer legally takes possession of the assets and assumes the liabilities of the acquiree). Not necessarily. The transaction is complete only after legal possession. Depending on how complicated the business combination is, the completion date can be some period of time after the passing of control.

3. **Recognise and measure the net assets involved in the business combination.** You need to know what identifiable assets are acquired and what liabilities are being assumed during the transaction. To do so, you follow the guidelines defining what constitutes an asset or liability per IASB's *Conceptual Framework for Financial Reporting* or the UK's *Statement of Principles* (referred to as the *Concepts and Pervasive Principles* in the new UK GAAP). For example, to be considered an identifiable asset, an item must have a future benefit that will contribute to future cash flow (see Chapter 11).

   You ignore goodwill for now, but you have to address any non-controlling interest in the acquiree. A *non-controlling interest*, also known as a *minority interest*, comes into play when another company owns part of the acquiree.

   The measurement part of this step pertains to how much the assets are worth and what the assumed debt of the liability is at fair value on the date of acquisition.

   Exceptions exist to the rules guiding this step. Some assets and liabilities are recognised and measured in a special fashion. For example, assets the acquiree is holding to sell are measured at fair value less cost to sell. For now, just remember the basics and worry about nuances if and when you take a financial accounting job dealing with business combinations.

4. **Recognise and measure goodwill or gain from a bargain purchase.**
You ignored goodwill in Step 3, and now it's time to pay attention to it!
Goodwill exists when the purchase price the acquirer is willing to pay
exceeds the recognised value of the acquiree's net assets.

I show you how to account for a business combination transaction
involving goodwill later in this chapter in the 'Grappling with goodwill'
section.

A *bargain purchase* exists in just the opposite circumstance: when the
purchase price is less than the fair value of the acquiree's net assets.
Newly qualified financial accountants and student accountants usually
assume this situation calls for recording negative goodwill as some sort
of contra-asset account. You don't. In a bargain purchase, you account for
the amount of the so-called 'negative goodwill' as income from continuing operations (see Chapter 10). Unfortunately under UK GAAP at FRS 10
Goodwill and Intangible Assets the situation isn't as clear cut (boo!).

Under the UK's FRS 10, any negative goodwill that remains after the fair
values of the acquired assets should be tested to see if it's actually worth
less than what's being paid for it (in other words, tested for impairment). On
the flip side, the fair values of the acquired liabilities should also be checked
carefully to see if any have been missed or understated.

Once the assets and liabilities have been double-checked (and sometimes
even treble-checked), then any negative goodwill is recognised on the balance sheet, directly underneath the goodwill heading and followed by a sub-
total showing the net amount of positive and negative goodwill.

The new UK GAAP will require any excess negative goodwill to be recognised
in profit or loss in the periods in which the non-monetary assets acquired are
recovered (an asset is recovered either by way of sale or by way of depreciation (depreciation being the method used to write off the cost of non-current
assets over their expected useful lives)).

Grappling with goodwill

Under the new rules put forth by IFRS 3(R), the acquirer in a business combination must recognise the assets it acquires plus the liabilities it assumes
(which together equal the *net assets*) plus any non-controlling interest in
the acquiree at their fair value at the date of acquisition. *Fair value* is what
an unpressured person would pay in an open market to acquire an asset or
transfer a liability.

To breathe a little life into this concept, Figure 17-1 shows an example of an acquiree balance sheet on the date of acquisition reflecting book and fair values for its assets and liabilities.

Figure 17-1: An acquiree balance sheet at the date of acquisition.

Balance Sheet	Book Value £	Fair Value £
Cash	20,000	20,000
Trade receivables	10,000	8,000
Inventory	50,000	65,000
Land	125,000	175,000
Buildings	225,000	225,000
Total assets	430,000	493,000
Trade payables	75,000	75,000
Ordinary £5 shares	75,000	75,000
Profit and loss account reserves (retained earnings)	255,000	
Total liabilities and equity	430,000	

The acquirer gave 30,000 shares (par value of £10 and fair value of £25) of its shares as consideration in the business combination to the acquiree shareholders. With this fact in mind, take a look at Figure 17-2, which shows the journal entry to record the business combination. Note that goodwill is the residual value between debits and credits.

Figure 17-2: The journal entry to record the business combination.

Journal Entry	£	£
Cash	20,000	
Trade receivables	8,000	
Inventory	65,000	
Land	175,000	
Buildings	225,000	
Goodwill	332,000	
Trade payables		75,000
Ordinary 30,000 shares at £10 per share		300,000
Share premium (30,000 at £15*)		450,000
	825,000	825,000

* £15 is the difference between par value of £10 and fair value of £25

Knowing what to do with goodwill under IFRSs

Amortisation is the method used to write off the cost of intangible assets over their expected useful lives, and goodwill is an intangible asset, right? Yep, goodwill is an intangible asset, but to throw a spanner in the works, if you're reporting under IFRSs you aren't allowed to amortise goodwill! Now don't panic if you're reporting under UK GAAP because amortisation is okay provided the goodwill isn't expected to have a useful life of more than 20 years (if it is, read on because the next bit is relevant in that situation). Goodwill doesn't just sit pretty on a company balance sheet forever; instead, it's tested annually for impairment, which means working out whether the amount of goodwill stated on the balance sheet is actually worth less than what it is carried at in the financial statements. This process is fairly complicated and is beyond the scope of this book, but if you're interested in finding out more, check out *IFRS For Dummies*, which is also written by me!

Reviewing Issues Affecting Mergers and Acquisitions

Accounting for business combinations has always been thorny. You have to decide whether to account for the transaction as a share or asset acquisition, what costs relating to the M&A are expensed in the income statement (see Chapter 10) and which amounts are taken to the balance sheet as assets or liabilities (see Part III).

In this section, I touch on issues affecting M&As that you may see in your advanced dealings with M&As, such as contingencies, payments made to employees as a condition of their employment and valuation.

Understanding contingent considerations

A *contingency* exists when an existing circumstance may cause an action to take place in the future depending on other events that have yet to happen and indeed may never happen. (I discuss contingent liabilities in Chapter 15.) In a business combination, a contingency means the *acquirer* – the business taking control – agrees to make payments to the acquiree in the future, depending on the outcome of an event that hasn't happened yet.

For financial accounting, the important aspect of contingent considerations is whether these future payments are accounted for as part of the purchase price or if they should be an expense reflecting after the M&A comes to fruition. One example of an expense is if part of the arrangement calls for key employees continuing employment in the new business. In this case, the payroll cost would be an expense.

An example of a contingency consideration that could be accounted for as part of the business combination is the handling of preacquisition contingencies involving assets and liabilities. For example, the acquiree has a contractual obligation to purchase an asset that was entered into prior to the acquisition. In this case, the asset needs to be recognised on the balance sheet as part of the business combination transaction. Any consideration that is contingent is valued at fair value (*fair value* is often referred to as *market value*).

Saying farewell to management: Golden goodbyes

Golden goodbye agreements guarantee key executives lucrative pay-offs if control of the company changes hands followed by a change in management. Sometimes management may negotiate these terms, which appear in a contract for employment, so they've covered themselves when accepting new employment. Let's face it: it would be a bit foolish to leave one well-paid job for another only to be let go in a couple of years if control of the company changes hands. In essence, a golden goodbye agreement is layoff insurance.

How an acquiring company handles these payments depends on the timing of the golden goodbye agreement. If the agreement was made prior to the mere whiff of an acquisition, and the employee will be saying farewell following the acquisition, the golden goodbye payment reflects as an expense on the target's books.

However, if the subject of the golden goodbye agreement comes up during the negotiation process between the acquirer and the target, it's an expense reflecting on the acquirer's books during the acquisition process. When might something like this happen? Well, perhaps the key employee is pretty crucial to the operations of the target business and the acquirer wants to make sure this person doesn't jump ship when the company changes hands.

Accounting for acquisition-related costs

If you've ever purchased a house or a car, you know that transactions like these usually carry a price. For example, the bank sorting out your mortgage probably required you to pay an arrangement fee.

Well, a business combination has a boatload of expenses relating to it. For example the lawyers involved in the deal will expect to get paid for their efforts and so will the accountants as well as other parties who are all involved in getting the deal to completion.

Using the acquisition method under IFRS 3 (R), all acquisition-related costs are expensed as they're incurred. (Previously, using the purchase method, these types of costs were allocated to the identifiable assets and liabilities, thus creating a situation where goodwill increased.)

Now, here's where a big difference exists between IFRS 3 (R) and UK GAAP at FRS 7 *Fair Values in Acquisition Accounting*. As I state above, all acquisition-related costs, such as legal and professional fees, are written off to profit or loss as they're incurred. However, under FRS 7 fees and similar incremental costs incurred directly in making an acquisition should be included in the cost of the acquisition, therefore creating an increase in goodwill. The new UK GAAP also requires the same accounting treatment as FRS 7.

Identifying other issues

To wrap up this section of the chapter, I explain two other issues you may have to account for in a business combination: corporation taxes and settlements when the acquirer and the acquiree have a preexisting relationship.

Recording income taxes

The provisions in IAS 12 *Income Taxes* and the new UK GAAP require the acquirer to recognise and measure a deferred tax asset or liability that comes about due to factors resulting from the business combination. This means that the acquirer has to account for any potential tax effects of temporary differences, carryforwards and any corporation tax uncertainties of an acquiree that exist at the acquisition date or that arise as a result of the acquisition. Here's what each of these issues looks like:

  ✔ **Temporary differences:** Deferred tax assets and liabilities can arise because there's usually a temporary difference between financial statements prepared using GAAP and those prepared for tax purposes. I cover this topic in much more detail in Chapter 18.

For now, a quick example of a *temporary difference* is when under GAAP the company uses straight-line depreciation (see Chapter 12) and for tax purposes uses a more accelerated method (such as *annual investment allowance*). Let's say the company is depreciating a desk costing £1,000 that it anticipates using for five years. Under the straight-line method, depreciation is £200 per year (£1,000/5). Using an accelerated method, the same desk has a depreciation expense in the first year of £500. (Note that I'm not using any particular accelerated method.)

So a depreciation expense difference exists in year one of £300, which leads to a corporation tax difference too. Eventually, the two depreciation methods will even out, with the desk being depreciated for £1,000 using either method – and the corporation taxes will even out as well. But until then, a temporary difference exists between the two.

✓ **Carryforward:** A *carryforward* occurs when the acquiree has taxable losses from prior periods that can be used to offset taxable profit in subsequent periods. For example, in 2012, the company has taxable net sales (see Chapter 10) of £1 million and tax-deductible expenses of £1.25 million, resulting in a taxable loss of £250,000 (£1 million less £1.25 million). If the company has taxable profit of £400,000 in 2013, its actual taxable profit is only £150,000 (£400,000 – £250,000).

✓ **Corporation tax uncertainties:** Uncertainties can result from many different events. One example would certainly be if the acquiree is under inspection by HM Revenue and Customs (HMRC) and the inspection isn't complete or the inspection results are being appealed as at the acquisition date.

IAS 12 requires the acquirer to recognise deferred tax assets and liabilities as a result of business combinations as an adjustment to goodwill or the bargain purchase gain. This will also be the case for business combinations that are accounted for under the new UK GAAP. Under the UK's FRS 19 *Deferred Tax*, deferred tax isn't normally recognised on positive fair value adjustments (also known as *revaluation adjustments*) to property, plant and equipment or intangible assets.

Handling preexisting relationships

In some cases, the acquirer and the acquiree have a business relationship prior to the date of acquisition. If you think about it, having some kind of relationship makes logical sense. Maybe one of the companies sells goods to the other, and it makes good business sense to combine the two companies.

If a business combination puts the kibosh on an existing relationship, the acquirer recognises a gain or loss on the transaction. In other words, a part of the overall consideration the acquirer gives to the acquiree includes an amount (either positive or negative) that's deemed to permanently end or *settle* the preexisting relationship.

Two types of preexisting relationships exist:

- **Contractual relationship:** If one of the parties provides inventory or other goods to the other, a contractual relationship exists. For example, the acquiree is an electronics manufacturer that has a four-year contract to provide an electronics retail company acquirer with laptop computers at a specified price and quantity.

- **Non-contractual relationship:** This type of relationship lacks the meeting of the minds you see when two parties sign a contract to provide a good or service for an agreed-upon price. A great example of a non-contractual relationship is when the acquirer and acquiree are the defendant or claimant in the same lawsuit; in other words, one is suing the other for copyright infringement (see Chapter 7).

How on earth do you handle preexisting relationships in all of these differing situations, I hear you ask. Well, if you're looking at a contractual preexisting relationship, you work out the gain or loss at the lower of the following:

- The amount by which the acquirer finds the contract to be favourable or unfavourable

- Any settlement provision in the contract

I can hear you saying, 'Wow! That makes perfect sense. Let's move on, please!' Not. I realise this subject is rather confusing, so I want to work through an example. Let's say the acquirer deems the contract terms to be unfavourable by £1 million, which gives the acquirer a loss of the same amount. But supposing the terms allow the acquirer to settle the contract for £250,000. Well, the loss is reduced to the lower of the two figures: £250,000.

Mercifully, the gain or loss for a non-contractual relationship is much easier to understand. You use fair value. In the example of the copyright infringement lawsuit, fair value is what an unpressured person would pay in an open market to settle the lawsuit. If you need to brush up on how to handle gains or losses, check out Chapter 10.

If some of the loss was already recognised as a *provision for a liability*, which is a noncurrent liability (see Chapter 8), the settlement loss has to be reduced. For example, if the acquirer has already recorded a provision in the amount of £200,000 relating to this lawsuit, the settlement loss is only £50,000.

Dealing with Investments in Other Companies

Companies often make investments in other companies by investing in the investee's (the company receiving the investment) net assets. The degree to which the buyer invests in the other company determines this transaction's accounting treatment in the buyer's books. Owning less than 20 per cent of the net assets in another business means you account for this as a simple investment. Owning between 20 and 50 per cent calls for using the *equity method*. When one business has over 50 per cent ownership in the other, which gives the investor a controlling stake, you have to prepare consolidated financial statements.

I discuss each method in turn, starting with simple investments.

Considering simple investments

A company may make two types of investment in another company depending on the investing company's intentions. The investor can make a long-term investment or a short-term investment.

Long-term investments are classified as fixed (or non-current) assets on the balance sheet and in UK GAAP these are initially recognised at cost and can remain on the balance sheet at cost (as per the Companies Act at SI 2008/4100 1 Sch 17). However, if the fixed asset investment has diminished in value and this diminution is likely to be permanent, the reduction in value must be charged to profit or loss.

If a business decides to account for a simple investment at fair value (using what's known as the UK's *Alternative Accounting Rules*), any fluctuations in the investment's fair value are taken to the revaluation reserve account in the equity section of the balance sheet.

Generally, those financial assets that are held-to-maturity and loans and receivables will be recognised on the balance sheet (statement of financial position) at historic cost under IAS 39 *Financial Instruments: Recognition and Measurement* and IFRS 9 *Financial Instruments*. All other financial assets are carried at fair value, with changes in fair value going through the income statement (with the exception of available-for-sale assets whose fair value changes go through *other comprehensive income* until the asset is derecognised, when it is then recycled through the income statement).

Current asset investments (those which the company expects to sell within 12 months of the reporting date hence *current*) are recorded at the lower of cost and net realisable value (NRV). As a result, any investment whose NRV is lower than cost must be written down to recoverable amount and the amount of the write-off is charged to profit or loss.

A current asset investment can also be carried at fair value, which will often be the investment's market value. If the investment is unquoted, the directors will determine its value. In the same way as the rule applied for fixed assets investments, any profit and loss arising from fluctuations in the investment's market value are taken to the revaluation reserve account on the balance sheet.

If reporting under IFRSs, any short-term investments would be classified as *held-for-trading* and would therefore be recognised at fair value, with changes in fair value going through profit or loss.

Utilising the equity method

You use the equity method when the investor's ownership in the investee is between 20 and 50 per cent. The equity method of accounting recognises that the investor is able to significantly influence that investee business. Because of this level of influence, the purchaser has to periodically adjust the carrying amount of its investment for the proportionate share of profit or loss less any dividends received. So the value of the buyer's investment increases when reporting its share of the profit from the investee. The value decreases when the investee pays out a dividends to the investor.

For example, let's say that ABC Limited purchases 40 per cent of the net assets of XYZ Limited for £100,000 on 1 January 2013. You record the purchase on the balance sheet initially at cost of £100,000. During 2012, XYZ pays out £10,000 in dividends to ABC and has total net profit of £300,000, £120,000 of which belongs to ABC (£300,000 × 40 per cent).

Using the equity method, ABC increases its investment in XYZ on the balance sheet by £110,000 (£120,000 – £10,000). At the end of the accounting period, ABC's investment in XYZ is valued at £210,000 (£100,000 + £110,000).

Consolidating financial statements

If one company owns more than 50 per cent of another business, a parent/ subsidiary relationship exists. When the parent owns more than 50 per cent of the subsidiary the parent is said to have *control* over the subsidiary. *Control* means that the parent is able to govern the financial and operating policies of the subsidiary. The parent, of course, is the more-than-50-per cent owner (acquirer), and the subsidiary is the acquiree. The parent has to use the equity method to account for its investment in the subsidiary. The financial statements of both are combined and shown together in the income statement (see Chapter 10), balance sheet (see Part III) and statement of cash flows (see Chapter 11).

The parent can have more than one subsidiary. And, wait for it! To make it even more convoluted, the parent could also be a subsidiary of another business.

Of course, like most things in life, accounting for this situation is easier said than done. This subject is so complex that I can't possibly cover it entirely in this chapter. But I want to cover the basics of how to deal with investments and transactions among the companies within the consolidated group.

Basically, you eliminate transactions taking place between parent and subsidiary, an example of which I show in Figure 17-3. In this example, you discover how to eliminate two different occurrences: investment in the subsidiary, and dividends.

Parent and Subsidiary Partial Consolidation Schedule

	Parent	Sub	Consolidation Adjustments		
			Debit	Credit	Consolidated
Investment in subsidiary	95,000	–		95,000	–
Ordinary shares	500,000	200,000	200,000		500,000
Retained earnings	725,000	75,000	75,000		725,000
Dividend received	50,000		50,000		–
Dividend paid		50,000		50,000	–

Figure 17-3: A partial consolidation schedule.

Here are your facts:

- ✔ The parent owns £200,000 of the net assets in the subsidiary, representing 100 per cent ownership.

- ✔ During the year, the subsidiary made a net profit of £75,000.

- ✔ The subsidiary declared and paid dividends of £50,000.

The partial consolidation schedule shows only the accounts affected by the consolidation process.

I also want to show you how to prepare journal entries (see Chapter 5) to eliminate sales and cost of sales transactions taking place between parent and subsidiary. This example deals with an intercompany sale of goods. Here are your facts about this transaction:

- ✔ The parent sells goods costing £5,000 to the subsidiary for £7,000 cash.

- ✔ The parent's gross profit (see Chapter 10) is 57 per cent.

✔ The subsidiary subsequently sells £2,000 of the goods it purchases from the parent to an unrelated third party for £4,000.

Figure 17-4 shows the three journal entries. The first reflects the sale on the parent's books. The second reflects the purchase on the subsidiary's books and the subsequent resale of some of the goods to its customer. The third reflects the consolidation adjustment, which has a two-fold effect:

✔ To eliminate the intercompany sale from the parent's books.

✔ To remove the overstated value of inventory from the subsidiary's books. This is worked out by taking the closing inventory in the subsidiary's books of £5,000 (£7,000 purchase less reduction in inventory of £2,000) and multiplying it by the parent's gross profit of 57 per cent.

REMEMBER

Consolidated financial statements show the financial position of separate legal entities as though they're one economic entity (this is for accounting purposes only; it doesn't, in itself, mean that the group has a legal existence). Who's interested in this sort of information? Any lenders or investors are interested because from their perspective, the separate business entities are one. Consolidated financial statements give the users a better picture of the business combination's overall financial health.

	Debit	Credit
Cash	7,000	
Sales		7,000
Cost of sales	5,000	
Inventory		5,000

To record the sale of goods from parent company to subsidiary in the parent's books.

Inventory	7,000	
Cash		7,000
Cash	4,000	
Sales		4,000
Cost of sales	2,000	
Inventory		2,000

Figure 17-4: *To record purchase and sale of goods in the subsidiary's books.*

Journal entries reporting any product sales between parent and subsidiary.

And tah-dah! Here are your consolidation adjustments:

	Debit	Credit
Sales	7,000	
Cost of sales		7,000
Cost of sales	2,850	
Inventory		2,850

To eliminate the impact of intercompany sale from parent to subsidiary.

Classifying Types of Reconstructions

Most of this chapter is about reorganising businesses through the process of business combinations. Before I wrap up this subject, I want to give you a heads up on two types of tax-free company reconstructions. This sort of thing occurs when a company transfers, sells or otherwise gets rid of a portion of its business. This is a hot topic because the shareholders may not be too keen on the idea of voting for a reconstruction structured so that it carries behind it a substantial tax effect.

Structuring such a transaction in order to make it tax-free would be a nice trick, wouldn't it? Well, the underlying fact is that HM Revenue and Customs looks at substance over form in this instance. When structured properly, such a reorganisation doesn't bring with it enough of an economic change to justify making it a taxable transaction.

I cover two tax-free reorganisations in this section: a hive-up and a group reconstruction. To make the explanation user-friendly, I use Company A and Company B to identify the parties in each example.

The purpose of this section is *not* to educate you in tax law and how to properly structure reorganisations. You'll cover that complex tax subject in your taxation studies, or you'll have other tax material that you can consult which will deal with such matters. Rather, I present this information so that If you hear one of these terms in your day-to-day work as an accountant, or as a student accountant, you'll have an 'Aha!' moment as you remember the association with mergers and acquisitions. Here are the two tax-free reorganisations:

- ✔ **Hive-up:** A tax-free hive-up takes place when one company (Company A) transfers most or all of its assets to another company (Company B). After this transfer takes place, Company A *liquidates*, which means it sells or otherwise gets rid of any remaining assets. Immediately thereafter, Company B is in control of Company A.

- ✔ **Group reconstruction:** With a group reconstruction, one company (Company A) transfers some of its assets to one or more of its controlled companies, which means Company A owns at least 50 per cent of the shares in Company B. After the transfer takes place, Company A transfers Company B's shares to Company A's shareholders and group tax relief is available.

Chapter 18

Accounting for Income Taxes

. . . .

In This Chapter

▶ Finding out why financial and taxable income may differ

▶ Taking a tax deduction for a net loss

▶ Comparing example book values and tax values

▶ Seeing how the balance sheet is affected by temporary differences

. . . .

*N*obody likes paying taxes. As you read this chapter, you may shudder at the mere thought of the last time you prepared and filed your own individual tax return. The fact is that there's no getting away from tax and the reality is that income taxes are a fact of life. Depending on your employment status, you may pay tax directly through your payroll via pay as you earn (PAYE) or, if you have any additional income, or are self-employed, you may have to pay tax via the self-assessment regime (which means you have to fill in a tax return each year).

Most businesses have to pay taxes, too. I say *most* because one type of business entity, a *partnership*, files an information tax return only. That business (the partnership) will show a tax return comprising of income and expenditure, which then results in a profit (or a loss). The individual partners will then pay tax on their share of the profit – the partnership itself does not pay tax. While preparing income tax returns may not be in the job description of a financial accountant, knowing how to account for income taxes is. Because financial information (for financial statements) prepared according to generally accepted accounting practice (GAAP; see Chapter 4) differs from financial information prepared for income tax returns, revenue and expense differences may exist between the two. In this chapter, you discover why the differences exist and why they're classed as either *temporary* or *permanent* differences.

In addition, you discover how to account for deferred tax, which directly relates to temporary differences. I also cover the issue of *timing differences* that will also give rise to deferred tax (particularly in the UK). I also discuss losses, which serve to reduce taxable profit in previous or subsequent years.

Finally, you see an example of how the same company has different profit before taxes using financial versus tax methods to record accounting transactions.

The amount of tax that a business pays is based on profit which is not to be confused with *revenue*. Revenue in the context of financial accounting is sales or turnover and I discuss the type of profit that is used to calculate tax in the next section 'Identifying Accounting Profit versus Taxable Profit'.

For the purposes of this chapter, I keep things simple and only stick to tax relating to companies. Any additional tax issues are best left to the tax people or your tax studies.

Identifying Accounting Profit versus Taxable Profit

A company's profit as computed using financial accounting often differs from its profit as calculated for tax purposes. That's because some items that are included in the financial statements of a company that make up profit or loss are often not allowable for the purposes of computing *taxable* profit or loss. These differences primarily arise because accounting standards may say one thing, whilst tax legislation may dictate another. Consider the following two sets of users:

- **Accounting standards:** As a financial accountant preparing or reviewing financial statements for a business, you follow the standards set by regulatory bodies such as the International Accounting Standards Board (IASB), which I explain in Chapter 4. A tax accountant, on the other hand, follows tax legislation issued by the government and applied by HM Revenue and Customs (HMRC).

- **Users:** As I note in many chapters in this book, the users of a company's financial statements are usually individuals and businesses. They may be considering whether to invest in or lend money to the company. The users of a corporation tax return, on the other hand, are usually governmental entities such as HMRC.

Figuring out accounting profit

You report accounting profit on the company's income statement (sometimes known as *profit and loss account*; see Chapter 10), which has different sections, starting with revenue and ending with net profit. The relevant section of the income statement for this chapter is the part fairly close to the end of the income statement, 'profit before tax'. This section is also known as 'profit on ordinary activities before taxation' or simply 'pre-tax profit'.

Profit before tax reflects the final result of subtracting all business-related expenses and losses from all business-related revenues and gains. You determine this type of profit before tax by following GAAP. In Figure 18-1, you see a portion of a company's income statement showing that it had profit before tax of £10,000.

Figure 18-1:
Financial
profit for
corporation
taxes.

	£
Profit before tax	10,000
Income tax expense	2,300
Profit for the year from continuing operations	7,700

Before you can arrive at the final total for the company's net profit or loss (known as *post-tax profit*), you have to reduce profit before taxes by subtracting a provision for the corporation tax the company will pay when it files its corporation tax return. In Figure 18-1, I assume a tax rate of 23 per cent (as that is the corporation tax rate that's expected to be in force in the UK in 2013/14), so the company's provision for income taxes line equals £2,300. Usually the amount of corporation tax due is worked out by preparing a separate schedule on file known as the *corporation tax computation* (commonly referred to as the *tax comp*). This tax comp takes profit before tax as reported in the company's income statement and adjusts it for items in the financial statements that aren't allowable for tax purposes (usually depreciation) and grants allowances that are allowable for tax purposes that aren't in the financial statements (such as capital allowances) to arrive at a taxable profit on which tax is then worked out using the relevant percentage.

The rate of corporation tax in the UK will drop again on 1 April 2014 to 21 per cent which was announced by the Chancellor of the Exchequer in his Autumn Statement on 5 December 2012.

Taking a look at taxable profit

Tax accountants work out taxable profit using rules other than GAAP; they use the Corporation Taxes Act 2010. Actually tax legislation in the UK is renowned for being extremely complex (in fact, some critics say the UK has the most complex tax system in the world!).

So what's the point of all this taxing malarkey? Before you start worrying about the government incurring all sorts of pointless items of expenditure, stop to consider how you got to work or to your college this morning. Did you take public transport? Or drive on a motorway? Have you recently been in hospital? Do your children attend a state school? Do you know anyone who receives Disability Living Allowance or Jobseeker's Allowance? All these aspects of our lives (and many more) are subsidised by the government through the taxes it collects.

Tax accountants report taxable profit on a corporation tax return. For a company, this is form CT600 *Company Tax Return*. You can download form CT600 from HMRC by visiting www.hmrc.gov.uk.

Like individuals, companies in the UK have a *sliding scale tax rate*, which means their tax rate goes up based on taxable profit. The amount of tax (at the time of writing) based on taxable profit is shown in Figure 18-2. For example, if the company has taxable profit on 31 March 2013 of £92,500, corporation tax (excluding any marginal rate relief that is outside the scope of this book), the tax charge would be £18,500 (£92,500 ×20 per cent).

Rates for financial years starting on 1 April

Rate	2012	2013
Small profits rate	20%	20%
Small profits rate can be claimed by qualifying companies with profits at a rate not exceeding	£300,000	£300,000
Main rate of corporation tax	24%	23%

Figure 18-2: Corporation tax rates.

Explaining why the two types of profits differ

Accountants use a bit of code to talk about the two ways in which business profit is calculated. The phrase *book values* refers to financial statements prepared using GAAP. The phrase *tax values* (logically enough) refers to calculations prepared for tax purposes. In some cases, the difference between book and tax values, such as profit figures, is huge: a business may have a high amount of accounting profit but have a negative taxable loss.

The gap between accounting profit and taxable profit is generally caused by three types of differences: temporary differences, permanent differences and loss carryforwards/carrybacks. I explain the first two here and the third in the 'Taking Advantage of Tax Losses' section, later in this chapter.

Tackling temporary differences

Temporary differences are items that will balance out over time so the book values and tax values eventually match. For example, a business reports some of its items of revenue or expense in one period for accounting purposes (because GAAP says it has to) and in an earlier or later period for tax purposes (because tax law says it has to). For this reason, accounting geeks may refer to temporary differences as *timing differences*.

Quite a few things can give rise to a temporary difference between book values and tax values. Here are four of the most common events:

- **Pension contributions:** A company may defer payment of its monthly pension contributions for a few months (for example, if it's experiencing cash flow difficulties), but in the year-end accounts it may recognise the pension arrears as a liability owed to the pension company, with the corresponding debit going to pension costs in the income statement, which will reduce the profit (or increase a loss). In the UK, pension contributions can only be deducted for tax purposes when the contributions are actually *paid*.

- **Depreciation:** Here's an example of the most commonly encountered temporary difference. For accounting purposes, the company uses a straight-line depreciation method, and for tax it uses a more accelerated method (such as a 100 per cent annual investment allowance, which means the company can write off the whole value of a qualifying asset for tax purposes in the year of acquisition). (See Chapter 12 for a full discussion of depreciation.) At the same time, financial depreciation methods may require the same asset to be written off over ten years. So, in other words, in some instances tax legislation may allow for writing off of the full cost of the asset in year 1 while for accounting purposes GAAP depreciation (in this case, straight-line over ten years) must be used.

- **Estimates:** Estimates are any expenses the company thinks is a reasonable amount to provide for in the financial statements. The main estimate that's generally not allowable for tax purposes is allowances for receivables (that is, bad debt provisions). Often a company will have an arbitrary percentage (often between 2 and 5 per cent) in mind of total receivables that it considers will not be recoverable; it then makes a provision for this bad debt in the accounts. General allowances against receivables are not allowable for tax purposes, but *specific* allowances (those attributed to specific customers) are. The company will not be able to make a deduction for tax purposes in its corporation tax return for general allowances until it actually incurs the cost.

- **Capital losses:** A company can buy and sell investments in other companies. However, if a company sells shares or other investments and has an overall loss on the transactions for the year, for tax purposes the company can't deduct this capital loss. Don't panic! The loss can be offset against any future capital gains. For financial accounting, the entire loss serves to reduce net profit.

Reviewing permanent differences

A *permanent difference* is an accounting transaction the company reports for accounting purposes but can't – and never will be able to – report for tax purposes. While GAAP permits reporting the transaction, tax legislation does not.

Quite a few accounting transactions lead to a permanent difference. In this section, I discuss five common ones:

- ✓ **Entertaining:** A company's directors or management may take its customers for a night on the tiles, or to a restaurant to thank them for their business. This type of entertaining is always disallowable for tax purposes. (However, staff entertaining up to a value of (at the time of writing) £150 per head which meets certain conditions is allowable.)

- ✓ **Clothes to meet a specific dress code:** Such clothes are not allowable for tax purposes because HMRC states that people must wear some sort of clothing regardless of the specific requirements of certain professions (these 'conflicts' are often coined *duality of purpose* in tax 'speak') and aren't allowable as a deduction for tax purposes.

- ✓ **Fines:** Fines for illegal activities aren't tax deductible, such as pollution or criminal acts. Certain penalties imposed by HMRC (such as those for late payment) are also disallowable for tax purposes.

- ✓ **Training costs:** Training costs that allow staff to develop new skills or knowledge aren't allowable for tax purposes as HMRC regards such new skills or knowledge as being of a capital nature rather than an expense.

- ✓ **Irrecoverable loan to a member of staff:** A loan made to a member of staff that's written off is not allowable for the purposes of tax (unless the trade in question is one of making loans).

Explaining deferred tax

Differences between expenses recognised in the financial statements versus expenses recognised for the purposes of tax due to temporary differences between book values and tax values are called *deferred tax assets and liabilities*. Only temporary differences lead to deferred tax assets and liabilities.

Say that a business has one or more temporary differences. For financial reporting under GAAP, the company has a corporation tax liability of £25,000, but its tax calculations show the business has tax payable of £16,000. The difference between the two is £9,000 (£25,000 – £16,000), and that amount is the company's deferred tax amount.

The calculation is fairly easy to understand, but how can you tell if the £9,000 is an asset or a liability? When tax expense is more than tax payable, the £9,000 is a deferred tax liability. It's a liability because the £9,000 represents income taxes that will be payable in the future after all the temporary differences even out. Because the amount represents money the business will eventually owe to the government, it is a liability.

If the figures in our example had been the reverse, with tax payable being £25,000 instead of £16,000, the £9,000 difference would be a deferred tax *asset* because tax payable would be less in the future after all temporary differences are reduced to zero. So at some point in the future, the £9,000 will serve to reduce the amount of tax payable to the Chancellor.

Taking Advantage of Tax Losses

A business has a taxable loss when deductions on its corporation tax return are more than in the accounts themselves. This situation doesn't necessarily have to start ringing the alarm bells. It can happen for many reasons that are relatively common, such as directors paying themselves a bonus at year-end based on pre-tax profit immediately prior to the bonus, or purchasing an expensive asset immediately prior to the year-end to take advantage of enhanced capital allowances that may be available (this is particularly the case when good tax planning has occurred prior to the year-end). For financial accounting, an accounting loss is an occurrence that's really noted only by investors and lenders. And depending on the facts and circumstances surrounding the loss, both sets of users may not be in the least bit dismayed. For example, many drug companies post net losses while doing the research to develop new drugs that will eventually be extremely profitable in the future.

For tax accounting, a taxable loss reduces the amount of tax the company has to pay on its profits in the past or going forward into the future. HMRC's rules regarding carrying the loss forward or backward are extensive. However, the next two sections provide the basic background of these two reliefs.

Identifying loss carrybacks

Should a business opt to carry a loss back to the prior year, it needs to indicate on the current year's corporation tax return (the year in which the loss arises) that it wishes to carry back the loss to the previous year as well as provide an accompanying letter to HMRC notifying it of the company's intention to carry back the loss. Once the loss is carried back it should produce an overpayment of corporation tax in the previous year, which will be refundable to the company. For example, a company has a taxable loss of $15,000 in 2013 and opts to carry back the loss to 2012, a year in which the company had taxable profit of $30,000. Notifying HMRC of the loss on the current year's corporation tax return and carrying back the loss reduces taxable profit for 2012 to $15,000 ($30,000 – $15,000), reducing corporation tax payable. The company will get a refund when HMRC processes the amended return. To put this expected refund in the books, you prepare a journal entry (see Chapter 5) debiting an asset account such as 'corporation tax refund receivable' and crediting income tax expense in the income statement for the tax effect of $3,600. Figure 18-3 shows how to work out the tax effect.

Tax legislation in the UK says that losses can only be carried back to the extent that they cannot be utilised against profits of the same period and the specified period is the 12 months immediately preceding the accounting period in which the loss arose. Losses can only be carried back against profits of accounting periods during which the same trade was being carried on.

	Year	Taxable Profit/ (Loss)	Tax Rate	Tax Paid
Figure 18-3: Calculating corporation tax refund receivable for a loss carryback.	2012	30,000	24%	7,200
	2013	(15,000)	23%	0

The taxable loss £15,000 in 2013 is carried back to 2012 which will trigger a refund of (£30,000 minus £15,000) £15,000 x 24% = £3,600.

Understanding loss carryforwards

A *carryforward* is when the company carries a loss forward to offset against taxable profit in subsequent years. This decision can happen when the company has no taxable profit in the prior year and has nothing to carry the loss back to.

For example, in 2013, a company has taxable net sales of £1 million and tax-deductible expenses of £1.25 million, resulting in a taxable loss of £250,000. If the company has taxable profit of £400,000 in 2014, its actual taxable profit after carrying the loss forward is only £150,000 (£400,000 – £250,000).

No letter to HMRC is needed in this case because the company reports the loss carried forward as a deduction on the tax return for the year in which it takes it (the company may attach a *loss memo* to the return showing HMRC how the loss has been utilised in the current year). To get this transaction in the books in the year the loss arises, you debit the 'deferred tax asset' account and credit 'deferred tax charge' in the income statement for the tax effect of £57,500. Figure 18-4 shows how to calculate the tax effect for this loss carryforward.

	Year	Taxable Profit/ (Loss)	Tax Rate	Tax Paid
Figure 18-4: Calculating corporation tax refund receivable for a loss carry-forward.	2012	(300,000)	24%	0
	2013	(250,000)	23%	0

Loss carried forward multiplied by the tax rate in 2013 of 23% equals £57,500.

	2014	150,000	23%	34,500

Total tax paid in 2014 after deducting the loss carryforward is £34,500.

Presenting a Side-by-Side Comparison of Book Values and Tax Calculations

Although I've done my best to keep my explanations simple and clear in this chapter, you may still find the difference between financial accounting and tax accounting confusing unless you can see examples of how both look using the same facts and circumstances. So before I end this chapter, I walk you through a simple comparison between a corporation tax return and income statement preparation. The comparison is laid out in Figure 18-5.

Comparison of Income Statement to Corporation Tax Return
For the Year-Ended 31 December 2012

Figure 18-5:
Comparing figures calculated for an income statement to those used for tax purposes.

	Income Statement	Tax Return
Revenue	250,000	200,000 (a)
Cost of sales	75,000	82,000 (b)
Gross profit	175,000	118,000
Distribution costs	43,000	30,000 (c)
Fine	25,000	0 (d)
Profit before tax	107,000	88,000
Income tax expense	24,610	20,240
Profit after tax	82,390	67,760

Here's a list of the temporary differences that exist for the example in Figure 18-5:

✔ Revenue contains some income which, under tax legislation, is taxable on receipt. However, GAAP requires the recognition of all revenue receivable (in other words, revenue is recorded when it's earned and realisable). The difference is £50,000, as shown on line (a).

✔ The company purchases new manufacturing equipment. Using the straight-line method, depreciation for the purpose of financial statements is £8,000. The tax authority has granted capital allowances on the same piece of equipment amounting to £15,000. Under GAAP, you take depreciation of manufacturing equipment to the 'cost of sales' account (see Chapters 10 and 12). This temporary difference reflects on line (b) of Figure 18-5.

✔ The allowance for receivables (also known as a *bad debt provision*), which is the amount the company estimates it will not be able to collect from customers, is £13,000. The company deducts this amount in the income statement as bad debt expense. It cannot have the deduction in its corporation tax return because it is a *general* allowance rather than a *specific* allowance. See line (c) of Figure 18-5 to spot the difference.

One permanent difference also comes into play. The company was fined £25,000 by the local council of the town in which its manufacturing plant is located for dumping toxic waste without a licence. This permanent difference shows up on line (d).

Look at the final three lines of Figure 18-5 to see how these temporary and permanent differences affect the company's profit after tax. Assume that its tax rate is 23 per cent. It's very interesting to see how the same company can have such a wide variance in post-tax profit depending on whether the financial accounting or tax accounting rules apply!

Taking Deferred Tax Liabilities or Assets to the Balance Sheet

In the earlier section 'Explaining deferred tax', I note that temporary differences create one of two balance sheet accounts: a 'deferred tax liability' or a 'deferred tax asset'. How do these two accounts show up on the balance sheet?

You classify deferred tax as current or long term depending on the specific asset or liability to which it relates. For example, the estimate for 'allowance for receivables' ties to trade receivables, which is a current asset. So this portion of the deferred tax will be current.

If the deferred tax doesn't specifically relate to any asset or liability, it's generally classified as a long-term (non-current) liability. Chapter 7 shows a complete balance sheet with these accounts.

You may be wondering whether you can offset a deferred tax asset and liability accounts. For example, your current deferred tax asset is £7,800 and your deferred tax liability is £5,400. Can you just show the difference of £2,400 (£7,800 – £5,400) as a deferred tax asset? The answer is it depends. FRS 19 *Deferred Tax* at paragraph 125(a) to (c) states that deferred tax debits and credits may be regarded as capable of being offset, and thus presented as a single net asset or liability only if:

✔ They relate to the same tax authority.

✔ They arise within the same taxable entities or within different taxable entities that are entitled to settle their tax liabilities on a net basis.

✔ The timing differences giving rise to a deferred tax asset reverse before or at the same time as those giving rise to a deferred tax liability.

IAS 12 *Income Taxes* takes a different approach in that the standard states that deferred tax assets and liabilities should be offset on the balance sheet only if the entity has the legal right to settle on a net basis and it's levied by the same taxing authority on the same entity or different entities that intend to realise the asset and settle the liability at the same time.

Seeing the Difference between UK GAAP and IFRS for Deferred Tax

Current UK GAAP at FRS 19 operates on a *timing difference* approach, which means that deferred tax is based on when income and expense hit the income statement (profit and loss account). IAS 12 *Income Taxes* operates on a *temporary difference* approach, which means that deferred tax is based on when assets and liabilities are received and settled, so IAS 12 is more balance sheet orientated.

The new UK GAAP, which is due to come into play for accounting periods commencing on or after 1 January 2015, will use a bit of a half-way house between the two – this will be known as the *timing difference plus* approach. Under this approach the current timing difference method will be enhanced to take into account additional deferred tax considerations relating to investment property revaluations, fair values (market values) on business combinations and unremitted funds being sent to the company from overseas subsidiaries or associates.

Chapter 19

Accounting for Leases

Most businesses need tangible, fixed assets (internationally known as *non-current assets*) for their day-to-day operations. Rather than shelling out the money to purchase all the necessary fixed assets, many companies opt to lease equipment instead. A major advantage to leasing rather than buying fixed assets is that leasing allows for 100 per cent financing, which greatly increases a company's cash flow (see Chapter 11).

In this chapter, you look at leasing from the point of view of both the *lessor* (the party owning the leased asset) and the *lessee* (the party acquiring the right to use the asset). You learn the operating and finance lease methods that a lessee uses to record leases, as well as the journal entries a lessee makes to record a lease in the financial statements under both these methods. You also receive a brief introduction to the classification of leases for the lessor. Specifically, I give you the lowdown on how a lessor handles operating, finance and sale and leaseback leases.

In this chapter, I cover everything you need to know to handle lease transactions, whether it be in your accountancy studies, or in your day-to-day work. You may also pick up some personal tips along the way – hurrah!

Reviewing Lease Basics

Whether a business is a small family-run company or a large motor vehicle manufacturer, it needs some basic *fixed assets*: tangible assets the company expects to use for more than a year. Common examples include computers, furniture and office fixtures, but depending on the type of business, the fixed assets required can be much more extensive. For example, a business making foodstuffs needs all sorts of mixing, cooking and packaging equipment. And a large retail clothing shop needs a significant amount of fixtures like display cases and shelving. (A retailer may also lease its shop.) As I explain in Chapter 7, on a company's balance sheet, such fixed (or non-current), tangible assets are grouped in a category called 'property, plant and equipment' (PPE).

Businesses won't always buy their PPE; sometimes they lease these assets. You may have entered into a lease yourself at one time or another. Maybe you're renting a flat or a car. Perhaps you rent your television and the terms of the lease say that, after the specified lease term, you pay a small sum and then become the owner of the TV.

Business leases are a bit more complex than most personal leases, so you can't always compare a business lease to a personal one. (However, if you've ever leased a car rather than financing it or purchasing it outright, you probably have some understanding of how convoluted the lease process can be.) When you rent a house for personal use, you have no claim to that house after your lease expires. But depending on how a business lease is set up, the company *could* be the eventual owner of a piece of leased equipment. The terms of the business lease also have an effect on how financial accountants account for the lease payments.

Identifying the advantages of leasing

Why would a business lease instead of buy its equipment? Here are some key motivators:

- **Ker-ching!** That's the sound of money shaking around in the company's piggy bank. A major advantage to leasing rather than buying is this: a company usually doesn't have to incur a large outlay of cash at the beginning of the lease the way it would have to with an outright purchase.

  In fact, many business leases come with 100 per cent financing terms, which means no money changes hands at the inception of the lease. Can you imagine what a boost to cash flow this can be? Of course, the business has to make the lease payments each month. But the assumption is that the company makes the payments from enhanced revenues it earns from the new equipment as a result of the lease.

- **Avoiding obsolete equipment:** Another advantage to leasing is working around obsolescence, which means the company anticipates frequently replacing the fixed asset. For example, swapping computer equipment certainly comes in handy for businesses which need to stay up to date with new and faster computer processing technology. The basic purpose of constantly updating computer hardware is to maximise employee productivity.

✓ **Having asset flexibility:** Say that the chief executive officer of a company decides to change the company car she's driving. Or say that the employee for whom a company leases a vehicle leaves the company. In either situation, with a leased vehicle the company doesn't have to worry about advertising the car for sale and trying to find a buyer; it just sends the car back to the leasing company.

✓ **Tax savings (possibly):** Depending on how the business structures a lease, tax advantages may be possible. I discuss this topic later in the chapter in the 'Looking at operating leases' section. For now, just remember that you treat operating leases like rentals, expensing the entire lease payment when the business makes it to the income statement.

✓ **Keeping the liability off the books:** Leases may provide *off-balance sheet financing*. This phrase means that the company's financial obligation (its *liability*, as I explain in Chapter 8) does not reflect on the balance sheet. This fact can affect a financial statement user's evaluation of how solvent the company is because that person will be unaware of the debt.

Off-balance sheet financing is a particularly prevalent problem where leases are concerned and much is trying to be done to stamp out the act of off-balance sheet finance.

Some additional economic advantages to leasing can come into play. For example, it may be the case that the equipment the business needs to make its products isn't available for purchase – the company that actually owns the equipment only wants to lease it. This situation may occur if the piece of equipment is highly technical or the company makes more money through leasing than through selling the item.

Introducing the lessor and lessee

Before I get into the nitty-gritty of accounting for leases, I want to provide a brief lease introduction. Don't worry – it doesn't involve anything too complex! You simply need to know who the cast of characters are in a lease. Knowing who's who in a lease transaction makes the subject easier to understand.

A lease always has two parties sitting on either side of the table: a lessor and a lessee. The *lessor* is the party who owns the fixed asset. The *lessee* is the party who wants to acquire the right to use the fixed asset. Consider deciding to buy another car and renting it out to your mate, Les: Les acquires the car to use it for social and business purposes and therefore is the lessee and you, as the owner of the car, are the lessor.

One interesting fact about leases is that the lessor doesn't necessarily own the fixed asset immediately prior to entering into a lease agreement. Sometimes purchasing the fixed asset is dependent upon finalising the lease agreement. In other words, part of the agreement is that the lessor commits to purchasing the leased asset. This situation may happen if the piece of equipment is expensive or not in high demand. Rather than keeping potentially leasable equipment in inventory that may become obsolete fairly quickly, the lessor advertises that it can lease the asset and then purchases the asset only when it has an interested potential lessee. This approach makes a lot of sense because it cuts down on the expense to store the equipment and increases the lessor's cash flow; the lessor doesn't shell out the dosh to purchase the asset until that asset is poised to become a source of revenue.

How a company accounts for leased assets differs depending on whether the company is the lessor or the lessee. Many of you reading this book may only have come across leases from the viewpoint of the lessee, so pay close attention to the next section. But to get the complete picture, make sure you check out the last section of this chapter, which gives you the lowdown on accounting for lease transactions from the standpoint of the lessor.

Accounting by the Lessee

Classifying a lease between a finance lease and an operating lease can be a tricky exercise. The correct classification depends on the *substance* of the transaction (by *substance,* I mean the commercial reality) as opposed to the legal form of the transaction. So it's not just a case of let's look at the lease agreement and there you have it – there's a bit more thought required. Clear as mud? Don't panic, keep on reading and the mud will start to clear. The lessee records the lease agreement and lease payments differently depending on whether the lease is a finance lease or an operating lease. The major differences between the two types of leases involve certain aspects of ownership and immediate versus delayed expensing to the income statement. Keep reading to find out what I mean.

Looking at operating leases

An *operating lease* has no characteristics of ownership and is, therefore, a walk in the park to account for. Now, when I say *no characteristics of ownership*, what I mean is that the *risks and reward of ownership* remain with the lessor. The risks of ownership are the costs of maintaining the asset if it breaks down, maintaining it routinely, and the cost of replacing the asset if it breaks down beyond repair. The reward of ownership is the income that the asset brings. Here's an example of how to account for an operating lease: Gabriella's Garments leases sewing machines for five years to make men's raincoats. At the end of the five years, Gabriella's Garments has no further obligation to keep or make payments on the sewing machines. Gabriella's Garments returns the machines to the lessor in the condition dictated by the lease agreement. The lessor also has to maintain the sewing machines during the five-year lease at its own expense on a periodic basis.

This type of lease doesn't affect the company's balance sheet as either an asset or a liability. The cost of the lease payments goes in the income statement as 'rental expense'. For example, if the lease agreement provides for a monthly lease payment of £5,000, each month the accountant at Gabriella's Garments debits 'sewing machine rental' (an income statement account; see Chapter 10) and credits cash at bank (a balance sheet account; see Chapter 7) for £5,000.

In other words, this transaction increases expenses by the total amount of the lease payment. Your cash account is reduced when the lease payment is made. Think that's too easy? Well, you'd be right because that's the extent of accounting for operating leases. Operating lease rentals are generally allowable for corporation tax purposes as well – bonus!

Walking through finance leases

Finance leases are quite a bit more complicated to account for than operating leases because they have characteristics of ownership. Here's what I mean: the lessee assumes all the responsibilities, benefits and risks of owning the leased asset. Therefore, the cost of the leased asset goes on the lessee's balance sheet as both an asset (property, plant and equipment) and a liability ('finance lease obligations').

Many companies operate under the misguided impression that as long as the lease agreement states it is an operating lease, they can treat it as such in their financial statements. Not true. If the lease agreement contains certain characteristics, it's deemed as being a finance lease. Financial accountants always ask to see any lease agreement for which they have to account. Company management could erroneously treat a finance lease as if it's an operating lease. The reason can be as simple as management not being aware that significant differences exist in the treatment of these two leases.

Operating lease changes are a-comin'

The amount of off-balance sheet lease obligations is estimated to be in the *billions* for publicly traded companies around the world. (Yikes!) For this reason, in 2010 the US standard-setters, the Financial Accounting Standards Board (FASB), and the International Accounting Standards Board (IASB) initiated a joint project to develop a new approach to lease accounting to ensure that assets and liabilities arising under leases extending 12 months after the balance sheet date are recognised in a company's statement of financial position (balance sheet). An agreement was reached on 13 June 2012 whereby some lease contracts would be accounted for under a similar approach to the exposure draft issued in 2010, meaning that the vast majority of leases which are entered into for periods of more than one year would appear on a company's balance sheet. At the time of writing, a standard had not been issued but is planned for issuance in mid-2013 (with a potential implementation date in 2015/16). If these proposals affect you, be sure to keep a close eye on www. iasb.org for further developments in this area as they're pretty radical changes.

Spotting characteristics of finance leases

Lease transactions are dealt with in IAS 17 *Leases* (if you're using UK GAAP, you'll need SSAP 21 *Accounting for Leases and Hire Purchase Contracts*). For consistency, I stick with the requirements of IAS 17, but SSAP 21 pretty much says the same thing as IAS 17 (with a bit of a difference that I look at later). To guide you in your lease identification task, here are the eight characteristics of finance leases in IAS 17 – only *one* of which needs to be met in order for the lease to be finance:

- **The lease transfers ownership to the lessee at the end of the lease term.** For example, ABC leases a machine from XYZ. After the signing of the lease, the machine is considered the property of ABC. Additionally, because ABC now owns this piece of equipment, it depreciates the equipment for financial statement and tax purposes. (*Depreciation* is the process of spreading the cost of the equipment over its useful life; see Chapter 12.)

- **The lease contains a bargain purchase option at the end of the term.** A *bargain purchase* means that the lease has a clause allowing the lessee to purchase the leased asset for an amount sufficiently lower than its expected *fair market value*, which is what an unconnected third party would pay for the same asset in an open marketplace on the date this purchase option comes into play.

You may be wondering how to determine the amount for 'sufficiently lower'. Unfortunately, generally accepted accounting practice (GAAP) doesn't give an exact formula for this figure. Financial accountants in practice take into consideration many factors, such as the age and condition of the asset, when setting a figure for the 'sufficiently lower' criteria.

✔ **The lease is for the major part of the asset's useful economic life.** *Economic life* is merely an estimate of how long the lessee thinks the leased asset will be useable for its intended purpose. So if the estimated economic life of the leased asset is 12 years, you treat a 9-year lease as a finance lease.

✔ **The present value of the minimum lease payments at the start of the lease is at least equal to substantially all of the fair value of the leased asset.** *Present value* means the current value (at the signing of the lease) of the total number of lease payments for the asset. Because this subject is a bit tough to chew, I explain it with an example – keep reading!

For the purposes of UK GAAP, SSAP 21 at paragraph 22 says that the present value of the minimum lease payments in a finance lease will normally be at least 90 per cent of the fair value of the leased asset. This differs from IAS 17, which does not prescribe a numerical benchmark guideline. However, the new UK GAAP, which is due to hit the streets in the UK for accounting periods commencing on or after 1 January 2015, also doesn't prescribe a 90 per cent benchmark.

✔ **The lease is of such a specialised nature that only the lessee can use it.** Where a company is in a relatively rare industry it may require assets that are bespoke to its activities. In this case, the leased asset is probably a finance lease.

✔ **If the lessee can cancel the lease, the lessor's costs associated with cancellation are paid by the lessee**. This arrangement is similar to a mobile phone contract – you find a better deal with another mobile phone provider and you cancel your contract early. The mobile phone company you're leaving charges you an early termination fee – this is the same as the early termination fee a lessor will charge a lessee and, if this is the case, the lease is indicative of a finance lease.

✔ **Gains or losses from fluctuations in the asset's fair value accrue to the lessee**. Here, any uplift in the asset's market value belongs to the lessee, not the lessor. On the flip side, any downward valuations also belong to the lessee.

✔ **The lessee can continue to rent the asset at the end of the term for a rental value that's substantially lower than market value.** Known as a 'peppercorn' rent, in this situation a lease term expires and the lessee continues to use the asset, but pays the lessor a rental that's significantly less than what an unconnected third party would otherwise have to pay.

Figuring present value

If you're a student accountant, the chances are your textbook contains a table for calculating the present value of an annuity of £1. An *annuity* is a series of payments made over time. You can freely download present value tables from the Internet. So, let's say you've been asked to work out if a lease agreement satisfies the fourth characteristic of a finance lease – that of having lease payments with a present value that's at least equal to substantially all of the fair value of the asset.

Here are the facts and circumstances of this problem:

- ✔ The fair value of the asset is £205,000.
- ✔ The lease term is for five years.
- ✔ The lease payments are £50,000 per year.
- ✔ The interest rate on the lease is 10 per cent. The *interest rate* is the rate of interest the company incurs if it finances a purchase rather than leases the asset.

Go to the table in the present value tables that shows the present value of an annuity of £1. Find the 10 per cent column, and go down that column until you get to Period 5. The number you will get to is 3.7908. Next, work out £50,000 multiplied by 3.7908. This calculation gives you £189,540, which is your present value of the lease payments. Is £189,540 substantially all of the fair value of the leased asset? Well, at 92 per cent (£189,540/£205,000 × 100) it sure looks that way! So you definitely have a finance lease.

Presenting a finance lease in the financial statements

In this section, I show you how to make journal entries (see Chapter 5) for a finance lease transaction and how to reflect a finance lease on the lessee's balance sheet.

Right, so first up: the journal entries, which I show in Figure 19-1. The journal entry is a three-part process involving recording the acquisition of the leased asset, divvying up the lease payment between capital and interest, and recording depreciation for the leased asset. For this example, I use the same facts that I use in the previous section on calculating present value.

Finance leases affect both the asset and liability sections of the balance sheet. Referencing the journal entries from Figure 19-1, you record the £189,540 leased asset in the fixed asset section (see Chapter 7) of the balance sheet. You also have to record the obligation to the lessor as a liability (see Chapter 8).

		Debit	Credit
1	Equipment	189,540	
	Finance lease obligations		189,540

To record the intitial acquisition

2	Finance lease obligations	31,046	
	Interest expense	18,954	
	Cash at bank		50,000

To record the annual lease payment. Interest expense equals £189,540 x 10%

3	Depreciation expense	37,908	
	Accumulated depreciation		37,908

To record annual straight-line depreciation. No residual value over the lease term of 5 years (£189,540 / 5).

Figure 19-1:
Recording a finance lease transaction.

Accounting by the Lessor

You'll probably only get involved with accounting for a lease as a lessee – unless you work for a company that specialises in leasing out assets. But lessees get more attention than the lessors, who tend to be left out altogether. So, while this subject goes beyond what you need to know for your day-to-day dealings with leases from the lessee's viewpoint, I want to give you a brief heads up on how to handle leases from the lessor viewpoint, so you can see the accounting issues from both sides of the fence.

The lessor decides how much it charges for leasing an asset and structures its lease based on many different criteria. Obviously, the most important criterion to the lessor is profit: how much this lease will increase its bottom line figure. The lessor also looks at the credit rating of the lessee and how long a lease term the lessee requires. For example, the lessor will probably charge a potential lessee with a bad credit rating more than it would charge a lessee with a good credit record.

Lessors have three major classifications of lease agreements: operating, finance and sale and leaseback. Just as it's easy for the lessee to account for an operating lease (see the 'Looking at operating leases' section earlier in this chapter), it's easy for the lessor to account for an operating lease. However, the accounting for both finance and sale and leaseback transactions is very complex. Due to the complexity of these transactions, if you're ever unsure of how to deal with these in real life, the best advice I can give you is to let your manager or another person with experience in this area deal with the accounting issues as they're prone to errors that can be very costly to sort out.

Operating leases

A lessor has to look at the precise criteria surrounding each lease to make sure it can account for a lease as operating. And what are these precise criteria? In a nutshell, they're as follows:

- ✔ **First, the lessor has to determine if the lease transfers any of the benefits of ownership to the lessee.** (I discuss what has to happen to satisfy this criterion in the 'Spotting characteristics of finance leases' section earlier in this chapter.)

- ✔ **If the first criterion is met, the lease has to pass a second test before it can be classified as operating.** To pass this test, both the following conditions have to exist:

- ✔ **The lessor has to be reasonably sure it will be able to collect the minimum lease payments from the lessee.** The bare-bones definition of the *minimum lease payments* is the minimum rental payments the lessor must pay the lease over the term. *Reasonably sure* means what a sensible person can expect to happen under normal circumstances. In other words, the lessor doesn't believe the lessee is going to close up shop and do a runner during the lease term.

- ✔ **The lessor has substantially completed all its requirements contained in the lease agreement.** For example, the lessor has delivered the leased equipment according to the terms of the lease. Additionally, any future costs associated with the lease are reasonably predictable. For example, the lease has a clause requiring the lessor to pay up to £500 for repairs taking place during the term of the lease.

Finance leases

A *finance lease* exists when these two criteria are met:

- ✔ The lease does not meet the criteria to be classified as operating.

- ✔ The lessor realises interest income, but not profit or loss, on the transaction.

The lessor's cost for the asset is the same as the fair (sometimes referred to as *market*) value of the asset, so the lessor's profit on the transaction is limited to the interest income it earns while the lease is in operation.

For example, Alex's Architraves Limited needs a certain type of equipment to make its architraves but doesn't have the money to purchase the equipment itself. Alex goes to a leasing company that agrees to purchase the asset and enter into a lease agreement with Alex's Architraves Limited.

In substance, this type of lease is the equivalent of an outright loan. The lessor uses an *amortisation schedule*, which shows how much of the lease payment goes to capital (sometimes called *principal*) versus interest, and recording the interest portion as revenue whilst reducing the amount of 'lease receivable' carried in its books by the capital amount.

Sale and leaseback transactions

A sale and leaseback transaction occurs when a company transfers legal title to an asset to a third party, but still retains use of that asset on a lease. The main reason a company will enter into a sale and leaseback transaction is to raise finance. The accounting treatment of a sale and leaseback transaction will depend on whether the leaseback is finance or operating.

Sale and leaseback as a finance lease

If the sale and leaseback is a finance lease, the substance of the transaction is that no sale has taken place (in other words, risks and rewards of ownership have not passed from the original lessee). Any excess of sales proceeds over the carrying amount of the asset subject to the sale and leaseback transaction (the profit on disposal) is not recognised as income of a seller-lessee. The profit is instead recognised as a liability (deferred) and released to the income statement over the life of the lease.

For example, ABC Limited disposes of an asset with a net book value of £70,000 and the sales proceeds are received at fair value of £120,000. The useful economic life of the asset is five years and there are five annual rentals of £28,000. On disposal, cash will be received of £120,000, which is a debit to cash at bank. You then remove the asset from the books by crediting fixed assets at net book value with £70,000 and the deferred profit of (£120,000 – £70,000) £50,000 is amortised over the lease term.

Finally, you'll then recognise a non-current asset of £120,000 with a corresponding lease payable of £120,000. Each year in the income statement you'll charge depreciation of (£120,000/5 years) £24,000. Interest will be charged to the income statement of (5 × £28,000) – (£120,000)/5 = £4,000, and you'll release the deferred profit over a five-year period at (£50,000/5 years) £10,000 per year.

Sale and leaseback as an operating lease

Where the sale and leaseback transaction is an operating lease, the substance of the transaction is that there is a sale and profit may be recognised. If the rentals and the sales price are established at fair value, a normal sale transaction has occurred and any profit or loss on disposal is recognised in the income statement immediately.

If the sale price is below fair value, any profit or loss is recognised immediately – *but* if the loss is compensated by future rentals at below market price, the loss is deferred and *amortised* (released to the income statement) in proportion to the rental payments over the period for which the asset is expected to be used. If the sale price is above fair value, the excess of fair value is deferred and amortised over the period for which the asset is expected to be used.

For example, assume that ABC Ltd has an asset with a book value of £70,000 and the fair value of the asset is £100,000. It would like to enter into a sale and operating leaseback arrangement and has been offered a sales price of £100,000 with a leaseback term of five years at £28,000 per year.

ABC will record the proceeds of £100,000 by debiting cash at bank. The credit side will go to fixed assets to remove the net book value of £70,000, with the remaining £30,000 going as profit on disposal of asset in the income statement. It will then pay a rental to the leasing company of £28,000, so the effect on the income statement is a £30,000 profit on disposal, with a £28,000 rental payment, showing a net uplift in profit of £2,000.

Chapter 20

Reporting Changes in Policies and Estimates and Correcting Errors

. . . .

In This Chapter

▶ Deciding on accounting policy alternatives

▶ Changing the way a company does its estimating

▶ Correcting mistakes

. . . .

*N*obody is perfect. It doesn't matter how hard financial accountants try to get everything just right, occasionally mistakes are made or notions about the best way to handle transactions change. For example, someone simply enters a transaction incorrectly (such as by transposing two figures – entering £989,000 instead of £899,000). Or maybe a company has been using a particular accounting method for years, but that method no longer provides the most accurate financial statement results.

This chapter explains how to deal with changes in the accounting policies a company follows (and the accounting methods it uses to apply those policies), changes in accounting estimates (a company's best guess about how future accounting transactions will pan out), and correcting mistakes that have been made. You might be thinking that the heading of this chapter allows lots of free will. However, as a financial accountant you'll realise that the idea of choice is really rather weighty (in fact the term *Hobson's choice* springs to mind) – do things right, or do them wrong and risk getting into trouble!

Coping with Accounting Changes

Sometimes the financial accounting staff at a business will be sailing along just nicely, doing their jobs when suddenly the whole transactional process comes to a grinding halt because the old way of doing things is no longer considered to give a true and fair view. When that happens, the company needs to change the way it accounts for various transactions. Two broad types of accounting changes are possible: changes in accounting policies and changes in accounting estimates. Confused about these types of changes? Well, you're not alone! That's why I cover each in turn in this section.

Correcting an error, which is an unintentional mistake, does not qualify as a change in accounting policy or estimation technique. To find out how to handle errors (which result in *restatements*), go to the 'Correcting Errors' section at the end of the chapter.

Reporting changes in accounting policies

Financial accountants use generally accepted accounting practice (GAAP; see Chapter 4) to record a company's accounting transactions and events, such as earning revenue, paying bills, and purchasing assets. But GAAP doesn't dictate only one way to handle accounting transactions. Depending on what's going on at the company, the financial accountant may be able to choose among many acceptable ways to handle the same accounting transaction or event. At certain times in the life of the business, it may make sense to choose a different accounting policy than the one that's been used previously.

How does a financial accountant or a company determine which GAAP are preferable to follow? The overriding concept is that whatever GAAP are used must provide a true and fair view (or present fairly in all material respects) the accounting for transactions reported on the company's income statement (profit and loss account), balance sheet and statement of cash flows (cash flow statement).

The accounting policies a company follows are the specific principles, bases, conventions, rules and practices applied by a company in preparing and presenting its financial statements that are in line with GAAP – most notably IAS 8 *Accounting Policies, Changes in Accounting Estimates and Errors.* If you're reporting under UK GAAP the equivalent standards are FRS 18 *Accounting Policies* (for both accounting policies and estimation techniques) and FRS 3 *Reporting Financial Performance* for error correction and prior period adjustments (the new UK GAAP deals with all of these issues in section 10). For example, in Chapter 12 I discuss *depreciation:* the method a company uses to spread out the cost of a non-current asset over its expected useful life. One of the accepted methods under GAAP for calculating depreciation is the straight-line method. Any company using this method would disclose that its accounting policy for property, plant and equipment depreciation is the straight-line method. (*Disclosing* means the company includes notes to its financial statements which spell out for the users anything that's not immediately apparent from the figures shown in the financial statements. I discuss explanatory notes and disclosures in Chapter 15.)

Keep in mind that a company cannot simply switch accounting policies in order to improve its bottom line for a given year. A business may switch accounting policies for only two legitimate reasons:

✔ The change is required by an accounting standard or interpretation.

✔ The change results in the financial statements providing reliable and more relevant information about the effects of transactions, other events or conditions on the company's financial position, financial performance or cash flows.

Next, I explain two ways of reporting accounting changes: the retrospective-effect method and reclassification.

Making changes retrospectively

When you change an accounting policy, you must apply that change retrospectively – that is going back to the previous period(s) reported in the financial statements and restating them as if the new accounting policy had always been in existence. You do this to make sure that the financial statements are comparable and consistent from one accounting period to the next. Here are three accounting policy changes you should know:

✔ Changing from the first-in, first-out (FIFO) method for inventory to another method; see Chapter 13 for the full lowdown on inventory.

✔ Changing accounting policies for long-term construction contracts (contracts that span more than one year).

✔ Changing accounting policies as required by an accounting standard change. (See Chapter 4 for an introduction to accounting regulatory bodies that could issue a professional pronouncement requiring such a change.)

Using retrospective application, you have to adjust the opening balance on retained earnings to what it would have been if you applied the accounting policy change retrospectively in all affected prior periods. This method sounds a lot more confusing than it is in practice.

Here are the steps you follow to apply a change in accounting policy retrospectively:

1. **Work out the effect of the accounting policy change, and adjust the carrying amount of any affected assets or liabilities to reflect the change.** For example, if the company changes its inventory valuation from FIFO to average cost (AVCO), the value of opening inventories will change. This will affect last year's closing inventory valuation and retained earnings and this year's opening inventory. See Chapter 7 for more information about assets and depreciation.

2. **Make an adjustment to opening retained earnings for the effect of the change.** So if net assets increase by £1,000 when you adjust the carrying amount of affected accounts, retained earnings also increases by £1,000. Wondering why both increase? I discuss this topic in Chapter 5, but the quick answer is that you increase assets by debiting them and increase retained earnings by crediting it. Every debit must have a corresponding credit, so if your debit increases net assets, a credit will have the same effect on retained earnings.

Reclassifying financial statement items

A *reclassification* occurs when you change a transaction from the way it was originally presented in the financial statements (known as a *change in presentation*). For example, you reclassify depreciation from overhead expenses to cost of sales, or you move the production director's annual salary from administration salaries to cost of sales. Reclassification is acceptable if the effect of the change will create a more accurate reflection of the accounting transaction.

When using reclassification, the business should also provide an explanatory note or disclosure in the financial statements (see Chapter 15). For example, an explanatory note may state that £200,000 of long-term debt was reclassified to short-term debt during the accounting period because management is choosing to pay the debt off early (in the next 12 months) instead of over the projected 60 months.

Switching to the FIFO inventory valuation method

Chapter 13 is all about inventory, so if you need more than a basic refresher on inventory concepts, check out that chapter before continuing to read this section.

Working out what's immaterial

Only material changes in accounting policy need to be applied retrospectively as accounting standards only deal with material issues, so what is *immaterial* then? Put simply, *immaterial* means the monetary amount in question is not substantive – that is, it doesn't have an effect on the user's decision-making process. What's material for one business may not be material for another.

For example, let's say that a change in accounting policy causes a difference in net assets of £50,000. On the face of it, this amount could be considered a large sum of money. (I certainly wouldn't mind winning that much in the lottery!) But what if the net assets for the business are £6 million? In that case, you would more than likely consider £50,000 to be immaterial at less than 1 per cent of net assets (£50,000 / £6m × 100). Financial accountants and auditors often use percentage guidelines to determine what's material.

A company can choose how to value its inventory. Two key methods for accounting for inventory are the first-in, first-out (FIFO) method and the average cost method (AVCO):

- ✔ **FIFO:** Using the FIFO method, the company assumes that the oldest items in its inventory are the ones first sold. Consider buying a pint of milk in the supermarket. The pints of milk with the most current sell by date are pushed ahead of the cartons that have more time before they go sour. The oldest pints of milk may not always be the first ones sold (because some people dig around looking for later sell by dates), but the business is basing its numbers on the oldest pints of milk being sold first.

- ✔ **AVCO:** Using the AVCO method, the weighted average cost of items held at the beginning of the year is calculated using the following formula:

$$\text{Weighted average cost} = \frac{\text{total cost of goods in inventory}}{\text{number of items in inventory}}$$

The weighted average cost is then used to value goods sold. However, a new weighted average cost must be calculated every time further inventories are bought during the year.

There is a further valuation methodology which exists in some GAAP, which is that of last-in first-out (LIFO). However, please be aware that this method is prohibited for companies that report under IFRS. For companies that report under UK GAAP, SSAP 9 *Stocks and Long-Term Contracts* does permit the use of LIFO, but doesn't particularly like it because it often results in inventories being stated in the balance sheet at amounts that bear little relationship to recent cost levels. However, a description of the LIFO method is as follows:

- ✔ **LIFO:** With this method, the company assumes that its newest items (the ones most recently made or purchased) are the first ones sold. Imagine a big display of chocolate bars in a supermarket. If a customer wants to buy one, he takes one off the top. As the supply of chocolate bars diminishes, the shop assistant adds more to the top of the old ones instead of moving the old bars of chocolate to the top of the pile. Therefore, the supermarket assumes that the newest items purchased are sold first, which is not always the same as the actual physical movement of the items.

What happens when a company changes its accounting policy to stop using the FIFO method and start using AVCO? Well, the company has to go back to the previous period reported in the financial statements and restate the inventory valuation as if the inventory were valued under the AVCO method which will result in a different closing inventory valuation in the previous accounting period, which will then affect the previous period's retained earnings. This is because the company has changed an accounting policy and accounting policy changes require retrospective application. Remember, if

AVCO produces an inventory valuation £5,000 higher in the previous accounting period, you'll have to uplift the inventory valuation in the previous period by £5,000 and then credit retained earnings to uplift those by £5,000.

The company making this change isn't required to do a full-blown disclosure in the notes to the financial statements (see Chapter 15). All that's required is to be shown in the notes to the financial statements how much of a change is taking place by using AVCO versus the prior method – both in net profit and retained earnings. Companies that have to disclose earnings per share (EPS) figures will also have to disclose the effect such a change has had on EPS. (See Chapter 10 for more information about both net profit and EPS.)

Changing a company's estimates

Accounting estimates are transactions a company enters into the financial records to reflect its best estimate about how certain transactions will eventually pan out. Sometimes, until a whole transaction comes to fruition, the company isn't 100 per cent sure how much revenue or expense to account for.

When a company decides on a method to calculate various estimates, the estimates (and the estimation technique used) are not set in stone. Sometimes unexpected future events affect the validity of the estimate, so changes in estimates are frequently made as new and better evidence is gathered.

Consider a personal example: Say that you're saving to buy a new car. You estimate you'll need to save £5,000 for a deposit on the car of your dreams. Nine months later, when you are ready to buy the car, changes in the economy and car prices cause your deposit to only be £4,000. Did you make a mistake by originally estimating £5,000? No, of course not. With the info you had available at the time, you made a valid estimate. You could not predict the changing conditions that created the difference in the deposit payment.

Reviewing types of business estimates

During your working life in accountancy, or during your accountancy studies, you will likely come across at least four major estimates:

- **The useful life of tangible assets:** *Assets* are resources a company owns. *Tangible* (or *fixed*) assets include property, plant, and equipment (PPE) like computers, desks, and manufacturing equipment. When a company purchases *long-term* tangible assets (those that have an expected useful life of more than one year), it has to depreciate them. *Depreciation* spreads the cost of a long-term asset over its expected useful life (see Chapter 12).

How can a company tell with absolute certainty how long it will be able to use an asset? It can't. Usually, its estimate is based on past experience or company policy. For example, the company usually trades in vehicles after they hit the four-year mark, so the expected useful life for depreciation purposes is four years. For manufacturing equipment, the expected useful life can be how long the company plans to make the product for which it purchased the machine in the first place.

Suppose the company institutes a cost-savings initiative dictating that its vehicles be traded in after *six* years instead of four. A sense of panic overcomes you! Fear not, I discuss how to handle this situation in the upcoming section "Handling changes currently and prospectively."

✔ **The residual value of a tangible asset:** Some methods of depreciation allowed by GAAP take into consideration the *residual value* of the tangible asset: how much a company assumes it can get for a non-current asset when the time comes to dispose of it.

For example, when the company trades in the company vehicle for a new one after four years, it estimates the old vehicle will have a trade-in value of £3,500. This amount is merely an estimate; the company won't actually know how much it gets until the transaction occurs. (You can read more about this topic in Chapter 12.)

✔ **Collectability of trade receivables:** *Trade receivables*, which I discuss in Chapter 7, is the amount of money customers owe the business for goods they purchased or services the company rendered to them. Unfortunately, every business knows that occasionally customers fail to cough up the cash.

In my experience, the main reason that customers fail to pay is *not* because they are unhappy with their purchase, but because they simply don't have the money. Sometimes, the intent is fraudulent from the start – the customer never had any intention of paying. And in some cases, business customers close up shop quietly in the night, never to be heard from again.

Whatever the reason for the uncollectible receivable, GAAP require that businesses extending credit to their customers estimate how much of trade receivables will eventually prove to be uncollectible. This step involves reducing both net profit, by increasing bad debts expense, and the book value of trade receivables for the amount of the estimate, by increasing the account called 'allowance for receivables' or 'provision for bad debts' account.

Contra accounts carry a balance opposite to the normal account balance. Because trade receivables normally has a debit balance, the contra asset account 'provision for bad debts' or 'allowance for receivables' has a credit balance. You can find more about the rules of debits and credit in Chapter 5.

✔ **Warranty costs:** When a company sells a product with a warranty or performance guarantee, it recognises the estimated cost of servicing the warranty in the same financial period the revenue from the sale is accounted for. You usually calculate the cost of the warranty by using an estimate based on recent experience. For example, in the last two years the actual cost of product warranties was 2 per cent of net sales, so the company uses 2 per cent of net sales for its current estimate.

Here's how to calculate the estimate: Say that gross sales are £10,000 and *sales discounts* or *discounts allowed* (any discounts the company gives to its best customers) are £2,000, making net sales £8,000 (£10,000 – £2,000). Two per cent of £8,000 is £160, which is the company's estimate for warranty expense.

See Chapter 8 for the full story about warranties. Because calculating the estimate for warranties is a critical aspect of many businesses (especially electrical appliance stores), in Chapter 8 I also walk you through facts and circumstances surrounding a typical warranty estimate transaction and show you the appropriate journal entries.

Handling changes currently and prospectively

Changes in accounting estimates (sometimes called a company's *estimation techniques*) have to be recognised currently and also prospectively if appropriate. This means that a change in accounting estimate is shown in the current year and all subsequent years (in other words going forward).

While the current and future financial statements show the effect of the change in estimate, no change is ever made to prior period financial statements. This is because a change in estimation technique is *not* a change in accounting policy (only changes in accounting policy are applied retrospectively). See the above section 'Reporting changes in accounting policies'.

A lot of folk starting out in the world of accountancy assume that a change in estimate will affect more than one year. To clear up this misconception, consider when a change in accounting estimate may only affect the current year. One example would be if the company originally estimates the useful life of a piece of manufacturing equipment to be ten years. When year eight comes around, the machine is on its last legs and clearly needs to be binned at year-end. Changing the useful life of the machine to eight years in year eight of its expected useful life does not affect any future periods – only the current period.

Correcting Errors

If you choose to pursue a career path as a financial accountant, you don't have to be perfect. That's quite a relief to see in print, I'm sure! However, you do have to handle any inadvertent mistakes in reporting accounting transactions in the financial statements to comply with GAAP requirements.

In this section, I explain the most common types of errors that occur in the financial statements, and I show you how to go about correcting them. The errors I refer to in this section are errors which have been made in prior periods because if you make an error in your current year's work you just sort it out and carry on as normal.

Looking at common types of errors

Inadvertent errors fall into three broad categories:

- **Arithmetical mistakes:** These mistakes occur when the financial accountant just makes a mistake with the calculator. A typical example is when you're totaling (sometimes called *casting*) a column of figures and you make a mistake adding them up; the mistake affects some aspect of data entry into the accounting software system, which then flows through to the financial statements.

    You could also make transposition errors, such as entering £959 into the accounting software instead of the correct figure £599.

- **GAAP mistakes:** GAAP errors occur in recognition, measurement, presentation, disclosure or just basically using an improper accounting method.

    - *Recognition* means determining how an accounting transaction or event affects the company's financials, and examples are littered throughout this book. For example, Chapter 10 discusses recognising revenue and expenses.

    - An example of *measurement* is determining an item's fair value. Using assets as an example, the *fair value* is the price a company could receive to sell an asset to an unrelated third party on a certain date.

    - *Presentation* means you show the transaction in the right way in the correct financial statement. For example, assets go on the balance sheet and revenue goes in the income statement, and not vice-versa.

- *Disclosure,* which I discuss in Chapter 15, means you give the users of the financial statements all the necessary information they will need when elaborating on financial transactions.

✔ **Interpretation of facts:** This error happens if the financial accountant misuses or misinterprets available information. For example, consider working out the residual value of an asset. Let's say the best information available at the time for residual value for a particular asset is that its worth at the expected date of disposal will be £5,000. The financial accountant unilaterally decides not to use this estimated figure but uses £10,000 instead.

Letting cancelling errors lie

When an error occurs that cancels itself out, (often referred to as a *contra*), management of a company (with the agreement of their auditors) may decide not to take any action.

For example, let's say the financial accountant screwed up recording depreciation in one year. Even though the depreciation entry in the second year was also incorrect, the two errors resulted in a zero net effect. If the books for both financial periods have already been closed, no further action may be necessary – especially if the error is immaterial. The financial accountant just moves on, making sure year three and all subsequent years are done correctly.

Even if the cancelling error is immaterial, if the books for year two aren't closed yet, you do have to adjust the opening retained earnings balance (see Chapter 9) for year two and take action to correct the error in year two prior to closing the books. Any direct corrections of errors to retained earnings are called prior-period *adjustments.*

Restating the financial statements

A restatement of the company's financial statements may have to be done for many different reasons. For example, the error in question is material, prior period financial statements are shown with the current year for comparison purposes, or the company's auditor deems a restatement necessary.

The restatement process consists of three steps:

1. **Adjust the balances of any assets or liabilities at the beginning of the first financial period shown in the comparative statements for the cumulative effect of the error.** Say that your first year is 2012, and at the year-end 31 December 2011, the cumulative effect of an error in the calculation of depreciation was £100,000. You adjust the book value of the depreciable asset(s) relating to the error by the £100,000.

2. **Take the second half of your Step 1 entry to retained earnings.** You do so because the error would have affected prior years' profit or loss, which would have transferred to retained earnings at the end of each year.

3. **Deal with the disclosure issues.** Your last step is to make sure the notes to the financial statements (see Chapter 15) detail the restatement, providing all the information surrounding the event, such as the nature of the error and the effect on net profit and retained earnings.

Keep all of this in proportion and consider the issue of materiality at all times. You don't need to write chapter and verse in the annual report if the bookkeeper inadvertently posted an invoice for motor expenses to the postage and stationery account. Significant changes and errors will need adjustment and disclosures, but insignificant over- or under-estimations or immaterial errors can simply be corrected in the current year with no major consequence.

Part VII
The Part of Tens

Go to www.dummies.com/extras/financialaccounting for online bonus content.

In this part . . .

- ✔ Gain insights into how companies may try to enhance their earnings.

- ✔ Lift the lid on how businesses try to hide bad news.

- ✔ Find out which industries may do their books differently to the norm.

- ✔ Go to www.dummies.com/extras/financial accounting for online bonus content, including an extra Part of Tens chapter: 'Ten Differences Between Some National Standards and IFRS'.

Chapter 21

Ten Financial Accounting Shenanigans

*F*inancial statement shenanigans centre around making a company's financial statements look fantastic, even when they aren't. The major areas of concern all artificially inflate the results of operations or reduce profits to keep the tax bill down. The company may report higher net profit than it should or manipulate its balance sheet figures, perhaps by underreporting liabilities or showing long-term assets as current. Why do companies mess around with their books and deviate from generally accepted accounting practice? Because they want to attract new investors or creditors by showing them great operating results. In this chapter, I reveal ten such manipulations.

Reporting Revenue in the Wrong Period

In financial accounting, income shenanigans usually result from reporting revenue early. The goal is to appease shareholders and provide justification for bonuses by showing higher-than-actual income. Also, management has a motivation to inflate revenue because high-ranking employees at most listed (or publicly traded) companies are rewarded by means other than their agreed-upon salaries. These reward systems allow for millions of pounds of incentive payments and share options to be given to those employees as they deliver faster and faster revenues and earnings growth – on paper at least.

With the accruals method of accounting, a company records revenue only when it is earned and realisable. For revenue to be *earned,* the job (whether it involves goods or services) has to be complete based upon the terms of the contract between the company and the customer. For revenue to be *realisable* means there is an expectation the company will be paid. Until both criteria are satisfied, a company can't record a sale to a customer as revenue in the income statement; see Chapter 10.

Massaging the Figures: Reporting Fictitious Income

When a company hires a tax accountant, it wants that accountant to legally apply tax legislation to reduce the company's taxable profit as much as possible (so it owes the least amount of tax). This is called *tax avoidance* which is legal (it's *tax evasion* that's illegal) but more aggressive tax avoidance schemes are becoming more morally and ethically frowned upon. When it comes to financial accounting, unscrupulous business owners will seek to increase net profit using means not allowed under generally accepted accounting practice (GAAP).

Creating fictitious income involves reporting sales transactions that lack economic substance (by *economic substance* I mean *commercial reality*). Sometimes a sales transaction may occur at face value but lack real intent. Two classic examples of this type of shenanigan are channel stuffing and side agreements:

- ✔ **Channel stuffing:** This takes place when customers buy more of one good or more goods than they could possibly need. Channel stuffing normally occurs at year-end. Put simply, it's a way for the company to artificially inflate revenue for that year. When this situation occurs, the unspoken agreement between the company and its customer is that the customer can return the unneeded good(s) after the first of the year for a full refund. The net effect is to artificially (and temporarily) inflate gross receipts.

- ✔ **Side agreements:** Another way to artificially (and temporarily) inflate a company's gross receipts involves *side agreements,* which are verbal agreements that change the terms of the sale. For example, a customer places an order buying 5,000 widgets at £100 per widget with the expectation that before the invoice is due to be paid, the price per widget will be reduced to £50. Again, this manipulation tends to occur especially at year-end so the company can inflate its reported revenue.

The first account in the income statement is always *revenue* (or *turnover*), which is the amount of income the company brings in doing whatever it's in the business of doing. Some accountants refer to revenue as *sales.*

Getting Income Classification Wrong

All money a company receives is not income. And sometimes, a company deliberately misclassifies money it receives in order to manipulate its financial statements.

For example, a business may get a loan from a shareholder or another third party, such as a bank. The loan amount should be recorded as a liability, but perhaps the business records it as income. Or the business generates funds by selling shares of the company. That amount should be recorded as equity, but again, the company may classify it as income.

A company may also try to boost its revenue by improperly adding to this category any profit made from a one-off sale of an asset (rather than classifying the amount as *gain on disposal of property, plant and equipment*). Another misclassification occurs if the business records interest or dividend income as a reduction of operating expense – for example, a reduction to interest expense – rather than as investment income.

You may be thinking, 'What's the big deal?' After all, the effect of these manipulations on the company's net profit is probably zero. The big deal (besides the possible fraudulent intent) is that misclassifying income statement items affects ratio analysis: a valuable tool used by potential investors and creditors for decision-making (see Chapter 14).

Failing to Record Liabilities

Liabilities are claims against the company by other businesses or by its employees, such as trade payables, unearned revenue (deferred income), and payroll accruals:

- **Trade payables** includes money a company owes its suppliers for goods and services it purchases in the normal course of business and anticipates paying back in the short term. For example, the company purchases inventory from a manufacturer or office supplies from a local stationers.

- **Unearned revenue** (sometimes referred to as *deferred income*) is money received from customers paying the business for goods or services they haven't yet received. An example of this is a deposit. For example, if you place an order for a pair of boots that a shoe shop doesn't currently have in stock in your size, the shop may ask you to pay a deposit toward the eventual sale before it places a special order for the boots.

- **Payroll accruals** are wages and other benefits earned by – but not yet paid to – employees. The accruals should be recorded in both the income statement and the balance sheet (see Chapter 8).

If a company doesn't record its liabilities, the effect is to show the company in a better light by increasing both *net assets* (total assets less total liabilities) and *net profit* (all income a company earns in an accounting period less all expenses the company incurs while making that profit).

Reporting Liabilities in the Wrong Period

Reporting liabilities in the wrong accounting period can be just as bad as not reporting them at all. This tactic is often employed at year-end to move items affecting the books in a less than positive way out of the current year and into the next. The ways to accomplish this manipulation are limitless. Here are just a couple examples:

- **Holding onto supplier invoices:** For example, the company may keep all supplier invoices it receives during the last 15 days of its accounting period in a drawer in the purchase ledger clerk's desk and save them until after the beginning of the next financial year. So for a 31 December year-end, all invoices a company receives after 15 December won't be entered into the accounting system until 2 January – which in this case is the next reporting period. This action distorts the financial statements by reducing current liabilities and increasing pre-tax profit for invoices that would hit the income statement.

- **Recording an inadequate warranty reserve:** If a company provides a warranty for the goods it sells, it also has to account for an estimate of how much it will eventually cost to service the warranty. Companies usually calculate the cost of the warranty by using an estimate based on recent experience; for example, recent warranty costs have been 2 per cent of net sales, so the company bases its warranty charge at 2 per cent as well.

  Suppose during the last month of the accounting period the company decides to use 1 per cent instead of 2 per cent for the warranty reserve. Then, it makes up the shortfall in the first month of the new accounting period. This action serves to artificially reduce liabilities and increase net profit – presenting a rosier picture than what is actually factual to the users of the financial statements.

Inflating Asset Values

Assets are resources a company owns (like inventory, property, plant and equipment) or investments (such as shares and bonds in other companies). Regardless of the assets' *fair value* – how much the assets would fetch in an open marketplace – most assets go on the balance sheet at their original historic cost. So, if a company owns an office building it paid £500,000 for, and the fair value of the building increases to £700,000, the company doesn't increase the value of the office building on its books for the additional £200,000 (if reporting under the cost model (which means the company reports assets at cost less depreciation) – it will do if reporting under the revaluation model (which means the company shows the value of its assets at market value at the end of each accounting period)).

Continuing with the building example, if appraisal valuation shows the fair value of the building increases by £200,000 and the company decides to add this increase to the books, there any many ways to hide the inappropriate change. Debiting an asset increases it, and for every debit there must be a credit (see Chapter 5). So if the company increases assets by £200,000, it also needs to credit an account for £200,000. To affect the books in a positive manner, the company could credit sales or owners' equity – both of which serve to artificially make the books look a heck of a lot better.

Here's another trick I see with new clients who don't know any better: A company may decide to ignore all *outstanding cheques,* which are cheques the company writes and releases that have not yet cleared through the bank. So when the year-end bank statement arrives, let's say ten cheques weren't cashed by the recipient in time to show up on the year-end bank statement. The company temporarily removes these ten cheques from the accounting records, adding them back in when they eventually clear the bank. This action artificially increases the year-end cash balance.

That being said, Chapter 9 discusses some investment-type assets that are adjusted to fair value. For example, *trading securities* – debt and equity the business purchases to sell short-term to make a profit – are initially recorded on the balance sheet at cost. Then as their fair value fluctuates, their monetary amount on the balance sheet goes up or down with any gain or loss going to the income statement. The business can't ignore a loss in value or inflate any gain in value.

Changing Accounting Policies Inappropriately

Accounting policies are the generally accepted accounting practice (GAAP) that financial accountants use to record a company's accounting events. For example, a company uses a specific accounting policy to charge depreciation (see Chapter 12) or value inventory (see Chapter 13). GAAP allows the financial accountant more than one acceptable way to handle many accounting events, so the company does have options.

However, there has to be a good reason for any change from one accounting policy to another. A company can't just willy-nilly switch back and forth between depreciation or inventory valuation methods (or any other GAAP for that matter) merely to increase the bottom line. For more about this topic, see Chapter 20.

For example, using the first-in first-out (FIFO) method of inventory valuation results in closing inventory of £300,000 and net profit of £100,000 for Village Shipping Limited in 2013. Village Shipping wants to show its investors a higher net profit for the year, so it switches to the weighted average cost method of inventory valuation for 2013, which increases closing inventory and increases net profit by £100,000. Higher net profit equals happy investors.

Failing to Disclose Related-Party Transactions

A *related party* is a business such as a parent company or affiliate that has direct or indirect control over another business. Most business transactions you'll see as a financial accountant are conducted at *arm's length.* That phrase means the company is conducting business with an unrelated third party. For example, if you subscribe to a magazine, the subscription order is an arm's length transaction: You don't know the publishers, and they don't know you. The price of the subscription is the same for you or someone in the office down the street.

Here's an example of a related-party transaction: A company loans money to one of its directors. This situation can be problematic on many levels, and especially if a verbal understanding exists that the director never needs to pay the money back. In this case, the loan incorrectly increases liabilities on the balance sheet, affecting investor and credit ratio analyses (see Chapter 14). Depending on the monetary amount of the loan, it may also affect the company's ability to pay dividends to non-related investors.

When parties to a transaction are related, the objectivity that naturally occurs in an unrelated third-party purchase or sale may be lost. Financial accountants must adequately disclose related-party transactions (see Chapter 15) so that users of the financial statements are aware these types of transactions exist. Related party issues are dealt with in IAS 24 *Related Party Disclosures* and for those guys who report under UK GAAP, it's FRS 8 *Related Party Disclosures* that you need.

Capitalising Expenses Inappropriately

Whether a purchase is *capitalised* (recorded on the balance sheet as a non-current (or fixed) asset) or *expensed* (recorded in the income statement as an expense) depends on both the monetary value and the type of purchase. Most businesses have a policy covering this decision; see Chapter 7. What a company can't do is decide to capitalise costs instead of expensing them to show a higher net profit.

For example, any costs that materially increase the life of an asset are capitalised. Routine repairs and maintenance costs are expensed. So for a car, rebuilding the engine (because it materially increases the car's useful life) is a capital cost. Oil changes and purchasing new tyres are expenses that have to be reflected in the income statement.

The distinction may not seem like such a big deal until you consider that large publicly traded companies may have thousands of cars. Misclassifying expenses as capitalised improvements can have a significant impact on the bottom line.

Hiding Reportable Contingencies

A *contingent liability* exists when a current circumstance may cause a monetary loss in the future. For example, the company has litigation pending that's not yet settled. If the monetary loss due to the contingent liability results in a legal or constructive obligation, is probable (in other words more likely than not) and the amount of loss that could be sustained is reasonably estimated, the company must show this loss on the financial statements as a provision for a liability.

For example, a company is nearing the end of tax inspection by HM Revenue and Customs (HMRC), and it is probable that the company will agree to adjustments increasing its tax owed plus interest and penalties. The amount of HMRC's assessment must reflect on the company's books to give investors and creditors an accurate picture of probable future uses of cash. (If the company pays the HMRC assessment, the amount of cash available for debt or investor payments will be reduced.)

Chapter 22

Ten Industries with Special Accounting Standards

1 bang on and on in this book about generally accepted accounting practice (GAAP) because it is such an integral part of financial accounting. While GAAP applies to most non-governmental entities, certain types of businesses must follow GAAP that are tailored to their specific industry. That's because the inherent nature of these industries may require modified accounting practices, financial reporting presentation, and required or recommended disclosures.

If you're a student accountant, some of these specialised instances of GAAP will probably be mentioned in your studies. Also, the info in this chapter will serve you well should you decide to work in one of these industries as a financial accountant. Keep in mind that in this chapter I simply scratch the surface of this topic. Should you decide to work with a business in one of these industries, you'll have to crack open your GAAP guide to get the full lowdown.

Airlines

Accounting for the airline industry is complicated because recognition of revenue and expenses can change depending on the type of airline: *legacy* (a major airline such as British Airways), *regional* (such as Flybe), or *cargo* (such as UPS). For example, some regional airlines' expenses are reimbursed by the legacy airlines using their services; therefore, the regional airlines don't record them as expenses. While more than a few accounting issues affect this complicated specialised industry, I want to address two biggies in this section: revenue recognition and handling airport slots.

- **Recognition of revenue:** Under GAAP, airlines have to account for flights paid for in advance as a liability until the conditions of the booking have been completed, which means the customer completes the flight as booked.

    If a passenger fails to use a non-refundable ticket, airlines can consider the flight closed the next day and record the revenue for this unused ticket. Exchangeable tickets not used within a certain time period set by the airlines are similarly accounted for as revenue. To arrive at a reasonable time period for determining when it is appropriate to record revenue on an unused exchangeable ticket, the airline looks to historic information that tells them how long in the past it took passengers to re-book their exchangeable flights. This time period can be between 6 and 24 months.

- **Landing and take-off slots:** These areas owned by airlines to enter and exit airports can be one of their largest assets on the balance sheet. While they have a physical presence, landing and take-off slots are accounted for as intangible assets (see Chapter 7). This treatment means their cost is initially taken to the balance sheet and then *amortised*: The cost is transferred to the income statement using an allowable amortisation method (see Chapter 7).

Finance Companies

If you ever took out a loan to purchase a car, you probably had dealings with a *finance company,* whose purpose is to lend money to both consumers and businesses. Examples of finance companies include banks, credit unions, and mortgage providers. Two specialised accounting issues that finance companies encounter are creating an provision (sometimes called an *allowance*) for loan losses and transferring receivables:

- **Provision for loan losses:** This provision has to be recorded in the financial statements when the finance company considers it probable that the loan is *impaired,* meaning it won't be paid back in its entirety. The provision is a reduction in the amount the company estimates that it will collect. Obviously, to determine the size of this provision, the finance company must be able to reasonably estimate the amount of impairment. It can't just stick any old figure in as a provision – there has to be some basis for its calculation.

✔ **Transfer of receivables:** When a finance company (perhaps in an effort to increase its cash flow) transfers a receivable to another finance company, it reports the transfer as a sale if it gives up all control over the receivable in question. Otherwise, if it retains some control over the receivable, the finance company keeps the receivable on its balance sheet as an asset. However, the receivable must be shown separately from other non-transferred receivables.

Franchisors

You're probably very familiar with the concept of *franchises*. What often happens is that a business that starts out on its own grows to be very popular. The original owners then start allowing other individuals to open shops using the same concept in other geographic locations. The parties to a franchise are the *franchisor* (the party granting the business rights) and the *franchisee* (the individual purchasing the right to use the franchisor's business model). A typical example of a franchise would be your local Costa Coffee.

Some special accounting issues for the franchisor include the fact that the franchisor does not recognise revenue until it has substantially performed all material services contained in the franchise agreement; for example, the franchise agreement may call for the franchisor to provide a certain amount of training to the franchisee. Also, if the initial franchise fee required at the time of signing the franchise agreement is significant in comparison to the *continuing fees* (usually a percentage of sales), the franchisor defers a portion of the initial fee (in other words, recognises part of the initial fee as a liability on the balance sheet), recording it as earned through future services rendered to the franchisee.

Oil and Gas Companies

This industry is all about mineral extraction and the production of crude oil. The job of this industry is to find areas that may contain natural resources (including natural gas), conduct some exploration, develop the areas (for example, put in oil wells), and acquire or produce the natural resource.

In IFRS the standard that deals with such industries is that of IFRS 6 *Exploration and Evaluation of Mineral Resources*. There is no specific equivalent in current UK GAAP and therefore companies reporting under UK GAAP must refer to FRS 15 *Tangible Fixed Assets*. In the new UK GAAP (which is planned for accounting periods commencing on or after 1 January 2015), such industries are directed to Section 17 *Property, Plant and Equipment* and Section 18 *Intangible Assets other than Goodwill*. Clear as mud? Well here are a couple of examples that may prove there is light at the end of the tunnel:

- Let's say a company finds land in the UK that it believes contains mineral deposits. The cost of acquiring the land (regardless of whether the drilling ever reaps any rewards) is *capitalised at historic cost,* which means it is shown on the balance sheet as an asset at the amount the company paid for it plus any other costs involved in its acquisition, such as legal fees.

- Any other costs that directly tie back to the successful discovery of any mineral/oil or gas reserves – for example, oil well drilling – are also capitalised.

- Any other costs are expensed as they are incurred.

Government Contractors

Another specialised industry that you may come across involves government contractors that provide goods or services to the UK government. The main accounting issue with this specialised industry is whether the contract between parties is structured as a fixed-price or a cost-plus contract:

- With a *fixed-price contract,* the price the government pays for completion of the contract is agreed at the signing of the contract. So, if the contractor incurs more costs than expected while fulfilling the contract, the contractor must take the extra costs on the chin.

- In contrast, a *cost-plus contract* allows the contractor to receive an agreed-upon price and to be reimbursed for allowable (or otherwise defined) expenses. The contract dictates which expenses fall into the allowable category. This way, both the government and the contractor acknowledge there may be unforeseen expenses or cost overruns that are crucial to the successful completion of the project.

Healthcare Entities

Examples of healthcare entities are hospitals, nursing homes, medical centres, and doctors' surgeries. A major accounting issue with this type of entity is the significant amounts of money healthcare entities may invest in drugs, linens, and other ancillary services. Because the amount of money is so large, proper treatment under GAAP is key to making sure financial results are accurate and understandable to the users of the financial statements.

Here are some specialised accounting issues in the healthcare field:

✔ Accounting for and reporting contingencies (see Chapter 8) surrounding medical negligence claims

✔ Accounting for revenue and cost recognition methods related to setting rates for services provided, working with third-party payers (insurance companies and BUPA), and contracting out certain services (such as x-rays and MRIs) to third-party providers

Film Production Companies

Motion picture accounting issues include how to account for the production, sale, licensing, and distribution of the films, associated DVDs, and product-related merchandise. The DVD and product-related merchandise aspects are pretty self-explanatory. But some issues are quite complex:

✔ **Production:** Motion picture production involves every step of making the film, from deciding on an initial concept to securing a script to releasing the finished product.

✔ **Sale:** The sale of a film takes place only when the master copy of the film and all its associated rights are transferred from the original owner to the interested buyer. After the sale takes place, the original owner has no right to any future profits.

✔ **Licensing:** Licensing means the owner allows others to show the film for a fee (like when you go to the Cinema).

Accounting for the film production industry can be quite daunting because it is very difficult to estimate earned revenue and related costs over the life of a film. To deal with this problem, the motion picture industry calculates an appropriate estimation method that, as accurately as possible, matches revenue and expenses to show the film's financial performance.

Not-for-Profit Organisations

These sorts of organisations don't have a profit motive when providing their goods or services; see Chapter 6. Accounting issues tailored to this type of entity include recognising contributions, which must be recorded at *fair value* (their value in an open marketplace). This step is easy for cash – after all, cash is cash! But it can get fiddly when a donor contributes assets such as property building or artwork. Many times a valuation has to be undertaken to properly value the contribution.

Another issue is the standard for financial statement presentation. Net assets and income statement accounts have to be broken down to distinguish those that have restrictions and those that don't. For example, a donor may specifically earmark money to be used only to support a specific program the not-for-profit provides – this money will be classified as restricted funds.

You might also come across *Community Interest Companies* (CICs) during your working life as a financial accountant. These are companies that are specifically designed for those who wish to operate for the benefit of the community, as opposed for the benefit of the company's owners (the shareholders). To be classed as a CIC, the company must pass a series of tests to make sure that the CIC is established for the purposes of the community and the profits made by the CIC are dedicated to these purposes.

House Builders

Specialised GAAP pertain to the costs a company (such as a social housing association) incurs when purchasing and developing land for rental – for example, developers who plow over trees and vegetation and level the land to build residential or commercial properties. Most costs a developer incurs are originally capitalised rather than expensed. Here are two examples of capitalised land development costs:

- ✔ **Pre-acquisition costs:** These costs take place prior to purchasing the land and will include legal fees for conveyancing costs to transfer ownership from the seller to the buyer.

- ✔ **Directly attributable costs:** These costs, such as the bricks and mortar used to build the properties that will be rented by the housing association, are incurred after the land is purchased and directly tie back to the project.

Computer Software

Here, I'm not focusing on a specific industry but on something that is employed in just about every industry: computer software. Accounting issues regarding software vary depending on whether a company buys software off the shelf to use in its business, purchases software from a developer for resale to others, or develops software in-house that is tailored to its specific business needs. (An example of developing in-house software is a manufacturer writing its own inventory software to monitor the numerous raw materials required to make its products.)

The primary issues with software revolve around revenue recognition and expense. For your everyday owner-managed business that purchases software off the shelf, the recognition of the expense is easy: The company follows its capitalisation policy, which usually means that if it plans on using the software for more than 12 months, the software cost is depreciated (written off to the income statement over its useful economic life) rather than immediately expensed if it is over the monetary benchmark capitalisation amount. The same holds true for retail stores purchasing software for resale to customers; they account for the software like any other inventory transaction.

But the accounting gets more complicated when the software is developed internally either for *proprietary use* (meaning for use only by the company that writes the software) or for sale to others (such as when a software developer sells a computer game to retail stores).

Index

• *B* •

• *C* •

About the Authors

Steve Collings, FMAAT FCCA is the audit and technical director at Leavitt Walmsley Associates, a firm of Chartered Certified Accountants based in Sale, Manchester in the United Kingdom. Steven trained and qualified with the firm and is also the firm's Senior Statutory Auditor. Steven qualified with the Association of Accounting Technicians in 2000 and then went on to qualify as an Associate Chartered Certified Accountant (ACCA) in 2005. In 2010 Steven became a Fellow of the Association of Chartered Certified Accountants (FCCA). Steven also holds the Diploma in IFRS from ACCA which he obtained in 2008 as well as their Certificates in IFRS and Certificates in International Standards on Auditing.

Steven specialises in financial reporting and auditing issues and has been writing professionally for several years. Steven is the author of *The Interpretation and Application of International Standards on Auditing* and *IFRS For Dummies*, both of which are published by John Wiley & Sons, as well as the author of other publications on the subjects of UK accounting standards, International Financial Reporting Standards and International Standards on Auditing. He is also the author of several articles which have been published in the various accounting media, primarily *AccountingWEB.co.uk*. Steven also lectures to professional accountants on financial reporting, auditing and Solicitors Accounts Rules. Steven won *Accounting Technician of the Year* at the British Accountancy Awards in November 2011.

Maire Loughran is a certified public accountant and a member of the American Institute of Certified Public Accountants. Her professional experience includes four years of internal auditing for a publicly traded company in the aerospace industry, two years as an auditor in the not-for-profit sector, and even some experience as a U.S. federal agent! Her public accounting experience includes financial reporting and analysis, audits of private corporations, accounting for e-commerce, and forensic accounting.

Maire is a full adjunct professor who teaches graduate and undergraduate auditing, accounting, and taxation classes. Interested in many different business-related fields, she has written *Auditing For Dummies* (a Wiley publication), a training manual for a Microsoft product, and a guide to starting a home-based business, as well as the Arts and Crafts Business Guide for About.com, a part of The New York Times Company.

Dedication

From Steve: I would like to dedicate this book to each member of my family and friends – particularly the Breary family who always make sure my weekends are not filled completely with writing tasks! I would also like to dedicate this book to Les Leavitt (managing partner at LWA) whose guidance and encouragement has enabled me to gain the knowledge and experience that is passed on to others in the accountancy profession through books such as this.

Author's Acknowledgments

From Steve: Writing a book is a project which brings with it a whole host of challenges and is certainly not a one-person project; the production of a *For Dummies* book requires the skill and expertise of an entire publishing team and this book, and my previous title, *IFRS For Dummies*, was certainly no exception. Writing the UK edition of *Financial Accounting For Dummies* has been a pleasure and therefore my most sincere thanks and gratitude goes to the Commissioning Editor, Claire Ruston, who got this project off the ground.

Every author of a book needs a strong and supporting publishing team behind them and the team behind *Financial Accounting For Dummies* have been just that. I would like to express my sincere thanks to Simon Bell (my project editor) for all his help and advice during the writing process. Caroline Fox (my technical reviewer) has, once again, done an outstanding job on the review of the manuscript with helpful advice and guidance throughout. The other guys on the publishing team also deserve a huge thank-you from me for all their help in taking the manuscript through the editing and publishing process and turning it into the finished product.

The support I have received from family and friends – particularly when deadlines are approaching, does not go unnoticed. My thanks go to Les Leavitt, the managing partner at Leavitt Walmsley Associates for his support and enthusiasm for this (and my other) book projects and for accommodating deadlines in with the work projects.

Finally, my sincere thanks go to you, the reader, who has picked up this book. I sincerely hope you find it helpful and a good reference guide to the world of financial accounting. Make notes in the margin and keep it close to hand to guide you through any complex issues you stumble upon during your journey through the world of financial accounting.

Publisher's Acknowledgments

We're proud of this book; please send us your comments at http://dummies.custhelp.com. For other comments, please contact our Customer Care Department within the U.S. at 877-762-2974, outside the U.S. at (001) 317-572-3993, or fax 317-572-4002.

Some of the people who helped bring this book to market include the following:

Acquisitions, Editorial, and Vertical Websites

Project Editor: Simon Bell

Commissioning Editor: Claire Ruston

Assistant Editor: Ben Kemble

Development Editor: Kate O'Leary

Copy Editor: Kate O'Leary

Technical Editor: Caroline Fox

Production Manager: Daniel Mersey

Publisher: Miles Kendall

Vertical Websites: Rich Graves

Cover Photos: © Tomislav Zivkovic / iStockphoto

Composition Services

Project Coordinator: Kristie Rees

Layout and Graphics: Amy Hassos

Proofreaders: Melissa Cossell, Jessica Kramer

Indexer: Estalita Slivoskey

FOR DUMMIES®

Making Everything Easier! ™

UK editions

BUSINESS

978-1-118-34689-1

978-1-118-44349-1

978-1-119-97527-4

MUSIC

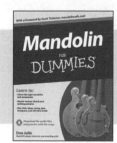

978-1-119-94276-4

978-0-470-97799-6

978-0-470-66372-1

HOBBIES

978-1-118-41156-8

978-1-119-99417-6

978-1-119-97250-1

Asperger's Syndrome For Dummies
978-0-470-66087-4

Basic Maths For Dummies
978-1-119-97452-9

Body Language For Dummies, 2nd Edition
978-1-119-95351-7

Boosting Self-Esteem For Dummies
978-0-470-74193-1

Business Continuity For Dummies
978-1-118-32683-1

Cricket For Dummies
978-0-470-03454-5

Diabetes For Dummies, 3rd Edition
978-0-470-97711-8

eBay For Dummies, 3rd Edition
978-1-119-94122-4

English Grammar For Dummies
978-0-470-05752-0

Flirting For Dummies
978-0-470-74259-4

IBS For Dummies
978-0-470-51737-6

ITIL For Dummies
978-1-119-95013-4

Management For Dummies, 2nd Edition
978-0-470-97769-9

Managing Anxiety with CBT For Dummies
978-1-118-36606-6

Neuro-linguistic Programming For Dummies, 2nd Edition
978-0-470-66543-5

Nutrition For Dummies, 2nd Edition
978-0-470-97276-2

Organic Gardening For Dummies
978-1-119-97706-3

12-47776–187x234mm

FOR DUMMIES®

Making Everything Easier!™

UK editions

SELF-HELP

Cognitive Behavioural Therapy For Dummies
978-0-470-66541-1

Creative Visualization For Dummies
978-1-119-99264-6

Mindfulness For Dummies
978-0-470-66086-7

LANGUAGES

Spanish For Dummies
978-0-470-68815-1

Polish For Dummies
978-1-119-97959-3

British Sign Language For Dummies
978-0-470-69477-0

HISTORY

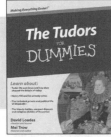

The Tudors For Dummies
978-0-470-68792-5

Medieval History For Dummies
978-0-470-74783-4

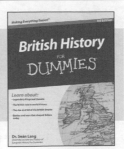

British History For Dummies
978-0-470-97819-1

Origami Kit For Dummies
978-0-470-75857-1

Overcoming Depression For Dummies
978-0-470-69430-5

Positive Psychology For Dummies
978-0-470-72136-0

PRINCE2 For Dummies, 2009 Edition
978-0-470-71025-8

Project Management For Dummies
978-0-470-71119-4

Psychology Statistics For Dummies
978-1-119-95287-9

Psychometric Tests For Dummies
978-0-470-75366-8

Renting Out Your Property For Dummies, 3rd Edition
978-1-119-97640-0

Rugby Union For Dummies, 3rd Edition
978-1-119-99092-5

Sage One For Dummies
978-1-119-95236-7

Self-Hypnosis For Dummies
978-0-470-66073-7

Storing and Preserving Garden Produce For Dummies
978-1-119-95156-8

Teaching English as a Foreign Language For Dummies
978-0-470-74576-2

Time Management For Dummies
978-0-470-77765-7

Training Your Brain For Dummies
978-0-470-97449-0

Voice and Speaking Skills For Dummies
978-1-119-94512-3

Work-Life Balance For Dummies
978-0-470-71380-8

12–47776–187x234mm

FOR DUMMIES®

Making Everything Easier!™

COMPUTER BASICS

978-1-118-11533-6

978-0-470-61454-9

978-0-470-49743-2

DIGITAL PHOTOGRAPHY

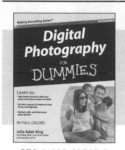

978-1-118-09203-3

978-0-470-76878-5

978-1-118-00472-2

SCIENCE AND MATHS

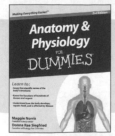

978-0-470-92326-9

978-0-470-55964-2

978-0-470-90324-7

Art For Dummies
978-0-7645-5104-8

Computers For Seniors For Dummies, 3rd Edition
978-1-118-11553-4

Criminology For Dummies
978-0-470-39696-4

Currency Trading For Dummies, 2nd Edition
978-0-470-01851-4

Drawing For Dummies, 2nd Edition
978-0-470-61842-4

Forensics For Dummies
978-0-7645-5580-0

French For Dummies, 2nd Edition
978-1-118-00464-7

Guitar For Dummies, 2nd Edition
978-0-7645-9904-0

Hinduism For Dummies
978-0-470-87858-3

Index Investing For Dummies
978-0-470-29406-2

Islamic Finance For Dummies
978-0-470-43069-9

Knitting For Dummies, 2nd Edition
978-0-470-28747-7

Music Theory For Dummies, 2nd Edition
978-1-118-09550-8

Office 2010 For Dummies
978-0-470-48998-7

Piano For Dummies, 2nd Edition
978-0-470-49644-2

Photoshop CS6 For Dummies
978-1-118-17457-9

Schizophrenia For Dummies
978-0-470-25927-6

WordPress For Dummies, 5th Edition
978-1-118-38318-6

12-47776-187x234mm

Think you can't learn it in a day? Think again!

The **In a Day** e-book series from For Dummies gives you quick and eas~~y~~ access to learn a new skill, brush up on a hobby, or enhance your personal or professional life — all in a day. Easy!

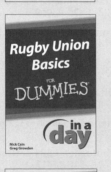